GRAND TOUR OF ITALY

Olive trees and orange groves at Salerno

GRAND TOUR
OF ITALY

By

ERIC AND BARBARA WHELPTON

Illustrated

London
Robert Hale Limited
63 Old Brompton Road S.W.7

First published 1956

PRINTED IN GREAT BRITAIN
BY WESTERN PRINTING SERVICES LTD, BRISTOL

CONTENTS

ILLUSTRATIONS

vii

ACKNOWLEDGMENT

The above illustrations are reproduced from photographs
supplied by the Italian State Tourist Office, London.

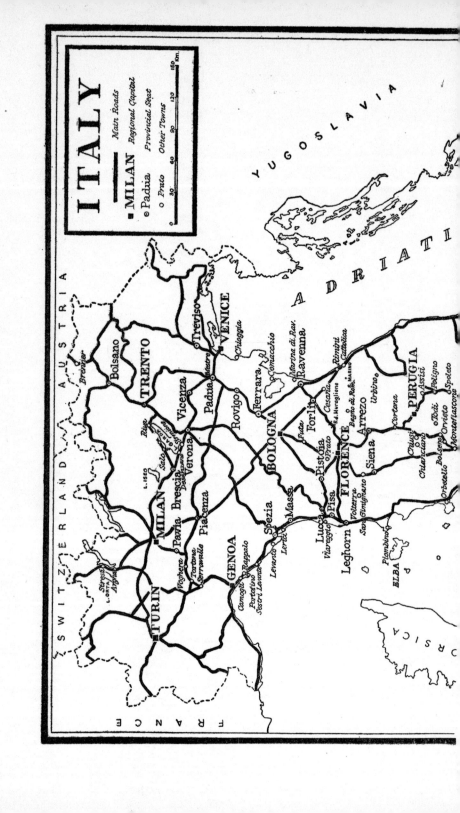

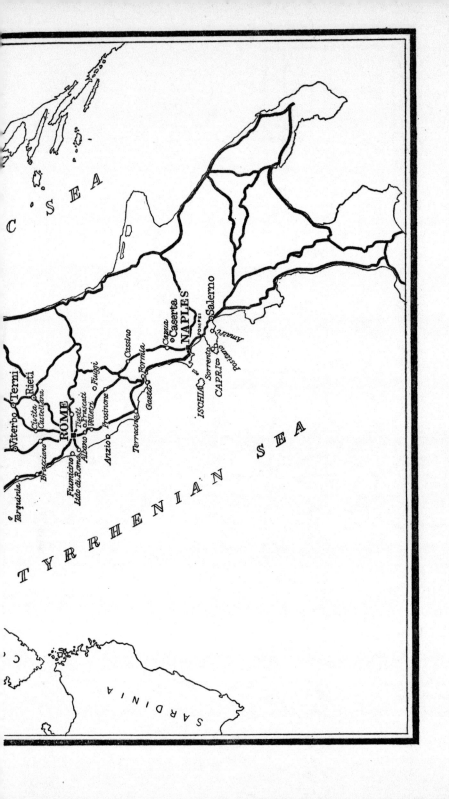

CHAPTER ONE

MILAN AND GENOA

SINCE I have always found Milan to be one of the least interesting cities in Italy, I feel sure that it is the right starting point for the Grand Tour, so that the traveller, as he progresses, may be filled with pleasurable anticipation of what still remains for him to see.

In any case, it is often necessary to stop a night in Milan, and so, with a few hours to spare, there is time to see the best of its attractions.

By road, or even by train, the first part of the Simplon route has its delights—how exciting it is to wind down the southern slopes of the pass, and to descend swiftly from the Alpine vegetation to the vineyards and olive groves on the shores of Lake Maggiore, and to pass from the trifling chalets of the heights to the well-composed architecture of the Lombard villages. Even in northern Italy, the scenery, the trees and the flowers combine to form a harmonious setting for the colour-washed houses, the tall steeples with their rounded belfries, and the castles perched perilously on their crags.

Usually the sun shines, and the air is warmer than in the valley of the Rhone only a few miles away where the sky is paler and the light is harder and less full of subtle tones than to the south of Simplon. Yet the waters of the lake are perhaps too vivid a blue, and the verdure is too lush for the landscape to be entirely satisfactory to a critical eye.

I have often broken my journey at Stresa to laze for a few hours on the bathing beach. If the weather is warm, I have hired a small boat, to row over to the Isola dei Pescatori, and to dine on the terrace of one of the *trattorie*.

If you are wise, you will try the *risotto a la Milanese*, for it is only in the north of Italy that they know how to make this dish which must be prepared with saffron—in Lombardy they do not know how to cook *pasta*. Then I would suggest the lake fish, of which there are many varieties not to be found elsewhere, but each of them

excellent. As for the wine, nothing can be better than the local white
wine on draught, for this is neither the meal nor the time for the
heavy, heating Chianti which comes from Tuscany, nearly three
hundred miles away, and costs far more.

There is a tiny village on the island, and then all around, beyond
the shining waters of the lake, the mountains form varied and fantastic outlines against the deep indigo of the starry sky. Nearer by,
a few lights twinkle on the Isola Bella, whose hideous, garish palace
attracts thousands of visitors in the summer-time. The garden with
its avenue of orange and lemon trees has considerable charm—there
are grottoes and well-disposed statues, fine vistas and terraces, but the
effect is marred by bad taste.

In their zest for the exotic, the gardeners have planted bamboos
and semi-tropical plants in the formal layout of parterres, aligned
hedges and bushes—the whole place suffers from one of those
nouveau-riche lapses that were fairly frequent in some stages of the
Italian Renaissance.

When the lake comes to an end, the *autostrada* begins, and on
either side of it, the horrors of modern publicity are displayed to the
full. The posters set at intervals of only a few yards are not only
large but in the worst of taste. Many Italians have protested against
this desecration of their country-side, but at present their efforts have
been in vain.

Except in the extreme south, the main roads here are very good,
and this blatant advertising covers a large part of their upkeep.

However, this particular *autostrada* passes through flat and altogether uninteresting country which is soon swallowed up by the
industrial suburbs of Milan.

I have sometimes avoided the Lake Maggiore route, and passed
through Orta, which is in a valley only a few miles to the west of
Stresa. This little town lies on the shores of a lake of the same name,
in a site of incomparable beauty. The main square with its medieval
town hall and seventeenth-century houses, is right on the water's
edge, facing an island with palaces, a castle and a complete little
village with a monastery and a church. All these are reflected faith-
fully on the smooth surface of the lake together with a green range
of mountains in the background.

At the back of the town, the narrow streets climb up the hillside
which is covered with gardens, orchards, and, further up, chestnut
forests.

In the spring and in the autumn, Orta is a peaceful place, though in the summer it is fairly crowded, but by a merciful dispensation, wheeled traffic is not allowed in the centre of the town.

Since Milan is the industrial and commercial capital of Italy, it is a modern city with skyscrapers, and huge and rapidly spreading suburbs. On all sides of the outskirts there are foundries, factories and textile mills. In the popular quarters, new blocks of workers' dwellings spring up on land where the mulberry-trees, the olive groves and the vineyards have only just been uprooted. At night the bright lights of the *autostrada*, and the railways, form long lines of radiance in the darkness.

Electric trains rush noisily to outlying places, crammed with commuters returning home after a long day's work in the city. Their employers race along the roads towards their villas in the hills and valleys of the Brianza, the shores of Lake Como or Lake Maggiore. In a sense, the true atmosphere of Milan is more like that of Paris or even Berlin than that of Italy.

As one advances, the analogy becomes more apparent, for three rings of broad boulevards enclose the centre of the city, and still broader avenues radiate out in all directions towards the countryside. Just as in Paris, the two inner rings of boulevards mark the site of the ancient ramparts; the larger one, the walls of the Austrian régime, and of the Roman Empire; the smaller one, the line of medieval fortifications of the first Sforzas, when Milan had shrunk after centuries of attacks, sieges and destruction.

Within the two or three square miles contained by the larger of these two rings of avenues, are to be found all the monuments of the past, and of course the Cathedral Square, which is still in a sense the social and commercial hub of the city.

The first impression of the inhabitants is that for the most part they belong racially to northern or central Europe, and ethnologically and historically this is quite correct, even though the southerners keep drifting in here in search of work in the factories.

Before the Roman Empire, northern Italy was held by the Cisalpine Gauls, and though in time they had to submit after the expulsion of the Carthaginians from the Peninsula, the Celtic strain remained. Eventually Milan became the second largest city in Italy, with such thriving commerce that the merchants and administrators could well afford to build themselves huge and splendid villas on the banks of the Lake of Como.

With the coming of the Barbarians, Milan was submerged repeatedly by successive tides of invasion only to arise once more in the fifth century when Theodoric reigned at Ravenna.

There were renewed incursions, first by the Goths, and later by the Huns, until eventually the Germanic Lombards occupied the greater part of northern Italy. As pagans and then, later, as heretics they were at variance with the Popes, who called in to their assistance the Frankish Kings with the strange and unforeseen result that Charlemagne not only subdued the Lombards, but was crowned Holy Roman Emperor in Rome in the year 800. For over a thousand years Italy was doomed to be dominated in varying degrees by foreigners, and it was not until 1860 that the Austrians were finally ejected from Milan.

In the late Middle Ages and in the early Renaissance, the city prospered under the tyrannical rule of the Viscontis and their successors, the Sforzas, who succumbed in the hard-fought duel between the French and the Imperialists.

In 1535, Charles V bequeathed Lombardy to his son Philip II King of Spain, and the Spanish misrule continued until 1713, when the whole province was handed over to the Austrians, whose administration was better, but not much less severe.

When General Bonaparte arrived after a succession of brilliant victories, he was greeted as a liberator, and his officers were fêted by the ladies of the aristocracy, although the newcomers did, in fact, enrich themselves at the expense of the population that they had come to deliver from supposed tyranny.

The greater prosperity which followed the unification of Italy in 1859 left its mark on the centre of the city which has preserved a nineteenth-century atmosphere in spite of the developments of the newer quarters. Huge arcades were constructed near the Cathedral Square, and the cafés here are still the focal point where people linger to chat, do business and watch the strollers who are to be seen at all times of the day.

The numerous millionaires have other resorts which come into fashion and disappear within the space of a few months, for the rich industrialists are cosmopolitans. Until the rise of the *haute couture* in Rome, the women bought their dresses in Paris, but the men patronize the tailors of Saville Row and drink imported whisky at a fabulous price.

The Milanese are adepts at money-making, but they are also good

Stresa. View of Lake Maggiore, the Isola Bella and the Alps

Pisa: the
twelfth
century
Cathedral

spenders and do not hesitate to gamble on the stock exchange or in their clubs.

At a first night at the Scala, the dresses and the jewels are as resplendent as in Paris or New York; the huge tiers of boxes are always crowded by spectators who, in many cases, rent them for the season.

The Victorians were filled with admiration for the cathedral with its countless pinnacles and lavish adornment of 2,300 statues. It is one of the largest churches in the world, but the architecture is devoid of any kind of composition or harmony—seldom has so much work and expense been devoted to a building with so little result. By day or by night this gleaming marble structure does indeed look like the conception of a pastrycook for a mayoral banquet.

The fact is that the cathedral and the rather gloomy streets of the centre are apt to give an entirely false idea of the æsthetic attractions of Milan.

If all the palaces, churches and ancient monuments were assembled together within a small area, the result would be a town which thousands of art lovers would be eager to visit.

The Church of San Lorenzo, for instance, was built at the same time and on the same plan as the Church of San Vitale in Ravenna. Though it was rebuilt subsequently, the sixth-century mosaics have remained intact.

Sant' Ambrogio is of even greater interest, though the nave was seriously damaged during the bombardments of 1943. Parts of the building date from the year 343, the rest was restored in the twelfth century. The coronations with the Iron Crown of Lombardy took place on the steps of the choir, and the High Altar is sheathed with panels of gold on which are depicted scenes from the life of our Lord. On the back there is a vivid presentation of the life of Sant' Ambrogio, which is, I suppose, one of the most complete records of costume and manners in the ninth century.

The fifteenth-century Abbey church of Santa Maria delle Grazie was badly damaged during the war, the cloisters were almost entirely demolished and the refectory reduced to a ruin, but the protective wall covering Leonardo's *Last Supper* fulfilled its purpose and saved the fresco from any serious deterioration. This painting has suffered from the atmosphere and from successive bad treatment, some of it in the shape of inexpert restoration, and is now only a shadow of what it must have been.

B

We know little of the reasons for Leonardo's long stay in Milan. It may be that, if Lorenzo de Medici had not sent him with a present to Lodovico Sforza, we should never have had this magnificent wall painting. Possibly Leonardo had already been commissioned to carry out the equestrian statue of Francesco, but whatever brought him, he spent seventeen years of the most productive part of his artistic life there.

His equestrian statue never materialized beyond the beautiful little bronze studies of horses, the countless drawings and the great clay model which was actually set up in the square but very soon perished. He was attached to the court and employed as an engineer, improving the city fortifications and "engines of war", experimenting with the possibilities of a flying machine and even making fantastic mechanical toys for the court children. Vasari tells us that he was "specially endowed by the hand of God himself" and that "this was seen and acknowledged by all men. . . . His gifts were such that his fame extended far and wide and he was held in the highest estimation not only in his own time, but also, and even to a greater extent, after his death; and this will continue to be in all succeeding ages. Truly wonderful indeed and divinely gifted was Leonardo da Vinci."

Despite his popularity and the satisfaction he seems to have given, he does not appear to have been very well paid by the Sforzas, for he sought commissions elsewhere and painted the *Virgin of the Rocks* as an altarpiece for the Church of the Conception for the Franciscan Friars. During the great building activity of the late fifteenth century, when Bramante was designing the sacristy and cloisters of Santa Maria delle Grazie, Leonardo worked on the painting of the *Last Supper* in the adjoining refectory.

However much the experts may lament the fading of this painting, it still remains to have a tremendous impact on all who see it, albeit they see it as through a mist. The dramatic force, the characterization and the movement are there, and the moment of great emotion as the words are said "One of you shall betray me". No one who has seen earlier Italian paintings of the same subject can fail to be impressed by the great changes in style and technique brought about by Leonardo's enthusiasm for experiment and for representing nature as closely as possible, for his passion for enveloping his landscape and figures in atmosphere instead of using a definite outline to separate them from the background. His predecessors arranged a conventional line of disciples along the table on either side of Christ. He groups them dramatically and makes them draw away from their Master in horror at the suggestion of betrayal, thus leaving him majestically isolated against the arched doorway and a vista of enchanting blue hills and rivers disappearing into the misty distance. We have a series of magnificent drawings for these heads at Windsor Castle and also sketches for the complete composition.

It is said that Leonardo never finished the head of Christ as he felt himself unable to define the divinity of the features. The head of Christ in the Brera gallery was not a study for the *Last Supper*, but a copy by one of his admiring pupils.

Here in the Pinacoteca housed in the Brera Palace is a collection of paintings by the pupils and disciples of Leonardo. The gallery definitely stresses the Lombard schools of painting, but it also possesses some outstanding works from Umbria and Venice. Francesca's *Madonna and Child with Angels* is serene and austere in its beautiful harmony of violet, blue and grey; Giovanni Bellini's *Pieta* is a magnificent composition of three tragic figures against a dramatic sky; Tintoretto's more flowing and gorgeous *Finding of the Body of St Mark* with its curves and flowing draperies and foreshortened figures dramatically catching the light. Perhaps to most people the greatest treasure of the Brera is Raphael's *Marriage of the Virgin* with its urbane figures dressed in glowing colours who step gracefully across the foreground, and smaller groups of figures lead one up the sweep of steps to the arcaded temple silhouetted against a soft blue Umbrian sky and the gentle undulating hills. There is very great satisfaction in the perfection of this painting, but to me it has a certain smugness and gives no feeling of the dramatic happening.

In the Poldi-Pezzoli Museum there is a delightful atmosphere of a private collection and its paintings are, for the most part, small and have an intimate appeal. The delicate and charming *Triumph of Bacchus* by Cima da Conegliano never fails to enchant me. A delightful triumphal chariot is drawn by gentle dusky leopards with red trappings, and blue mountains sweep down to the sea against a golden sky.

Lovely, naive primitives with golden backgrounds and glowing colours are a source of delight, and landscapes shimmering under warm blue skies decorate the backgrounds of religious subjects. Among a series of lovely portraits is the fascinating *Young Woman* by Antonio Pollaiuollo, her clear-cut profile against a pale blue sky flecked with clouds.

Barely a hundred miles separate Milan from Genoa, and the road is not of outstanding interest, that is to say, in comparison with the delights that await the traveller in other parts of the peninsula. In one of his books, D. H. Lawrence declares that the Italian highways are mournful and desolate beyond description.

Nothing could be further from the truth. I can find charm and beauty even when passing through the flat plains of Lombardy with their wide sky-lines and vistas of the distant Alps stretching endlessly on the northern horizon. Then also the rustic architecture of the villages is full of character, and the colour-washed houses are admirably composed; the eves of russet-tiled roofs overhang stone terraces built above huge round gateways.

In the fields, the vine, the mulberry and the olive combine to form the harmony of vegetation which is so peculiar to the Mediterranean, where even the foliage falls into classical patterns of ornamentation.

Along the side roads, yokes of oxen drag their creaking chariots, urged on with the same cries that have been used for three thousand years. In Italy, perhaps more than anywhere else in Europe, there is a sense that, in spite of invasions and countless political changes, the essence and life of the countryside is unchanging, that the peasant rather than the aristocrat or the town dweller is the true heir of the greatness that was Rome.

In Tuscany, for instance, I have found that the hills and the valleys are still called after the gods of mythology even though on the maps they have less resplendent names. Oaths too are of ancient origin, for they still swear by Bacchus or by Jupiter or use those complicated phallic terms of abuse which are to be found among the more scabrous Latin authors, but must indeed descend from the Priapic cult of the Etruscans.

In the north these traditions have nearly vanished or have been so attenuated that they have nearly disappeared, but the countrymen are still gripped by the unchanging spirit of the earth that they till so laboriously.

However, the industrial zone of Milan now stretches most of the twenty-two miles to Pavia, a town which boasts of the oldest university in Italy; founded first of all in 825, and then refounded in the fourteenth century.

The huge Certosa, sheathed in multicoloured marble, has little or no æsthetic attraction for me, even though the ornamentation of the interior is lavish. In its general lines this structure, designed by Giovanni Amadeo (or Omodeo), possesses some harmony, but the whole effect is spoilt by the excessive use of decoration, and the chapel is in the amorphous Gothic of the Mediterranean, which does not bear comparison with the medieval architecture of the northern countries of Europe. However, this monastery was the second in importance of the Carthusian Houses, and as such it may merit some attention, but the pictures and statuary that adorn it are the work of secondary artists of no great genius or talent.

The tomb of St Augustine in the cathedral was designed and constructed by Venetian artists in the fourteenth century.

However, Pavia is not without a certain picturesqueness, for the shell of the fifteenth-century castle is still standing, and it is agreeable to stroll along the ramparts on a clear day when the snowy peaks of the Alps can be seen gleaming in the distance.

Voghera, the next town of any size on this road, has nothing to attract the attention of the traveller, but soon after leaving it, the grey-green foothills of the Apennines bring the monotonous flatness of the Lombard plain to an end.

The approach to Genoa is not an easy one, for steep ranges of mountains guard it from the north, but it is thanks to the protection of these mountains that the Republic of Genoa survived for so many years, whereas the states of the plains were doomed to early extinction.

In the eleventh and twelfth centuries many of the towns on the shores of the Mediterranean were practically independent and self-governing even though, in theory, they owed allegiance to Byzantium or to the Holy Roman Emperors. From Ragusa to Marseilles these small maritime republics flourished and waged war on each other until they were gradually eliminated.

So, for instance, Amalfi, which had grown so rich by trading with the Levant, was annexed by the Norman Kings of Naples in 1131.

The Genoese, on the other hand, swallowed their nearest neighbours, such as the small Republic of Rapallo, but their main pre-occupation was to overcome their principal commercial rivals the Pisans.

Having driven them out of Corsica and Sardinia, the Genoese finally destroyed their enemies at sea when Admiral Doria routed their fleet at the Battle of Meloria. Then he followed this success by filling up the mouth of the Arno so that Pisa could no longer be used as a port.

In the two succeeding centuries, the Genoese attained immense power and wealth, partly by transporting many of the crusading armies to Palestine, but largely through trading with the Levant and by establishing settlements in North Africa, Syria and even the Crimea. Since they were primarily business men, they did not quarrel with the Saracens and they maintained commercial relations with them even when they were fighting against their fellow-Christians.

In the last years of the thirteenth century and throughout the fourteenth century, the Genoese strove with the Venetians for the mastery of the eastern Mediterranean, until finally they were defeated at the Battle of Chioggia and had to abandon their project to dominate the Adriatic.

Nevertheless, the prosperity of the Genoese did not appear to be seriously impaired, and the wealthy merchants and aristocrats built themselves immense palaces in the city, and splendid mansions in the countryside.

The seizure of Constantinople by the Turks was the cause of the decline of both Venice and Genoa, though the great Admiral Andrea Doria saved his city from the clutches of the Emperor Charles V, and held the fleets of the Barbary Corsairs at bay.

In the seventeenth and eighteenth centuries, the Republic became little more than a pawn in the great rivalries between France, Spain and the Empire. The rebellious Island of Corsica was offered to the British, who declined to buy it, and so it was sold to the French, and thus Napoleon acquired a new nationality the year that he was born, and he lived to see the city of his oppressors annexed by his adopted country in 1805.

In 1815, Genoa was made part of the Kingdom of Savoy and Sardinia, and the last vestiges of its independence disappeared.

In the first half of the nineteenth century, a number of English and German travellers came to winter in Genoa, attracted by the mildness of the climate, the natural beauty of the scenery, and the picturesqueness of the city before it was submerged by modern buildings and industrialization.

At Albaro, now only a twenty minutes' walk from the Brignole station, Byron rented a large pink-washed villa, the Casa Saluzzo.

He arrived from Pisa with five carriages, several servants, a monkey, some dogs and wagon loads of furniture.

He was accompanied by his mistress, the Countess Guiccioli and her family, the Leigh Hunts with all their children and, of course, Trelawny, who was to follow him on the last fatal expedition to Greece.

The Casa Saluzzo can still be seen, standing in a rustic setting, not more than two hundred yards away from the main road with its surging noisy traffic and urban houses.

Some years later, Dickens and his large family also spent a few months at Albaro in a nearby villa, and he, like Byron, was enchanted by the beauty of the landscape, the romantic aspect of the ancient palaces and country houses scattered among the orchards and vineyards.

In the present day, Genoa is a busy modern town which stretches for over fifteen miles along the coast, for the steep hills and mountains prevent expansion inland.

Villas and blocks of flats have been built on the slopes up to the heights which are crowned by extensive seventeenth-century fortifications. Broad avenues wind up through these suburbs, which are more easily reached by a funicular and some half-dozen lifts that are strung along at intervals on the north side of the city.

The funicular from the Piazza Zecca goes a thousand feet or more up to the Righi from which there is a magnificent view of the town and of the surrounding countryside. Behind are the grey, stony ranges of the Apennines, and on either side the hills are crowned with stone fortresses.

Below, through a veil of smoke, the church towers and rooftops of the town are massed together, dominated by the three or four new skyscrapers of which the Genoese are inordinately proud. Then comes the massed shipping of the harbour where the huge ocean liners are berthed as well as merchant ships from all parts of the world.

To the east, and to the west, the coast, with its background of hills, merges into far-off horizons, and the grey slopes turn to deep blue and violet in the distance.

The Righi is a pleasant place in the day time, when the sun is shining brightly and spreading its radiance on the violet surface of the sea. It is pleasant also on a warm night, when the landscape is spangled with the lights of the city, and the gleam of those of the suburbs that stretch along the coast for so many miles.

In spite of all the changes of the past, Genoa is still something of a capital, or at any rate of a great commercial centre such as Liverpool or Hamburg.

The Piazza de Ferrari, the hub of the town, is a large and busy square, with a surge of buses, trolley-buses and cars, with a constantly moving crowd, in which men predominate. The Genoese are, in fact, traders and businessmen with their eyes constantly turned towards the sea, for their shipping is still their greatest source of revenue. Columbus was born here, and his house is shown to visitors with great pride, although he had to seek his fortune in Spain.

On the fringes of the old town, there are streets of massive and splendid palaces which are profusely decorated with the paintings of secondary artists. So, the narrow Via Garibaldi is lined with large seventeenth-century mansions, most of which are now counting houses and banks, but the largest of all, the Palazzo Bianco, is a museum given up to French, Dutch and Italian pictures.

The Palaces of the Via Balbi are still more imposing, for here can be seen the former Palace of the Doges, the University, the splendid residence of the great Andrea Doria, and the Palazzo Durazzo, which was turned into a Royal Palace.

Nevertheless, in spite of all these imposing and monumental buildings, the art and architecture of Genoa never attained great heights—it would be in fact foolish to linger long here if there is any possibility of going on to Florence, Rome and the beauties of the south.

However, I have always enjoyed wandering through the medieval town which lies between the Via Garibaldi and the harbour. The narrow lanes, or *caruqi* as they are called, are full of movement and full of interest though they are rarely visited by the casual traveller.

As in the past, entire streets are given up to a single craft, as for instance, the Via dei Orifice, which consists mainly of goldsmiths' shops. No guide is required in this quarter, for it is more agreeable to pick out for one's self the fine old carvings over a doorway, the monumental stairways perceived by a glimpse into a small courtyard.

In the course of wandering through the maze of alleys in this ancient quarter, one encounters, quite unexpectedly, the Piazza San Matteo which is surrounded by thirteenth-century palaces that are faced with black and white marble. A large mansion on one side was presented to Andrea Doria as a reward for his many victories over the enemies of the Republic.

It is a building of the greatest elegance, with tall Gothic windows supported on slender stone pillars, and an open loggia on the third floor.

The great Admiral is buried in the crypt of the Church of San Matteo in a tomb surmounted by stone cherubs and adorned with classical motifs. The style is apt enough. A Renaissance character, he was born in the last years of the Middle Ages, and his dwelling is a medieval one, but his sepulchre reflects the style of the new epoch in which he distinguished himself so greatly.

The black and white marble facings of the Cathedral of San Lorenzo always leave me wondering whether I really like this form of decoration—at times I loathe it, at others I can tolerate it. The architecture of the church is Gothic, but the pillars which support the arches are Classical, yet the effect is not too incongruous. The gold-plated fifteenth-century Ark of St John the Baptist is worthy of attention, but the greatest treasure of the Cathedral is the Sacro Catino, a shallow cup that was brought back from the Crusades, and was believed to be made from a single emerald.

The most notable building of the town, however, is the Banco di San Giorgio, a thirteenth-century palace on the quayside. St George is the patron saint of Genoa, and the bank named after him helped to bring great prosperity to the city, for it was one of the first credit establishments of its kind and became very powerful. This corporation not only owned fleets and house property, but also had its own colonies, and something like a private army and navy.

Doubtless the fact that Genoa was a free port assisted its operations, and in the harbour zone, people of races and all religions could dwell without fear of persecution.

Much of the picturesqueness of this ancient quarter has been lost, but some fifteenth-century houses have been restored in the Via Sotto Ripa. In the arcades of this street there are sailors' taverns and restaurants where the best of the local dishes are served at reasonable prices. The fish soup is fair only, but the squid (calamai) are excellent, the local white wine on draught is refreshing and palatable.

I am also partial to the red mushrooms and the *pasta* cooked with *pesto*, a sauce prepared with basil, oil, garlic and strong cheese which is aromatic to say the least of it.

CHAPTER TWO

GENOA TO FLORENCE BY ROAD

I ALWAYS leave Genoa with some regret for I like the Ligurians, although they cannot be said to be typical Italians.

Reserved and thrifty, they are often accused of being mean and cold-blooded by their southern neighbours, but I cannot say that that has been my experience.

It is true that they care little for display, and that a Genoese millionaire may walk to his office in order to save a tramfare, but they are, in fact, both kindly and hospitable to strangers.

Like the Milanese, they are cosmopolitan and have many contacts in other countries, but, unlike them, they hate spending money and gambling, and they prefer a quiet life.

The local dialect is not a pretty one, and since they are not talkative or excitable, the Genoese are apt to irritate the southerners who enjoy a flow of words and the display of their emotions.

One of the pleasing attributes of the Genoese and of their fellow Ligurians is that they keep their promises and are business-like, perhaps almost too business-like, for I do not mind the adaptability and the readiness to please of many of the other types of Italians.

The fact is that the Ligurians are an ancient race who have kept their own peculiarities throughout the three thousand years of their history. The racial type changes as soon as you reach the frontiers of their province, about twenty miles to the south of Spezia.

The railway journey from Genoa to this town is one of the most tantalizing in Europe, for the track has been literally carved out of the rock, and more than a hundred tunnels have to be passed. The landscape is enchanting; just as one is beginning to enjoy the view of a small harbour surrounded by whitewashed fishermen's cottages, the whole scene is blotted out, to be replaced a few minutes later by a rocky bay with a sandy beach covered with brightly coloured umbrellas that shade groups of sunbathers.

If you have not come by car, and you have time to spare, it is possible to go by road on one of the comfortable buses that cover the whole of Italy.

Centuries ago, the Roman armies and their predecessors marched and counter-marched along the coast road which was part of the Via Aurelia, one of the great highways that started from the Capital. When, in time, it fell into decay, travellers from the north found it easier to journey southwards by sea from Genoa as far as Civita Vecchia, Viareggio or Leghorn according to their destination.

The small schooners that transported them sailed only by day and put in for the night at one of the little harbours that are strung along the coast at convenient intervals. As a rule, the course was not far from land, for in these regions, storms spring up with surprising suddenness as Smollett discovered to his cost.

It was Napoleon who finally rebuilt the coast road, but in recent years it has been still further improved, which is just as well, for the flow of traffic is always considerable and there are many built-up areas.

As I have already explained, the suburbs of Genoa extend for many miles, and they have enveloped a number of little fishing-ports which have not altogether lost their original character. So every few miles there are glimpses of small harbours, with fishing-boats swaying in the blue water and nets spread out to dry on quays that gleam in the white sunlight.

So within a few minutes of leaving Genoa, the villages of Sturla and Boccadesse contrast surprisingly with the blocks of flats and the villas on the slopes behind them. Further up the hillside the olive groves and orchards are, I am afraid, fast disappearing through the onslaughts of the speculative builder.

Quarto dei Mille is noted not only for its orange groves, but because it was from here that Garibaldi set out for the conquest of Sicily with his immortal thousand men in May 1860.

The expedition was unofficial and so the strange army had to be marshalled in a fairly circumspect manner, but the local police were sympathizers of the cause of Italian Independence, and they turned a blind eye to the whole operation.

Though it is, practically speaking, a suburb of Genoa, Nervi still keeps its character as a winter resort with large hotels, groves of palm trees, carob trees and eucalyptus.

The climate here is so mild that semi-tropical plants grow in great profusion, and in the early spring, the gardens are ablaze with golden mimosa in full flower.

Since the ground slopes steeply up at the back of the town, the vineyards, the orange groves and the olives are only a few hundred yards away. Higher up, the hillside is covered by dense chestnut forests, and at intervals, the red rooftops of villages cluster round tall white church-towers surmounted by small tulip-shaped domes.

To the south, the Portofino Peninsula juts right out into the sea, and its cliffs rise sheer up from the water's edge and merge into densely wooded hills two thousand feet high.

Beyond Nervi, the Via Aurelia deviates a little from the shore, bypassing Sori and Bogliasco, two little villages with a line of white-washed houses curving round a small harbour. Neither of these places has been developed for tourists, and in each of them you can find inexpensive pensions and modest hotels. The more sophisticated travellers tend to hurry on to Rapallo or Santa Margherita.

I have never been attracted by Recco, the next place on this road, but I do like Camogli, with its ancient ten-storeyed houses rising straight out of the sea, and mirrored in the smooth water of the port. Steep narrow streets and alleys and even flights of steps lead up to the gardens and vineyards above.

A town with a long tradition of seamanship, it is now little more than a modest resort for painters and quiet people from Genoa— there are no grand hotels or new-fangled bars, but the road comes to a stop here, and the traffic cannot descend to the water's edge.

For those who like rock bathing in clean water or long walks across country, there is the Peninsula of Portofino at hand.

Santa Margherita, on the other side of the isthmus, is a largish town, which has the general aspect of other Riviera resorts. The climate is mild, there are avenues of palm trees, and in the summer-time it is crowded with visitors and day-trippers from all parts of northern Italy.

The five miles of coast to Portofino have been mercifully protected from the speculative builder, and so the road passes through a beauti-fully wooded landscape, where the steep rocks and tall trees are reflected in the inlets and creeks below. The vegetation is profuse; large masses of bougainvillæa flow over the sides of walls and houses like purple cataracts; roses bloom here ten months a year.

Portofino itself is the idealized fishing-village set at the bottom of a small narrow bay from which gardens and woodlands rise on either side. Fishing-boats and large yachts moored at the quayside almost touch the tables and coloured umbrellas of some half-dozen cafés. On the heights above there is a castle, a large sixteenth-century villa and an ancient church, where according to the legend, the bones of St George were laid to rest.

A forty minutes' walk across the hill leads to San Fruttuoso, a small twelfth-century monastery built at the end of a narrow wooded creek. It was selected to be the burial place of the Dorias, and the tombs of six admirals of that name are to be seen here.

A handful of fishermen and their families still live in the little hamlet, which also has a pleasant inn and a small bathing-beach, but in the height of summer, the place is always full of visitors, and even then, in the morning, you can have it all to yourself.

Rapallo, separated from Santa Margherita by two miles of headland, is far smarter than its neighbours, and certainly less crowded though more expensive.

The winter climate is so mild that, like Nice or Cannes, it has a number of winter residents, some of them writers, poets and painters.

The town is on the shores of a wide bay with a background of high mountains. Cafés and smart hotels line the water's edge, but Rapallo is an old town, with narrow streets, some ancient palaces, and two or three large churches of architectural merit.

A cable car transports passengers up to the Sanctuary of Montallegro, two thousand feet above the sea level. The church and monastery were built as a shrine for a Byzantine Madonna of rare beauty which was found in the wreckage of a Dalmatian ship in the sixteenth century.

The view from this place is one of the most beautiful along the coast, for it comprises not only Portifino but also the whole of the gulf down to the Peninsula of Sestri Levante, and it is claimed that, on a clear day, it is possible to see the snow-covered peaks of Corsica in the far distance.

On leaving Rapallo, the road to the south rises rapidly to pass through olive groves and vineyards, planted on the steep slopes of a mountain. On one side, the rocky peaks tower above the highway, on the other the sea eddies and ripples in the bays and inlets far below.

A winding road descends to the little village of Zoagli, which was totally destroyed by bombing during the Second World War. Two small pebbly beaches next to the pinewoods in this valley provide reasonably good bathing.

A little further on, the Via Aurelia swoops down suddenly to a broad plain which extends for perhaps a dozen miles. Although the sands are good, there is nothing to make one dally at Chiavari or Lavagna, two of the most uninteresting towns it is possible to find in Italy.

On the other hand, Sestri Levante, at the far end of the bay, is charmingly situated on a small peninsula which projects far out into the sea. A castle on the wooded heights of this headland completes the composition of the landscape. The old town set on the narrow isthmus has a fishing harbour on the south side, and on the north side an esplanade facing the wide gulf which stretches as far as Portofino.

At Sestri, the highway leaves the sea to pass through olive groves and vineyards; then there is a climb through oakwoods to successive ridges covered with pines. From time to time it is possible to get a glimpse of a distant bay, at the far end of a long valley. Since there is no through coastal road, some of the enchanting little resorts can only be reached by train.

Others such as Levanto, Bonassola and Moneglia are linked up with the Via Aurelia and are really pleasant places for an overnight stay, since each of them has good bathing and is undisturbed by the noise of through traffic.

Levanto is a charming little town with remains of medieval fortifications, the ruins of a castle, and a really beautiful church.

The *Cinque Terre*, five little fishing ports built perilously on the side of the cliff, have small harbours, and terraced vineyards going right down to the water's edge. All five, Monterosso, Vernazza, Corniglia, Manarola and Riomaggiore, have remained unspoilt because they are inaccessible by road and have no real beaches. Each of them has little inns and taverns overlooking the sea, frequented by painters, writers and other people who value peace and quiet. The local wine is exceptionally good, though it is rarely sold outside this part of Liguria.

For a long while past there have been plans to build a coast road between Sestri Levant and Spezia—how soon these plans will be realized I cannot tell, but in the meantime the motorist has to use the Via Aurelia which passes through really beautiful country.

From the top of the Bracco Pass (altitude 2,000 feet) there is an astonishingly wide view of the Apennines, often snow-covered in winter, and the distant Carrara Mountains. A little further on the road descends, and here the prospect is of the Bay of Spezia, deep blue when the sun is shining and fringed with the white houses of towns and villages.

Spezia itself is a naval base, and is on the whole an unattractive town, rebuilt after the merciless bombardments of the last war.

Lerici, on the south side of the bay, is a charming little town with a ruined castle and fragments of the old fortifications. Shelley spent the last few weeks of his life at San Terenzo near by in a small white house right on the shore, and it was at this time that his friend Byron swam the six or seven miles to Porto Venere, a place of great antiquity and beauty on the northern arm of the Gulf of Spezia.

The colouring and light at Lerici are singularly brilliant. The atmosphere is usually clear and the climate is mild. I have always enjoyed stopping here for a meal on the quayside which has a prospect of the whole coast as far as Porto Venere and the Island of Palmaria.

On leaving Lerici, the road climbs up a steep hill and then descends to the Magra, the river which marks the boundary between Liguria and Tuscany.

Apart from its massive castle and ancient cathedral, Sarzana, the first town beyond the bridge, is noted because it is believed that it was the home of the Bonaparte family before they migrated to Corsica in the fifteenth century.

From here to Pisa there is a clear run of thirty-six miles by a straight road and over flat country. The rather featureless towns and villages succeed each other at close intervals, but the scenery is not unattractive. For the whole of the way on the left-hand side, the Carrara Mountains rise up against the horizon, with their white marble crags and cliffs that look as if they were covered with snow.

At a lower level, on the foothills, there are castles, walled towns and fortified villages built far inland so as to be safe from the raids by the Normans, the Saracens, and later, the Barbary pirates.

On the plain live the workers who shape and carve the marble brought down from the quarries on the heights. Then finally along the sandy shore a succession of resorts have been built among the pinewoods so that there is now an almost continuous seafront for over fifteen miles.

Of these places, Forte dei Marmi, one of the first of the series, is frequented by wealthy Florentines, whilst Viareggio, at the far end of the line, is a kind of Margate or Atlantic City, crowded with people of all classes throughout the summer.

Despite its jerry-built villas and huge hotels, its serried ranks of bathing huts and umbrellas and its loudspeakers that blare hot music unceasingly, Viareggio has a history, for the harbour with its swaying schooners was once the only port of the tiny Republic of Lucca.

The body of Shelley was washed up on the sands, and it was on the then deserted shore that Trelawny burnt the corpse with ceremony in the presence of Byron, Leigh Hunt and a group of officials and soldiers.

Puccini is another eminent man associated with Viareggio, for he lived there for some time and spent the last years of his life at Torre del Lago in a villa built on the shores of the small lake of Massaciuccoli, only a few miles away in the depth of the coastal pine forest.

A few miles further on, the trees become scarcer on approaching Pisa, and the Dome of the Baptistry, the Leaning Tower and the Cathedral can be seen above a strip of the old town wall. To the north, a double range of deep blue mountains form a background to the distant belfries and rooftops of Lucca.

And, indeed, the first reaction of the traveller from Lucca is that the two cathedrals are almost exactly alike in design, the chief difference being that at Pisa a fourth row of graduated columns fills the triangular pediment surmounting the building.

The cathedral at Pisa has also the great advantage of being seen from all angles as no other building touches it.

The actual grouping of the Cathedral and Leaning Tower, the Baptistry and the Camposanto is magnificent. Surrounded on two sides by the ancient city wall, the Campo dei Miracoli is surely a field of miracles, it is a place apart, cut off from the traffic of the town, its velvety lawns spread like a carpet under these lovely marble examples of the genius of the Romanesque and Gothic architects of Tuscany.

In the daytime the perfect proportions of the creamy marble buildings rise from the quiet green of the grass and shine against the brilliant blue sky but, if you are fortunate enough to see them in the moonlight, the domes and columns gleam with an unearthly beauty against the dark sky and the details are thrown into strong relief by the deep violet shadows.

Florence: view from the
Piazzale Michelangelo

Florence: the Ponte Vecchio with the Tower of the
Signoria in the background

The cathedral was begun in 1063 on the site of the ancient Basilica of Santa Reparata to commemorate the victory of the Pisans over the Arabs. After the great naval victory at Palermo, the Pisans brought back such rich spoils that they were able to speed up work on the cathedral, but it took more than half a century to build and was not consecrated until 1118. Certain modifications were carried out to the apse and the façade in the thirteenth century, but it is almost certain that the later architect respected Buschetto's original design, for the whole building has complete architectural unity.

The ancient bronze doors opposite the camapanile, cast in the late twelfth century, represent scenes from the life of Christ. The panels are simply and beautifully designed and dramatically tell the story, but they also take their place in the design of the doors as a whole, balancing one with another, weighted by the double panels at the base with their strange little palm trees leaning in opposite directions, and completed above by double panels of figures and trees.

The interior of the cathedral gives the impression of immense size partly because the double aisles increase the feeling of space. They lead to the half-dome above the altar which is decorated by the huge mosaic of Christ with the Virgin and St John. Influenced by Byzantine mosaics the figure of Christ is rather stiff and forbidding and lacks the majesty of true Byzantine art, but the figure of St John has a grace of line and depth of feeling in contrast to the hard formality of the rest of the design.

The lovely pulpit by Giovanni Pisano shows the break-away from the conventional Byzantine composition and is full of movement and naturalistic touches. The panels representing *The Last Judgment* are in very high relief, the figures, almost in the round, show an extraordinary variety of movement and emotional feeling. There are delicious naturalistic details in the panels of *The Nativity* and *The Adoration of the Magi*: beautifully observed trees, horses, sheep and dogs, all showing the newly-awakened Tuscan enthusiasm for countryside and natural forms.

In the sacristy, Giovanni Pisano has left us one of the most beautiful ivory Madonnas in the world. Her body curves gracefully backwards to take the weight of the Child, lifted shoulder high; her robe flows in simple, long lines broken by the gentle curve of a bordering fringe.

The Leaning Tower rises from its own square of grass a few yards from the cathedral and is more interesting as a piece of architecture

c

than because it happens to lean very considerably. Romanesque in style, it repeats in glowing marble, tier upon tier of the slender pillars and rounded arches of the Cathedral façade. We see these again in the circular Baptistry but contrasted with Gothic details and additions of the fourteenth century.

Within the baptistry is the famous pulpit carved by Niccolo Pisano, father of Giovanni, and leader of the Gothic movement in sculpture: the movement away from rigidity towards naturalism. This glorious pulpit is hexagonal and raised on seven columns, six at the angles and one in the centre. Three of the outer columns rest on the backs of lions in Lombard style; the centre one is supported by a group of figures. Between the carved arches rising from the Classical capitals are Gothic figures supporting the panels of *The Nativity*, *The Adoration*, *The Circumcision*, *The Crucifixion* and *The Last Judgment*. Perhaps the loveliest is the beautifully composed *Nativity*, much more impressive in its architectural unity than the looser composition of Giovanni's work in the Cathedral. Niccolo's figures, too, have more dignity and repose and are obviously the work of a great master, though they have not the gentle charm of his son's.

Beyond the Baptistry and the Cathedral are the walls of the Campo Santo, the straight long lines broken by the sharp black-pointed cypresses rising from the cloistered lawns within. Later than the other three buildings and Gothic in style, the Campo Santo is in perfect harmony with them, and the four buildings show the gradual development from the Romanesque to the Gothic from the twelfth to the fourteenth centuries.

The Campo Santo was very badly damaged during the Second World War and many of the frescoes spoilt beyond repair, but fortunately the famous painting by Traini of *The Triumph of Death* has been saved and is now to be seen in a room off the cloister. This fourteenth-century painter has dramatized the story to the full and the fresco has a wealth of lovely detail as well as many amusing realistic touches. What is left of the colour gives some idea of its former glowing beauty. The fine lines of the building, massive outside contrasted with the slender elegance within, still remain and, through the traceries of the high Gothic arches, we can look on to the green lawns with their flowering bushes and tapering cypresses. There is a feeling of peace and timelessness and a certain melancholy about this ancient burial ground to which more than fifty shiploads of sacred earth from Jerusalem were brought in the beginning of the thirteenth century.

There are interesting fragments of paintings, ancient sarcophagi and early carvings to be found in the ambulatory.

The melancholy air of the Campo Santo seems to envelop the whole of Pisa, although it is indeed a beautiful city in a beautiful and harmonious setting. Perhaps it is because of the long centuries of slow decline that followed the destruction of the Pisan fleet at Meloria, or perhaps the reason is only a climatic one.

Although the new town round the station was destroyed in the last war, the old town on the banks of the river Arno was fortunately spared from great damage, and the bridges have by now been rebuilt.

The streets to the south of the cathedral have preserved their ancient character. Many of the old palaces have survived from the past, including the splendid Archbishopric.

In the Piazza dei Cavalieri, a sixteenth-century palace stands on the site of the tower of hunger where Count Gherardesca and his two sons were starved to death because he was believed to have betrayed his state to the Genoese in the last stages of the struggle for supremacy.

The main feature of this square, however, is the huge and nobly proportioned Palazzo dei Cavalieri, where the knights were instructed before receiving the accolade. The façade is decorated in bright colours and, inset in deep niches, are busts of the Grand Dukes of Tuscany. Nearby also is the Palace of the Knights of St Stephen with the Church of their order, on whose walls and ceiling frescoes depict the principal achievements of the members in their fights against the Turks.

The Arno with its jade green waters flowing slowly between stone embankments holds even more melancholy and sadness than the rest of Pisa, for the life of the town is centred round the new quarters further south.

Huge ancient palaces are reflected clearly on the smooth surface of the river, and there is the feeling that all movement and activity have departed from them.

Some of these mansions date back to the Middle Ages, others, including the Palazzo Upezzinghi, belong to the Baroque period.

In the early nineteenth century, Pisa was a health resort, and so Byron came here and set up house with the Leigh Hunts at the

Palazzo Lafranchi. He arrived with his mistress, the Countess Guiccioli, his dogs, his monkeys and a large retinue of servants who quarrelled incessantly. Shelley also wintered in Pisa, but the group of poets and their womenfolk was far from being a happy one.

The little Church of Santa Maria della Spina, on the same side of the river, was built in the thirteenth century, but over-restored in the nineteenth century. Its Gothic architecture is much admired by the Italians, though in fact this style is so foreign to them that it is rarely successful. The interior is worth visiting because of the remarkable statues of Nino Pisano and, in particular, a beautiful effigy in painted wood of the Madonna suckling the Child Jesus.

In the Museo Civico are many lovely early works by Tuscan artists of the twelfth and fourteenth centuries, and a delightful gentle *Madonna Adoring the Child* by Gentile da Fabriano, who seems to have wandered about all over Italy carrying out commissions.

The distance from Pisa to Florence is little over forty miles by the old road that follows the Valley of the Arno and passes through Empoli.

Since the trains are frequently crowded beyond endurance, it is more agreeable to do this journey by one of the comfortable C.I.A.T. coaches or one of the long-distance buses of the local transport companies.

Then the Arno road passes through a succession of towns and built-up areas, and the scenery is frequently screened by houses. The motorist cannot do better than take the *autostrada* that links Viareggio with Florence. Even though the distance is greater by ten miles, the time taken will be considerably less.

This highway bypasses Lucca, a town which is ideal for an overnight stay since it is far more cheerful than Pisa, and has a charming intimate atmosphere.

In the Middle Ages Lucca was a City State like Florence, then, after a brief period of domination by Pisa, it became a Republic with territories that included a brief strip of the coast near Viareggio, and some of the mountainous region behind it.

In 1799, the French occupied the whole of northern Italy, and in 1805, Napoleon created the Grand Duchy of Lucca for his sister Eliza Bacciochi. After the Battle of Waterloo, the former Republic was allotted to the Dukes of Parma, who ceded it to Tuscany in 1847.

The old town is still encircled by a complete ring of seventeenth-century ramparts on which have been planted broad avenues of trees.

Life within the walls is very animated, for Lucca is the centre of the olive oil industry, and the country people flock to the town to do business or to go to the market.

In spite of the many social and political changes, there is still the impression of small capital, for the Grand Ducal Palace fills up one side of the main square, and next to it is the charming Regency theatre built by Napoleon's sister.

The eleventh-century cathedral with its thirteenth-century façade like that at Pisa is an outstanding example of Romanesque architecture. Below the triple row of arcaded galleries is a magnificent equestrian statue of St Martin which is gracious in its composition and natural simplicity. The portals are decorated with bas-relief by Niccolo Pisano.

Chief among its treasures of art are the recumbent statues of Ilaria del Carretto by Jacopo della Quercia, the Volto Santo, an eleventh-century figure of the Crucifixion enshrined in a small temple designed by Civitali in 1482.

There are several other churches of note in Lucca, but perhaps the town's greatest charm is to be found in the narrow streets lined with medieval houses and palaces, and even towers and castellated buildings. The unpretentious taverns serve good healthy country food at moderate prices, and, until now, few tourists visit the city.

The *autostrada* is disfigured by countless posters, but it passes through pleasant scenery. On the northern side, some of the lower ranges of the Apennines succeed each other all the way to Florence.

The highway bypasses Montecatini, the most popular of Italian spas which has the broad avenues, the luxury shops and exhibition style buildings typical of such places all over the world.

Pistoia, twenty miles further on, is also bypassed, but it would undoubtedly be considered an art city of the first order were it not so near to Florence with its vastly superior attractions.

Seen from a distance, it has indeed some resemblance to Florence, for it lies in a plain at the foot of high mountains, and a domed church rises from among the red rooftops.

Next to the cathedral, with its tall thirteenth-century tower, there is also a black and white marble Baptistry, and there are many medieval palaces, but the finest of these are the Palazzo del Comune and the Palazzo di Giustizia in the Piazza del Duomo.

But Pistoia is noted most of all because of the lovely della Robias on the façade of the cathedral and the Ospedale del Cappo, which is a dependence of the Hospital of Santa Maria Novella in Florence.

CHAPTER THREE

FLORENCE

MANY people claim that Florence is the most beautiful city in the world, a claim difficult to dispute, for, apart from the splendour of its monuments, the great charm of its ancient streets and palaces, it is in a setting which seems to have been designed by nature as a background for the finest creations of man.

Unfortunately the approaches to the Tuscan capital do not tend to give the right impression of the wonders that it has to present, for the roads from the west pass through industrialized suburbs, and from this side, the traveller cannot see the domes, towers and belfries that form such a magnificent silhouette against the sky.

The first sight of Florence should be from the Piazzale Michelangelo, a square on an eminence two hundred feet high, on the south bank of the Arno, and yet quite near the centre of the city.

From the wide terrace, or better still from the steps of the Church of San Miniato a little further up, there is an astonishingly wide vista of the town and of the countryside.

Nearby the groves of cypresses and evergreen trees slope steeply down to the remaining strip of the ramparts with which Michelangelo encircled the city in the sixteenth century.

Then, beyond these walls, the red tiled roofs of a line of massive old palaces do not screen the jade green waters, or the glistening granite embankments on the north side of the river.

Two or three hundred yards inland the huge grey nave of the Church of Santa Croce dominates the surrounding houses, and its ugly, pencil-shaped belfry lunges upwards into the sky.

A little way to the left, Brunelleschi's deep orange dome and the gleaming marble of the cathedral stand out more sharply against a dark background of distant hills, whilst Giotto's tall square tower half hides the smaller dome of the Baptistry.

The battlements of the Signoria, the fortress residence of the medieval magistrates, rise up above the ridged roof of the Uffizi, the government offices of the Grand Dukes, and the line is con-

tinued by the buildings on the Ponte Vecchio, the most famous of
the old bridges that span the river.

The three-hundred-foot-high tower of the city fathers swells out
into more battlements near its summit, and is surmounted by the
open belfry of the *Vacca*, the deep-toned bell whose pealing
announces tidings of joy or sorrow to the citizens of Florence.

In the distance there are more domes, more huge palaces rising
out of russet rooftops, and here and there remain some of the grey
stone towers that served as strongholds and places of refuge in the
far-off days when the factions of the Black and White, the Guelf
and the Ghibelline, waged ceaseless war upon each other in the
narrow streets of the town.

At sunset, a golden radiance lends enchantment to the whole city,
and the old walls take on a roseate hue, the tiles glow a fiery red
and the black of the cypresses is turned to a warm brown.

The surface of the river glistens like silver, and the hills become
purple in the distance, whilst far away to the right, the mountains
of Vallombrosa become violet in the slanting rays of the sun.

Down in the valley, deep bells peel, and their ringing is echoed
by the shriller tones from village churches in the countryside.
Beyond the city in the grey-green of the olive groves, rise the towers
and walls of castles, and the huge villas built long ago by Florentine
patricians.

Windows gleam like diamonds in the fading light, but quickly
yet imperceptibly, the sky deepens, the stars appear and seem to
grow nearer, and the night comes upon us all too fast.

Fiesole, high up on the hill beyond the town, is crowned with a
diadem of brightness above the sparkle and flickering radiance of
the plain.

Fiesole, in fact, is more ancient than Florence, for it was an
Etruscan stronghold, inhabited long before the Romans settled on
the low-lying land of the riverside.

The town grew to importance under the Empire, but fell into
decay during the Barbarian invasions to rise again as a free city in
the eleventh century, and to become prosperous when the nobles of
the region left their estates to take part in the commerce of the town.

Under this arrangement the Florentines grew rich, in spite of the
constant dissensions that prevailed between the principal families of
the city. Apart from the personal rivalries and feuds there was the
problem created by the fact that the small republic was not strong

enough to do without the support of the Pope or the Emperor, and so, according to their allegiance, the people were either Guelf or Ghibelline, and the power shifted frequently from one party to the other.

Each time that there was a change, the leaders of the defeated faction were murdered, exiled, or forced to go into hiding.

Sometimes the Emperors were able to garrison Florence or place it under the jurisdiction of one of their nominees, but whenever the Imperial power was diminished, a popular rising would re-establish the Guelfs.

Within the city, the constitution of the Government was gradually modified, first of all to counter the influence of the nobles, and later, that of the richer merchants who were known as the *popolo grasso*, as opposed to the *popolo minuto*, who belonged to the guilds.

The guilds or *arti* gradually dominated the political scene, and in time, the number of the lesser guilds was augmented so that the *popolo minuto* was able to overthrow the *popolo grasso* who were nobles or merchants allied to the nobles.

In practice this meant little more than the fact that the representatives of the lesser guilds could take part in the government of the city, and some of these representatives were as rich as, if not richer than, the leaders of the aristocratic factions which they had dominated.

The great patrons of the Renaissance, therefore, were of the urban middle classes, and if their artistic sense was impeccable, their taste was not.

The strangest feature of the history of Florence is that, despite the turbulence of her citizens, continuous civil wars and revolts, and wars with the neighbouring city-states, the Florentines became wealthy. At first the main source of their wealth was the weaving and dyeing and selling of the wool from their own countryside. As in England, the production and sale of wool led to the creation of banks, for some debtors required credit, and others were afraid to send their gold by sea or by road.

So the Florentine financiers not only played an important rôle in commerce, but even in international politics, for the Peruzzis made loans to Edward III to enable him to pay for the expenses of his campaigns in France.

The English King never paid his debts and the Peruzzis were ruined, but they had taught the world that wars could be waged on credit, a lesson that has resulted in many millions of unnecessary deaths in the centuries that followed.

The thirteenth century had been a period of great prosperity for Florence, and for a while artists such as Cimabue and Giotto and Duccio flourished. New walls were built round the city, and Giotto's geometrical tower was built near the Baptistry, as well as the Palace of the Signoria.

Towards the end of this century, the dissensions between the Guelf and the Ghibelline were such that many citizens were put to death or exiled. Among the latter was the poet Dante who spent the last twenty-one years of his life as a refugee in different towns of northern Italy.

In 1348, the Black Death swept through Europe, taking a heavy toll of the population of Florence, and killing off three-quarters of the inhabitants of Siena which had been, until then, one of her principal rivals in Central Italy.

In the fifteenth century, the territories of the Republic were enlarged by the annexation of Pisa together with the region that lies immediately to the south of that city.

Gradually the democratic character of the administration disappeared to be replaced by oligarchic rule. For a while, two great families, the Albizzi and the Medici, strove for the domination of Florence, but in the end, Cosimo de Medici became the supreme authority. Though untitled, his wealth and power were such that he lived in a princely manner in the Palazzo Riccardi which he had constructed as well as the Church of San Lorenzo and the Monastery of San Marco.

He and his son, Lorenzo the Magnificent, are famous because they were the patrons of many of the greatest artists of the Italian Renaissance, and it was largely through the munificence of these two members of the Medici family that Florence became one of the greatest art centres that the world has ever known.

The Republic had extended its activities to the sea, and her ships traded with all parts of Europe, sailing from the stronghold of Leghorn, the base of the new and formidable navy. Amerigo Vespucci, a Florentine mariner, was destined to give his name to the mainland of America which he was to discover.

Lorenzo's successor, Piero, was unable to withstand the occupation of Florence by Charles VIII, King of France.

Shortly after the French withdrew, the monk Savonarola was

made lawgiver and introduced a theocratic government in which Christ was held to be Head of the State, which was ruled by an assembly of a thousand councillors.

Savonarola then began to put into practice the puritanical doctrines that he had been preaching for the past five years—the Carnival was forbidden, games and musical instruments were destroyed, and books and sensuous pictures were burnt on pyres in the squares of the city.

After three years of this strange régime, the Florentines grew tired of austerity, and the monk on his side grew more exacting and authoritative. At last he questioned the authority of the Pope and was excommunicated for refusing to desist from preaching.

Eventually Savonarola was seized by the mob, tortured, then hung and his body was burnt in the Piazza Signoria.

After various vicissitudes the Medici returned to Florence, and in 1532 Alessandro was made an hereditary duke by the Pope, and the title was held by the family until its extinction in the first part of the eighteenth century.

Cosimo I, who succeeded Alessandro, maintained the traditions of his predecessors, Cosimo *Pater Patriæ* and Lorenzo the Magnificent, by patronizing the arts. He founded the Academy of Florence and commissioned or bought many of the pictures and statues which are now in the Uffizi Gallery.

In 1569 he was created Grand Duke by the Pope, and was confirmed in this rank by the Emperor Maximilian II.

The territories of the Grand Duchy had been gradually extended by purchase, by conquest and by treaty, so that Tuscany now comprised Siena, Arezzo and Cortona, as well as some seventy-five miles of the coast that lies to the south of Pisa and to the north of Viareggio, which was still held by the Republic of Lucca.

In 1735, the Grand Duchy passed to Francis Duke of Lorraine, the husband of Maria Teresa. The first of the Habsburg princes were good rulers, and so under their reign Tuscany was one of the happiest and most prosperous of the Italian states.

At the beginning of the nineteenth century, Napoleon created the Kingdom of Etruria into which was incorporated the Grand Duchy, which he eventually revived for his sister, Eliza Bacciochi.

The Habsburgs returned in 1814 and remained in Florence until it became the capital of United Italy in 1860.

In 1871, the Government was transferred to Rome, and Florence was reduced to the level of a provincial city, but during the eleven years that had elapsed, some of the finest features of the city had been destroyed.

The greater part of Michelangelo's ramparts was pulled down, and many ugly buildings erected. The hideous Piazza della Repubblica was planned on the site of the historic old market, though this horrible piece of planning was not carried out until many years later.

For the past fifty years, the Fine Arts Department of the Italian Government and the local authorities have collaborated successfully in their efforts to preserve the ancient monuments of the city and also to prevent them from falling into decay.

If the country highways are marred by unsightly posters, the towns on the other hand have been kept clear of the signboards and tasteless advertising that so frequently mar the streets of ancient cities and villages in Great Britain. Shop signs and other forms of publicity are taxed and restricted to the minimum by effective legislation, and proprietors who alter and disfigure old buildings are compelled to restore them to their original condition at their own expense.

Fortunately the greater part of Florence has kept its original character, and most of the fine patrician palaces and the picturesque narrow streets of the centre have much the same aspect as they had a hundred and fifty years ago.

In spite of the wholesale destruction wrought during the Second World War throughout Italy, Florence escaped fairly lightly thanks to the policy of the Allies, who decided to encircle the town instead of attacking it frontally.

All the bridges except the Ponte Vecchio were blown up by the Germans before they retreated, and a number of buildings on either side of this bridge were completely destroyed.

The damage was restricted, but the houses wrecked on the river front were ancient and picturesque, and they have been replaced by structures that are in keeping with the surroundings, but are not complete restorations of what was there before.

From the scenic point of view the loss is irreparable even though the view of the Ponte Vecchio with its background of palaces, hills clothed with cypresses, and distant mountains is still incomparably beautiful. The pattern of the landscape has been completed so skilfully by the hand of man, and its harmony is such that one realizes at once why this countryside was so often used by the Florentine painters as a kind of backcloth to their religious pictures.

Here on the banks of the Arno, the light is clear, the colours are always strong yet mellow, and everywhere one is conscious of the splendid natural setting which adds so much to the charm of this unique city.

The destruction of the bridges was a great loss, and especially the wrecking of the Ponte Trinita whose arches of mellowed marble can never be replaced, however skilful the reconstruction may be.

The Ponte alla Carraia, designed by Ammanati in the sixteenth century, had already been rebuilt several times, but the main lines of the original plan had been kept, and have been used in the latest reconstruction.

The Cathedral and Baptistry are in the centre of Florence standing probably on the site of the Forum of the Roman city that flourished for so long and then disappeared leaving no traces after the repeated passage of Barbarian hordes.

Nevertheless, the Piazza San Giovanni is still the real hub of the town, for the Piazza della Repubblica, two or three hundred yards further south, is in fact a place for strolling or conversation at one of the numerous cafés that line the sides of the square.

I am inclined to think that most northerners experience a slight shock when they see the Cathedral, the Baptistry and Giotto's tower, for each of these three buildings is sheathed in the white and dark green marble that is quarried at Prato ten or twelve miles away.

So when the sun is shining, the walls, statues, pinnacles and towers gleam dazzlingly against the deep blue sky, and Brunelleschi's red dome soars upwards in the background behind them.

An architect of the greatest originality, Brunelleschi began as a silversmith, then he became a sculptor, and it was only after his designs for the doors of the Baptistry had been rejected that he found his true vocation.

As Pope Pius the Second observed, life in Renaissance Italy was extraordinarily fluid: a valet could become a king, and indeed men changed their trades and professions with the greatest of ease.

After a short stay in Rome, which doubtless inspired him to study the methods and the monuments of the ancients, Brunelleschi returned to Florence.

It was then that he planned the dome which some of his predecessors had thought of erecting, but recoiled before the technical difficulties of a project that was hard to realize with their limited knowledge of engineering problems. Indeed, one of these architects had suggested that a cupola should be built round a gigantic mound of earth which was to be removed once the structure was completed.

Brunelleschi's dome surpasses in height the Dome of St Peter's and is therefore the tallest of its kind in the world, and it was the first large cupola to be erected for many years.

It was a great triumph of engineering, but this technical achieve ment is dwarfed by the æsthetic success that was realized. It would be difficult to think of Florence without the beautiful dome of Santa Maria dei Fiore which rises so majestically from its rooftops and can be seen from all sides and from very far away. But Brunelleschi also built the huge and gloomy Pitti Palace, the Church of San Lorenzo which houses the statues of Night and Day by Michelangelo, and lastly, the lovely Pazzi Chapel at Santa Croce and the beautiful Church of Santo Spirito that so many casual visitors to Florence fail to see.

As I have already explained, the Baptistry of San Giovanni is older than the Duomo, and until the second half of the eleventh century it was actually used as a cathedral. No one knows precisely when this octagonal building was constructed—some authorities even suggest that it dates back to the sixth century, but it seems probable that it belongs to a later period, and was still quite new when reconsecrated in 1059 by Pope Nicholas.

Despite the constant changes in taste, the bronze gates remain among the greatest wonders of the world of art. The south gate was carried out by Andrea Pisano in the middle of the fourteenth century and depicts scenes from the life of St John the Baptist in a series of panels designed with the utmost restraint and simplicity. No confused background detracts from the dramatic impact of the figures and their beautifully wrought draperies.

The northern and eastern gates were both carried out by Lorenzo Ghiberti, who spent forty years of his life over the work. He obtained the commission in competition with many of the most famous sculptors of his time and the result proves that the judges were not mistaken.

The northern gate is the earlier of the two and by far the most satisfying æsthetically, in the sculptor's restrained use of the medium and in his respect for the limitations of his art. He depicts the events of the New Testament without any superfluous details and with superb dignity. He balances this austerity with the framework of the door which is decorated with a riot of delicate natural forms, flowers and birds and plants. Here he shows the effects of his early training as a goldsmith and his love of the delightful forms to be found in the countryside around him.

In the eastern gate, by far the more popular of the two, he lets his exuberance run away with him, not only in the borders, which are a miracle of foliage, fruit, birds and even an enchanting little squirrel munching a nut, but also in the panels themselves illustrating scenes from the Old Testament.

He goes far beyond the realm of sculpture and tries to depict in bronze things which can better be expressed in paint. He renders landscape, architecture, and perspective, both aerial and linear, with equal confidence. His questing Renaissance spirit sought to overcome the problems of realistic representation in bronze, and what Paolo Ucello had discovered about the use of perspective in painting he could interpret in relief.

The eastern gates are certainly a magnificent technical achievement and, of course, the amazingly realistic representation of detail has great popular appeal. There is no denying that these gates are most impressive in their original gilded splendour restored by cleaning, and Michelangelo, whose authority can hardly be questioned, acclaimed them as worthy to serve as the gates of Paradise.

Admittedly the façade of the Cathedral of Santa Mario dei Fiore is a very poor nineteenth-century imitation of early Tuscan art and it is very easy to be put off by the unpleasant colour and gloom of the interior. But, if you are seeking clean soaring lines, harmonious proportions, a feeling of space, unity and grandeur, you cannot but be satisfied with the design.

The walls seem empty, but it does give us a chance, rare in a cathedral, of admiring the bare architectural structure. Yet there are still individual works of art to delight us—the lovely Pieta which Michelangelo created in his old age, expressing deep tragedy and despair, the light blue and white of della Robbia's two plaques and the two magnificent equestrian frescoes painted by Ucello and Castagna.

The glorious *Singing Galleries* designed by Donatello and Luca della Robbia were removed into the Cathedral Museum in the seventeenth century, where it must be admitted they can be seen more easily, as can also the figures of the prophets recently removed from the Campanile. It is interesting to compare the work of the various sculptors—the strong movement of Donatello's dignified prophets, the lively robust flow of movement in his *Cantoria*, the gentle sweetness and grace of Luca's angels and the restful repose expressed by Andrea Pisano in his King David.

Assissi: the Church of St. Francis and the Umbrian hills

The Roman Forum: the Arch of Septimus Severus and the Temple of Mars

CHAPTER FOUR

FLORENCE (*CONTINUED*)

THE Uffizi was designed by Vasari in the sixteenth century to serve as administrative offices for Cosimo de Medici. The ancient church of San Pietro once stood on this site and some of the frescoed columns can still be seen.

Many people with only a few days to spare in Florence experience a feeling of dismay at the size of this gallery and at the number of paintings and pieces of sculpture of the first importance that it contains. They are afraid of getting tired and confused and of missing some of the things they had come especially to see. There is no need to despair for, after all, it is not so very difficult to concentrate on thirty or forty of the greatest treasures. They are all familiar from reproductions and one has only to glance quickly round each room on entering and single out the main paintings.

Although the gallery has works of art from many countries, the most important part of the collection is devoted to the Tuscan schools and it is as well to concentrate on these and the few outstanding pieces of classical sculpture rather than spend too much time over the Venetians which can be better studied in Venice, and the foreign schools whose principal collections are elsewhere.

The best of the classical works are in the Hall of the Tribune. There you will find the lovely, cream-coloured *Medici Venus*, a third-century Greek work; a kneeling slave of very lovely proportions; a group of wrestlers and the *Dancing Fawn* which is, perhaps, the most popular statue in this room. It has a lovely rhythmic movement and a strange, haunting smile.

You will find the paintings arranged chronologically and in schools, so it is comparatively easy to trace the development of painting from the thirteenth century and throughout the golden age of Tuscan Art and also have a little time to spare for the more famous works of the other schools.

It is interesting to compare the three early Madonnas by the Sienese and Tuscan schools. Cimabue's *Madonna* still has the stiff

D   49

conventional composition of the Byzantine school, but there is life in the faces of the Madonna and Child and a certain variety of pose among the angels who are grouped with a feeling of rhythm. These figures are already more than symbols. Giotto's interpretation of the same theme is a great advance in naturalism: the Virgin and Child are human, living people, capable of emotion; the angels have expressive faces and all the figures are solid with the third dimension stressed. It is difficult for us to realize what a revolutionary idea this was. In place of symbolic cold figures, the Bible characters are depicted as real solid people with emotional feelings. Sometimes, instead of a golden—heavenly—background, real trees and sky and landscape are introduced. From this time onwards the Gothic spirit in painting, architecture and sculpture was to take the place of the Romanesque and the Byzantine, and later, to blossom out into the full enquiring spirit of the Renaissance which sought to solve all problems connected with the realistic representation of nature.

Duccio's *Madonna* shows the Sienese love of rich colour, of delicate and harmonious design and of a certain gentleness of expression. Particularly lovely is the arabesque of the border to the Virgin's robe which flows over her knees and down to her feet on the steps of the throne. Simone Martini's *Annunciation* glows with gold and luminous colour and shows a wonderfully delicate touch.

In the fourteenth-century room, how lovely is the *Adoration of the Magi* by Gentile da Fabriano! The composition is perhaps rather overcrowded, but what marvellous detail and how lovingly he has painted the animals and birds and flowers, the patterns of the brocades and silks, the Child stretching forward to touch the head of the bearded king. Below, set in the frame, are small scenes from the New Testament delightfully observed—in particular the *Flight into Egypt*.

Fra Angelico's *Coronation of the Virgin*, with wonderful angelic figures bursting with heavenly song, glow against the radiance of the golden sky, in glorious soft shades of violet, olive green and pink in contrast to earlier painters' brilliant primary colour.

In the fifteenth century we have Masaccio's statuesque dignified figures, with long lines of heavy draperies, simple, dramatic and solidly formed.

If you have had a surfeit of religious pictures you can enjoy the lively movement of Ucello's *Battle of San Romano*. Astonishingly solid, wooden-looking rocking horses leap about; brilliant scarlet and golden lances cut across the composition; animals and figures prance over the felt hills; horses, riders, broken lances and pieces of armour lie precisely foreshortened and show Ucello's passion for solving problems of perspective. For me this picture is a constant source of delight with its mixture of exuberance and precision.

The charm of Filippo Lippi's graceful *Madonna* with the beautiful folded hands and the curiously ugly angels who lift up the child, prepares us for the even more rhythmic grace of Botticelli's two paintings—*The Birth of Venus* and the *Coming of Spring*.

These glorious, joyous paintings show fully Botticelli's wonderful mastery of line. The *Coming of Spring* is a miracle of grace and light, airy movement. A faint spring breeze trembles through the fragile draperies; delicate flowers bestrew the ground trodden by the bare feet of nymphs. The whole picture is a unity of continuous flowing lines leading to the graceful figure of Spring. The same qualities are to be found in the *Birth of Venus*, but the salt sea air flutters the garments and catches the ripples of the green-blue sea. Pink roses are lightly thrown across the picture and the fresh blowing breezes are here instead of enchanted, shadowy woods.

Botticelli's *Adoration of the Magi* is a glow of colour and gorgeous raiment. All the magnificence of Renaissance Italy is being laid at the Child's feet and the right-hand figure in the golden cloak is Botticelli himself, the portrait of a man who delighted in the pagan fantasies as well as being intensely religious, who loved colour and light and a dancing line, but who was also deeply moved by the fanatical outbursts of Savonarola.

The smaller scale of Francesca's portraits of the Duke and Duchess of Montefeltro, the statuesque repose of their calm faces and the delicious decorative Umbrian background are a welcome relaxation after the overwhelming greatness of Botticelli's genius.

We are again staggered by the genius of Leonardo in the half-finished, faded *Adoration of the Magi*, an unbelievably accomplished work carried out when he was still young, which already reveals his mastery of atmosphere and aerial perspective.

Raphael shows us all the ease and grace of the Umbrian school: the calm restful lakes, the feathery trees, the serene face of the Virgin, the charming affectionate gestures of the children stroking the goldfinch. The softness of the colours and the gentle grace are perhaps a shade cloying, but one cannot really fail to be moved by such perfection and it makes even greater the astringency of Michel-

angelo's robust strength, his mastery of form and composition, and
the terrific impact of life in his *Holy Family*. It is the work of a
sculptor interested more in form than colour, more in the problems
of anatomy and movement of the human figure, than in the
subtleties of light on landscape or the decorative value of flowers and
plants.

Gentle and charming is the warm glow of the flesh in Correggio's
Virgin Adoring. A warm-blooded gentle Virgin, lovingly kneeling
over a real baby, more human and lovable than Raphael's.

This brings us to the soft luxurious richness of the later Venetians,
flooded with golden light, always stressing colour, glowing, living
flesh, brilliant rich draperies.

Titian's warm, glowing *Venus* with the little dog is here, and the
famous *Flora*, whose warm flesh contrasts with the white gown and
the silky auburn hair falling over the rounded shoulder.

Veronese's dramatic *Annunciation* with its brilliant lighting,
whirling draperies and angel-filled clouds, is very different from the
Florentine interpretation of the same theme. This is the work of a
man primarily interested in paint and light, as were all the
Venetians, whereas the Florentines, frequently trained as sculptors
or goldsmiths, always clung to an outline and the concise explana-
tion of form. In the inevitable struggle between form and colour the
Florentines chose form and the Venetians colour, with the resultant
sacrifices.

Quite near the Uffizi is the Palazzo del Podesta or the Bargello,
the ancient Palace of the Podesta, which contains the national collections of sculpture and the minor arts.

This austere battlemented castle was for a time used as a prison
and takes its name from the Bargello or chief jailer. It contrasts
oddly with the elegant slim tower of the lovely little church of the
Badia where we can see Mino da Fiesole's gracefully designed tomb
to Count Ugo with its perfectly proportioned classical lines relieved
by delicately wrought garlands and a fine roundel of the Virgin
and Child in the semi-circular arch. Here also is the famous
Vision of St Bernard by Filippo Lippi, who manages to convey
an intensity of feeling into the composition although it is rather
crowded.

But it is in the Bargello that we find the works of the greatest of
the Florentine sculptors. The ground-floor rooms have collections of
armour and some early works by Michelangelo, the *Drunken*

Bacchus and a lovely roundel of the *Virgin and Child* as well as a portrait bust of the master by an assistant.

We have to cross the rather forbidding arcaded courtyard and climb the monumental flight of steps to reach the great Council Hall where there is a magnificent collection of Donatello's work. The arresting figure of St George, taken from its niche in the Orsanmichele, dominates the whole room. We turn to the sad gaze of the pathetic-looking figure of John the Baptist with beautifully modelled hands and arms and the decorative curls of the coarse hair of his goatskin. In contrast the bronze David, naked but for his curious little helmet, is vitally alive and suggests continuous flowing movement.

Here you can see the two panels submitted by the final contestants for the commission to carry out the bronze gates of the Baptistry: *The Sacrifice of Isaac* by Brunelleschi and Ghiberti.

It is interesting to compare Donatello's *David* with the one by Verocchio in another room. This latter is serene and sophisticated— a portrait of a charming boy in a close-fitting, beautifully designed tunic, standing confidently triumphant over the head of Goliath.

Here in the Bargello it is a delight to wander from room to room and get a complete picture of medieval and Renaissance Florence. There is a superb collection of della Robbia's coloured terracottas, of ceramics and ivories, of furniture and of medals with portraits of the great figures of the time. There is even a fresco—a portrait of Dante—attributed to Giotto, in the chapel.

On the other side of the river is the enormous yellow, rough-hewn stone Pitti Palace. Originally designed for Lucca Pitti, by Brunelleschi in the fifteenth century, it was considerably extended and a courtyard was added in the sixteenth century and, in the eighteenth century, the wings on to the square.

It has magnificent collections of china, majolicas, ivories and jewellery, but the visitor with but a few days to spare has only time to see the famous picture gallery.

It is an extraordinarily varied collection, as it was assembled over centuries by royal dukes including the Medici and the archdukes of Austria, each with a different taste in painting. The rooms themselves are sumptuously decorated, many of them with painted ceilings and elaborate carvings and furnishing. I think it is a particularly tiring gallery, for it is too large to give the feeling of an intimate private collection in a lovely house, and, as a national collection, it is badly lighted and confused. It does, of course, hold some outstandingly lovely paintings.

In Titian's *Concert* the expressive head of the young man is turned slightly away from us and the darkness of his dress accentuates the light on his hands and face. Perugino's *Deposition* is rather cloying in its sweetness but has a beautiful background.

Raphael's *Madonna del Granduca* is touching in its simplicity but the famous *Madonna of the Chair* is spoilt for me by the over-complacency of Mary, though the Child is lovable enough. The group, already a little restricted in the circular panel, is completely crushed by the massive and elaborately decorated frame.

One cannot help marvelling at the accomplishment of the well-known *Saint Sebastian* by Sodoma, although it misses any great inspiration. The body of the saint is skilfully balanced with the twisting tree, the angel floats gracefully in the air and the strange misty landscape recedes perfectly into the background, yet there is a touch of sentimentality which breaks the dramatic effect.

After so much looking at pictures, it is a delightful rest to wander in the Boboli Gardens, which form a perfect setting to the Pitti Palace and relieve it of some of its austerity.

The classical garden with its amphitheatre is used for outdoor performances. Great terracotta vases, delightful nymphs, terraces and fountains, contrast with informal paths that lead up the hillside over which the gardens are spread. There are wonderful views of the Palazzo Vecchio, the cathedral and Giotto's tower through cypress, ilex and pine trees which cast their long shadows over the sandy paths and the green lawns.

Although both the Uffizi and the Pitti contain representative collections of Italian paintings, we must look in churches, palaces and monasteries if we want to see the best of some masters' work. For Masaccio we have to go to the Brancacci Chapel in the Carmine, for Fra Angelico, to the monastery of San Marco, and for Benozzo Gozzoli, to the Medici Chapel in the Riccardi Palace.

The Church of the Carmine is only a few minutes' walk from the Pitti Palace on the same side of the river. At first sight it is rather a dull church with no especial architectural attraction, but the little Brancacci Chapel has inspired painters from all over the world who come to see the frescoes by Masolino, and his pupil, Masaccio. Here, beside the work of his master, one can study the majestic, dramatic compositions of Masaccio who was born at the turn of the fifteenth century and is the earliest of the masters of the Florentine Renaissance. Although he died at the age of twenty-eight, his influence on painting was tremendous. He breaks away from the suave elegance of the fourteenth century and, influenced by the splendid achievements of the Florentine sculptors, more especially those of his older contemporary, Donatello, he treats form three-dimensionally in brilliant light and shade and he infuses his characters with a dynamic force and an imposing dignity.

The Expulsion from the Garden of Eden is one of the miracles of the world of painting. No one can fail to be moved by the desperate tragedy of the two despairing human beings cast into the desolation outside the Garden of Eden and we cannot but agree with Vasari who said that here, in the Carmine, was to be found "the real cradle of beautiful painting".

To see the work of the other outstanding genius of the early fifteenth century, we have to cross over the river to the Piazza San Marco and to the monastery where Fra Angelico lived and painted, which is now a permanent museum of his work.

Masaccio and Fra Angelico were entirely different personalities, but they had this in common: they were both passionately interested in the technique of painting and in discovering new and better methods of expressing themselves. Masaccio found out how to simplify his figures and give them monumental solidity, at the same time making them intensely dramatic and often tragic; Fra Angelico was happy to express gentleness and saintliness, but he was also a magnificent draughtsman and one of the greatest colourists of any time or school. His glorious tones of pink and green, violet and purple had not been used by earlier painters and they have a subtlety which has never been surpassed. He is often thought of as the painter-saint—which he certainly was—but it is less often realized what great discoveries he made in the use of delicate and brilliant colours perfectly harmonized together.

Here in the monastery of San Marco we have a chance to see some of his work in its original setting, for here we have not only the famous altar-pieces by the Dominican painter, but also the frescoes painted on the walls of the cells.

Not far away, in the Palazzo Riccardi, is the small windowless Medici Chapel where Benozzo Gozzoli painted by torchlight the glorious processional *Adoration of the Magi*.

He took this opportunity to record in the journey to Bethlehem portraits of the Medici family, the Emperor Palealogus, Sigismondo Malatesta and a self-portrait among the cortège of Florentine notabilities against a background of the Tuscan countryside. Especially lovely is the young Lorenzo da Medici, magnificently dressed, astride his white horse, gay with almost oriental trappings.

These frescoes are far removed from the grandeur of Masaccio's work and the delicacy and piety of Fra Angelico's, but they reveal superb craftsmanship and a lovely sense of design.

Nearby, the rough brick façade of San Lorenzo, designed by Brunelleschi, has the look of a well-proportioned, unfinished or even temporary structure. In its austere but impressive interior are some late works by Donatello, and preserved in the New Sacristy are the world-famous Medici tombs by Michelangelo. *Night* and *Day*, *Twilight* and *Dawn* are too familiar by copy and photograph for me to describe them. Better to free one's mind from all preconceived ideas about these superb sculptures and let the impact of the originals have its own fresh effect on us.

You cannot stay in Florence without seeing two copies of Michelangelo's *David*—one in the Piazza Signoria and one in the Piazzale Michelangelo, but for the original in its colossal perfection, you have to go to the Academy of Fine Arts where it is set up in a rotunda and very well lighted. To me it is almost terrifying in its perfection and vitality—it is living flesh recreated in marble. Only a giant like Michelangelo could do this without breaking the limitations of sculpture.

Just behind the Accademia, the Piazza della Santissima Annunziata is one of the most beautiful squares in Florence, and, in its own individual way, of Europe, and yet it is characterized by the greatest simplicity.

It is surrounded on three sides by arcades and decorated with busts of Medici Grand Dukes. The equestrian statue of Ferdinand I is by Gian Bologna, the sculptor from the north of France who achieved fame in Italy.

Over the arches of the Foundling Hospital are the roundels of the Circumcision of the Holy Child by Andrea della Robbia—touching little portraits of a baby in blue and white glaze that can be seen in reproduction in nearly every country in the world.

Over the door of the chapel of the Hospital is an Annunciation by Lucca della Robbia.

From a distance, the immense Church of Santa Croce appears to be so hideous that there is little inducement to approach it, and far less to go inside. Nevertheless, every serious student of Italian art and history should visit what Byron called "the Westminster Abbey of Florence". Within its walls are buried Galileo, Michelangelo, Machiavelli and Manin, the gallant defender of Venice, as well as such distinguished foreigners as the Duchess of Albany and King Joseph Bonaparte.

For centuries the principal families of Florence used Santa Croce as a place of sepulture and, in some cases, their tombs are in chapels which were specially constructed for the purpose.

In the Middle Ages, the Florentines played the game of *calcio* or football in the vast square that extends in front of the church.

Even from nearby, the exterior of Santa Croce is unprepossessing, for the tall, thin, pointed tower is hideous, and the marble façade, erected at the expense of an Englishman in the nineteenth century, is tasteless.

Once through the portals, the impression is a different one, for this church is, next to the Basilica at Assisi, the most important building erected by the Franciscans, and it was begun in the last years of the thirteenth century. The Italians seldom knew how to interpret Gothic architecture, but here it is at its best—the flat wooden roof rests on simple pointed arches of noble proportions, and little attempt is made at useless ornamentation.

Since there are no less than seventy tombs and many monuments, I must content myself by pointing out only the most noteworthy as, for instance, the magnificent bas-relief of the *Annunciation* by Donatello and the large Crucifix by the same sculptor.

In an oval, on the right of the main entrance, a Madonna and Child by Rossellino is a full relief in which all the tenderness of motherhood is expressed with the reverence due to this subject.

On this side also is the entrance to the fourteenth-century cloisters that lead into the Pazzi Chapel, designed by Brunelleschi and decorated with medallions by the della Robbias.

Though Giotto painted frescoes in four of the chapels of Santa Croce, most of his work has been effaced by time.

In the Peruzzi Chapel, however, we may still see one of the masterpieces of this great artist, the *Scenes from the Life of St Francis*, which is without any doubt the greatest treasure in this church.

In a neighbouring chapel, a pupil of Giotto's executed mural paintings of the *Life of San Silvestro*, but in this case, though the technical skill is great, the inspiration and feeling are lacking.

The Church of Santa Maria Novella is, in a sense, the sister church of Santa Croce, for it was built in the same century and in much the same architectural style. The exterior has not suffered from any form of restoration, and the excellence of its proportions is such that Michelangelo expressed the greatest admiration of its beauty.

The immense square in front of the church was used for chariot racing, a sport that was revived in the seventeenth century.

Santa Maria contains such a wealth of art treasures that here again I will only mention two or three of the most notable.

On the wall, to the right of the main entrance, Masaccio's *Crucifixion with the Saints* is rightly considered to be one of the masterpieces of Florentine painting.

Another picture of note is Duccio's *Madonna* in the chapel of the Rucellai family.

But the Green Cloisters, despite the sad state of the frescoes, remain the chief point of interest in Santa Maria Novello. The strange green, grey and white of these marvellous paintings by Ucello, only a shadow of what they once were, show his remarkable command of composition and his feeling for space. His austere figures intensify the drama of the great stories of the *Creation, The Flood,* and *The Expulsion from the Garden of Eden.* He also invests all the animals with the same kind of nobility expressed in the horses of his famous battle pieces—one in the Uffizi, another in the National Gallery—and everywhere in these faded pictures, the direction of his lines and his knowledge of linear and aerial perspective combine to lead our gaze into the furthest depths of the composition.

If you have time to spare and are interested in Etruscan art, there is a wonderful collection in the Archæological Museum, but it is not the subject of a casual visit. Once you pass through the charming garden into the galleries you find the exhibits of such absorbing interest that you will have to return again and again, and it will probably inspire you to prolong your stay in Italy in order to visit the Etruscan tombs and see the original wall paintings.

CHAPTER FIVE

LIFE IN FLORENCE : THE VIA TORNABUONI :
THE CHARM OF OLD STREETS : THE CASCINE :
THE SOUTH BANK OF THE ARNO : THE
PIAZZALE MICHELANGELO : FIESOLE :
THE COUNTRY SUBURBS

FOR the past two hundred years, travellers of all nationalities
have visited Florence, and many of them settled in the city or
in villas in the neighbouring countryside. They were attracted,
not only by the monuments and treasures of art, but also by the
cheapness and pleasantness of life in Tuscany. So, for instance, in
1847, the Brownings were delighted to discover that for less than
two hundred and fifty pounds a year they could afford to rent a
comfortable flat, keep a carriage and two horses and a manservant
as well as two or three maids. Food of excellent quality was
abundant and inexpensive, and the middle-class British and Americans could mix freely with the Florentine aristocracy.

There were, of course, certain disadvantages, for the heat in
summer is excessive. In winter the climate is cold and damp, as an
icy wind blows down from the snowy heights of the Apennines, and
the huge rooms of the old palaces with their marble floors are difficult to warm. However, in the spring and in the autumn, the air is
mild, the sun shines on most days and the blue skies and clear light
enhance the beauty of the buildings and of the landscape.

So, for just over a hundred years, between 1830 and 1930, there
was a large colony of foreigners in Florence, and of these some four
or five thousand were British or American. The Anglo-Saxons had
their own doctors, chemists, bakers, bankers and house agents, and
even, at times, their own newspapers.

Not only did they bring a lot of money into the town, but they
restored many fine old palaces and villas, and contributed hand-
somely to local charities and institutions.

When I was young, for some years I edited an English paper in
Florence. I lived in an old house in the Costa San Giorgio, a steep

alley that climbs straight up the hill at the southern extremity of the Ponte Vecchio. From the window of my room I could see the tall tower of the Signoria, Giotto's tower, and the hills of Fiesole on the far side of the valley. In the summer, nightingales sang in the tiny garden, and, at the back, there was the noise of the slums, the shouting and the quarrelling, and of course the serenading of ladies that went on until the early hours of the morning.

In the evening I used to dine very frequently at the Nuova Toscana, a pleasant tavern in the Piazza Signoria, because it was there that men of letters such as Norman Douglas, Scott Moncrieff, Reginald Turner, Aldous Huxley and Ezra Pound congregated.

The food was cheap and good, and the wine really excellent, and so the hours would pass pleasantly, especially if the weather was warm enough for us to sit at one of the tables outside.

Sometimes the moon shone on the marble statues in the Square, and the clear light would bathe the huge figure of Neptune rising out of the fountain in the centre, and the equestrian effigy of Grand Duke Cosimo I, by Giovanni Bologna, who came, it is believed, from Boulogne in France.

The Loggia dei Lanzi was named after the Swiss lancers of Cosimo I, but the fine round arches, supported on well-proportioned pillars, were erected in 1336, two hundred years before the Duke began to reign.

The Loggia is composed of three open arches that enclose a platform raised by steps above the level of the Square.

Of the many statues that are sheltered under the vaulted roof, the most noteworthy are Cellini's triumphant figure of Perseus holding up the head of Medusa, and the *Rape of the Sabines* by Gian Bologna.

Near the entrance of the Palazzo Vecchio stands a copy of Michelangelo's *David*, and opposite, Bandinelli's *Hercules and Cacus* to serve as sort of gateposts to the entry. The stone lion, the *Marzocco*, was the heraldic symbol of the city of Florence, and in the Middle Ages, prisoners were made to kiss the backside of this animal as a sign of submission.

The cool shaded courtyard is surrounded by arcades with Renaissance decorations. In the centre of the fountain by Verrocchio a lively Cupid plays with a dolphin.

I have had frequent occasion to visit the interior of the Palace, for during the Second World War it was used as the headquarters of the Allied Control Commission. The immense Council Hall of the Five Hundred is decorated with scenes depicting incidents in the history of Florence. They are interesting as records, but dull as paintings, for their creator, Vasari, was an indifferent artist though an excellent historian.

The chapel, where Savonarola spent the night prior to his execution, is notable because of the fine frescoes on the walls and ceiling by Ghirlandaio.

In the latter part of the sixteenth century, the Signoria became the residence of the Grand Dukes, and so a wing was added by Vasari and also a corridor through the Uffizi and over the Ponte Vecchio to give direct communication with the Pitti Palace.

Incidentally, some of the shops that line the sides of the Ponte Vecchio are worthy of attention, especially the jewellers whose pearls and diamonds are so valuable that they have to be lowered into special safes buried in the bed of the Arno.

The Via Borgo San Jacopo was badly damaged during the war, but it is here that you will find silversmiths whose families have been plying their trade for centuries, and they are such good craftsmen that they will make almost anything to order, or do the most complicated repairs.

The lacemakers and embroiderers are to be found in most streets of the centre, but some of the best of them have shops on the north bank of the Arno, and the same is true of the leather merchants who not only follow the traditional designs, but make handbags and pochettes in the prevailing fashion.

A few hundred yards from the northern extremity of the Ponte Vecchio is the Mercato Nuovo, commonly called the *Porcellino,* because of the bronze statue of a wild boar on the steps of a fine sixteenth-century loggia which shelters the stalls where flowers and straw hats are sold.

In the days of the Republic, debtors could find asylum here when they were pursued by their creditors, and, embedded in the pavement, is a round stone on which the bankrupt were forced to sit.

This stone is shaped like the wheel of the *Carroccio,* the chariot which the medieval Florentines took into battle as a kind of emblem and rallying point, but also because the presence of this vehicle was believed to be a portent of victory.

Or San Michele or field of San Michael was originally an open Loggia built in the thirteenth century, but a hundred years later the walls were built in to form a chapel for the principal crafts of the city. The guilds are therefore represented by statues of their patron saints, so there is a St Mark for the linen drapers and a St Peter for the butchers, both of them by Donatello. St Peter for the bankers and St John and St Stephen for weavers are the work of Ghiberti.

The splendid altar serves as a shrine for a Virgin by Bernardo Daddi, who was one of the leading exponents of the School of Giotto.

The windows of this small chapel are also of the fourteenth century and their vivid colours bathe the interior with a mystic light.

In Florence, however, there are so many monuments of note that few visitors can spare the time to see them all, and in a sense the street scene is of such attraction that it is a pity not to spend hours in wandering casually through the city to enjoy the beauty that can be found at every corner. So, for instance, I like to stroll down the narrow Corso, and its continuation, the Borgo degli Albizzi, where some of the finest of the patrician palaces cast deep shadows over the busy movement of shopper and vehicles. When the traffic is too dense, one can turn into the little lanes to seek out the old-fashioned *trattorie* patronized by the peasants who bring in their produce from the neighbouring countryside. The fare is abundant and good, especially the steaks, the mushrooms (fungi), and dishes such as kidneys or breast of chicken fried in butter.

In such places the wine on draught is of the best, though in my opinion far too strong to be drunk in quantities before nightfall, for when the sun is high it is apt to make me very sleepy.

Despite the charm of these old and rather popular quarters, I find that after a while I am ready to turn to the elegance of the Via Tornabuoni, the Bond Street of Florence which starts at the northern extremity of the Ponte Trinita. Here, though this thoroughfare is far from broad, there is relative space, quiet and dignity, and in spite of changed times, the atmosphere is an aristocratic one. The shops display rather expensive goods, but they are in the best of taste and attractively arranged.

If the middle classes congregate in the Piazza della Repubblica, and the bulk of the tourists take their drinks in the Piazza Signoria, the élite is to be found in the Via Tornabuoni.

At twelve o'clock the remaining members of Florence's oldest families come to Doney e Nipoti, the oldest and the smartest café in the town, and certainly the most exclusive. The well-dressed habitués have known, liked or hated each other for many generations, but here at any rate survives the urbanity of a past age. The place figures in many nineteenth-century memoirs—the Brownings and the Landors mingled with English lords, Austrian princes and Italian counts to discuss duels and racing or the scandals of the Grand Ducal Court over a glass of Marsala or of Vermouth.

Times have changed, for millionaires and expatriates of wealth prefer to sun themselves in the West Indies or in Florida. Russian Grand Dukes live modestly on the Riviera, and exiled monarchs seek refuge in Portugal. Nevertheless, a few staunch habitués still linger to drink potent Negroni or Scotch whisky, and nibble delicious barquettes of caviar or foie gras, and enjoy good conversation.

Giacosa's, on the opposite side of the street, provides more or less the same amenities, but it is the traditional haunt of the smarter Anglo-Saxon residents and their Italian friends, and so the drinks flow a little faster and the verbal comments are rather slower, though the writers and painters of pre-war days have long since disappeared, and their fame, alas, has dwindled too.

Nevertheless, the Via Tornabuoni still preserves its ancient charm and character for smartness—the dressmakers who make their debut here may well, like Schiaparelli, open up branches in Paris, London and New York, though she did begin in Florence.

In this street also there are two of the best bookshops in Europe, but the Via Tornabuoni takes its real atmosphere from the splendid palaces that line it continuously on either side.

At the northern extremity, the Palazzo Antinori in the Square of the same name was built in the fifteenth century and faces the Baroque church of Sant Gaetano.

Further on the left-hand side of the Via Tornabuoni, the huge mass of the Palazzo Strozzi overshadows all its neighbours, for it was intended to be the largest and most splendid patrician residence of the city. The rough-hewn stone façade is adorned with immense wrought-iron lanterns of a pattern which has been copied in every part of the world.

The palace opposite, at the angle of the Via della Vigna Nuova, was the home of a wealthy but mysterious Scottish nobleman who settled in Florence in the sixteenth century.

Continuing southwards past the porches where women sell their flowers, along the deeply shaded street one comes upon the small Piazza Trinita with the splendid baroque church and on to the riverside where the battlemented Palazzo Spini and the house of Alfieri face each other.

It is delightful to stroll along the Lung Arno Corsini in the full sunshine, and enjoy the view of the mellow tinted houses on the opposite bank and, rising above them, the towers and domes of churches, the hills crowned with cypresses, large villas and ancient castles.

The huge cream-coloured Palazzo Corsini with its terraces, its lines of statues set at intervals on the edge of its flat roof, lends a touch of dignity to the scene, for the medieval Florentines were austere. Their successors in the early Renaissance were perhaps too exuberant, too anxious to display their wealth and power, but in the decline of the seventeenth century came the measure and order which has a pleasing quality of its own.

As one progresses to the west, the streets grow wider, the buildings more modern, for this is the airy Cascine quarter where live the Florentines who have grown weary of the chill halls of the ancient palaces, and the stuffiness of the older regions of the city.

The Cascine is a fine park by the riverside. Once the private property of the Grand Dukes, it was laid out as pleasure gardens by the Princes of the House of Lorraine.

In the nineteenth century, fashionable people used to drive here in their carriages, and so in the day-time the Cascine was the meeting-place of Florentine society.

I have never liked this park, for the foliage of the evergreens is dull and dusty, there are few flowers, and I infinitely prefer walking on the hills outside the city.

In any case, I have always found that Florence itself is ideal for strolling, especially in the early morning and at night.

I am particularly fond of the Oltr' Arno, the quarter that lies on the south bank of the river, and especially of the district that stretches between the Via Guicciardini and the Via dei Serragli.

The Borgo San Frediano that lies to the west of it is a slum, certainly less dirty than in the past, but it is necessary to pass through it in order to reach the Church of the Carmine, with its noted frescoes.

Years ago I lived for some months in the Piazza Santo Spirito, and I still have memories of the summer nights when there was tinkling of guitars under the trees through which could be heard the soft trickle of the fountain. On one side, the white fiddle-shaped façade of the church built by Brunelleschi, stood out clearly against

Rome: the Fontana di Trevi

The façade of
St. Peter's and
Bernini's
colonnade

an indigo sky spangled with stars. The darkness concealed the shabbiness of the palaces without hiding their noble proportions. Few tourists frequent this square, for there is nothing spectacular to see, nothing to publicize, and yet the harmony of Santo Spirito has given me lasting pleasure, and I never fail to come here whenever I am in Florence.

In the late evening too, when the rush of traffic has died down, one can enjoy glimpses into dimly-lit old courtyards with massive wrought-iron gates, and splendidly designed lanterns suspended under huge doorways. Immense stone coats of arms are placed high above each portal, and the broad overhanging eaves cast deep shadows over the narrow streets such as the Via Santo Spirito, the Via Maggio and the Via Maffia.

Since my tastes are simple, I often drop into one of the wine shops for a plate of spaghetti, a hunk of cheese and some fruit with a half fiasco of draught Chianti which is sometimes rough but always palatable with a meal of this kind.

The local customers are usually very friendly, and their curious sing-song Tuscan dialect is quite pleasing in spite of the harsh guttural C's which give their speech a quaint intonation.

If the reconstruction of Florence in the nineteenth century was foolish and lacking in taste, some excellent planning was accomplished on the fringes of the city.

Outside the Porta Romana, the southern exit of Florence, a new area of parks and villas was laid out through which wind broad avenues planted with elms, oaks, chestnuts and cypresses. These Viale dei Colle (hillside avenues) twist and turn up the hillside until they reach the broad Piazzale Michelangelo from which there is the view of Florence described fully in Chapter Three.

A beautiful avenue of cypresses leads up to the Church of San Miniato, built in the eleventh century in honour of a Florentine saint who was martyred in the third century.

The whole structure, inside and out, is encased in light-coloured marble, but the effect is pleasing and far from garish. Next to the cathedral at Pisa, this building is in fact one of the finest examples of Tuscan Romanesque, because of the excellent harmony of its proportions and interior decoration.

At the far end of the choir the huge mosaic representing Our Lord crowning San Miniato is Byzantine in character though it was in fact executed in the fourteenth century.

E

The cypresses of the old cemetery, the oaks and pines of the nearby groves make a fitting setting to this beautiful church in its really admirable site.

The view from the terrace outside the main porch is even more comprehensive than the prospect from the Piazzale Michelangelo below.

By great good fortune, the nineteenth-century architects who planned the development of Florence were wise enough to preserve a green belt around the city, and they took care to ensure that the greater part of the farmland remained untouched.

So, in most directions, enchanting country is within easy reach of the centre. For instance a narrow alley named the Costa San Giorgio leaves the southern extremity of the Ponte Vecchio, passing under an archway to climb steeply through a picturesque slum and reach one of the old gateways of the city six hundred yards further on. From this point it is known as the Via San Leonardo, a lane that passes between pink-washed walls overhung with branches of olives and other fruit trees. The big wrought-iron gates of ancient villas afford glimpses into courtyards and gardens. In places, a fold in the ground opens up vistas of small farms, bounded by Michelangelo's massive ramparts, and beyond them the towers and spires of Florence. By crossing the Viale dei Colle, this walk can be continued right up to the heights crowned by the Torre del Gallo, but all the way there are villas, gardens and little farmsteads.

On the summit of the hill, a turn to the left leads to still more open country, for the rustic road follows the line of a high ridge with vast expanses of olive groves on either side. To the south there are the rolling hills and dales that stretch for many miles towards Siena. To the north, the vineyards and orchards appear to descend right down to the edge of the Arno. The hills and mountains across the valley are turned to deep blue or violet by the distance. Indeed the landscape with its features of cypresses, church towers, castles and huge medieval villas contains all the elements that the Renaissance painters employed as backgrounds for their religious pictures —Nature here has been almost too abundant with her gifts, but man has known how to use them well.

The return to Florence can be made by going on through the little hamlet of Arcetri, and then descending the hill to the eastern suburbs of Florence.

On the south side of the Arno, the village of Bellosguardo to the west of the Porta Romana is another delightful objective for a walk in the early morning or afternoon, and here again, there are farms, villas and castles, and another magnificent prospect of the town and its surroundings.

Fiesole, perched a thousand feet up above the river valley, can be reached by a trolley car that winds up the steep road past immense villas, gardens and olive groves. After about twenty minutes, the bus glides into the square of the ancient little city which is in fact older than Florence itself, for it was an Etruscan Citadel, and ruins of the massive walls still remain.

A Roman theatre in a beautiful rustic setting of hills and farmland is used in the summertime for performances of classical plays and modern tragedies.

The Bishop's Palace was erected in the eleventh century at the same time as the beautifully proportioned little cathedral. Nearby, the town hall is decorated with the coats of arms of the local notables, for Fiesole was at one time a little republic, administered in much the same way as Florence.

In the summertime, tourists come in large numbers to visit the monastery or simply to drink or eat at one of the restaurants and enjoy the view from their terraces that overlook Florence and the Valley of the Arno.

A country lane through gardens and villas descends to the gates of Florence, and since it is a short cut, the trip takes little more than an hour. I have used this route many times, sometimes in the height of summer, at other times in winter when the snow lent a strange and exciting magic to the landscape, but I have enjoyed it most of all in June when the nightingales sing on every tree, and the air is spangled with fireflies.

Another excursion which I can commend is to take a rather rough path across to the woods that surround the Castle of Vincigliata, which was at one time the stronghold of Sir John Hawkswood, noted English condottiere in the Middle Ages.

From there field paths lead to Settignano, a delightful village which has not been commercialized as much as Fiesole.

When the weather is propitious there is nothing that I like better than to take a trolley bus out into the country and dine at a little *trattoria*. The food is simple but good, the wine is excellent and the innkeepers kindly and hospitable. Nearly all these places have out-door terraces or gardens where one can eat a meal at leisure in a really attractive setting.

Of the other outings that I can suggest, one of the most agreeable is to go eastwards on foot along the south bank of the Arno to one of the several riverside taverns with gardens by the waterside. The Florentines seldom use this track because of the snakes that rustle through the grass, but in the daytime these reptiles are easily avoided.

Further afield the Carthusian monastery at Galluzzo is a charming example of a medieval monastic house.

Baroque ornamentation has been added to the Gothic structure but the result is not altogether displeasing. The Certosa, as it is called in Italian, is situated on the top of a high hill which has to be climbed on foot, but the gardens and cloisters are cool and shady and the monks make and sell a liqueur from the same recipe as the French Chartreuse.

I am allergic to golf, but I have nothing against the Florence course, which has been laid out among pinewoods and hills ten or twelve miles out of the town. The clubhouse is up to date, the swimming pool is superb, and British and American visitors are given a warm welcome.

CHAPTER SIX

FLORENCE : AREZZO : TRASIMENE : PERUGIA : ASSISI : SPOLETO : TERNI : ROME

THE shortest and most convenient road from Florence to Rome passes through Siena, Pienza, Montepulciano, Orvieto and Viterbo, but since it is my intention to describe this route in a subsequent chapter, I will content myself with mentioning its existence.

Then also, whenever I did not wish to return to Florence, I have sometimes made my way home from the Italian capital by the Adriatic coast or along the shores of the Tyrrhenian Sea by Civita Vecchia, Grosseto, Leghorn and Genoa.

However, if I had to plan an itinerary, I should use the two inland routes which offer far greater scenic and artistic attractions. The coastal road from Rome to Leghorn is only moderately interesting and in places the landscape is really dull.

Once or twice I have effected a successful compromise by going to Siena first of all and then taking a reasonably good, cross-country road to the Lake of Trasimene and continuing to Rome through Perugia and Assisi.

Nevertheless, if I were on my first trip to Italy, I should hate to miss seeing the Valley of the Upper Arno, Arezzo, Orvieto, the Lake of Bolsena and the Lake of Bracciano.

In Central Italy most of the secondary roads are viable, but it is just as well to find out beforehand if they are under repair or in a poor condition. I am always glad to avoid using the great highways, especially when, as in Italy, they are disfigured by hideous posters. As a rule, most country inns and taverns north of Rome are clean and serve adequate food, though the meat may be tough and heavily flavoured with garlic. The *pasta* are always good, but the quality of the wine varies considerably from place to place.

In towns such as Arezzo, Siena, Perugia, Orvieto and Viterbo, there are plenty of restaurants of different categories, but the further one goes to the south, the more they tend to deteriorate in the smaller places.

In Italy, as in France, I have always found it more practical to have a picnic lunch, bought at a *rosticceria* where a large variety of cooked meats are sold and placed, on request, in cardboard containers. Many of these shops also stock fruit, wine and cheese, bread and cakes, and bottles of mineral water flavoured with genuine fruit juice can be obtained almost anywhere. All these mineral waters are delicious, but it is easier and cheaper to buy them from a local spring, for there are spas in every province of Italy.

In village inns, omelettes are frequently made with olive oil, but if the oil is sound the result is palatable. Personally I do not care for the omelettes to which artichoke leaves have been added, for these vegetables are tough and stringy, and the green part tastes like old rope.

For the first few miles the road follows the Valley of the Arno, in this region, a broad fast stream on a rocky bed with pools and shallows where peasants fish and seldom make a catch. The scenery is typical of the landscapes which the primitive Florentines used as backgrounds to their religious pictures.

Long lines of black cypresses climb up the slopes of silvery-grey hills surmounted by battlemented castles or red-roofed villages. Monasteries lurk in hollows or perch on inaccessible heights; peasant women with babies and watching cattle form Nativity scenes under the spreading eaves of pink-washed cottages, whilst their husbands lash straw with their whirling flails.

A twist or turn of the road and the river reappears, spanned by the curving arch of an ancient stone bridge, and, on the banks, rustle the tall reeds from which fifteenth-century Elders may have watched Susanna bathing her white limbs in the brown rippling waters of the stream.

In the background rises the dark green mass of Vallombrosa, still clad with the dense shady forests of oaks and chestnuts that Milton admired so much. In winter the snow-covered slopes attract the skiers from Florence and Arezzo; in summer visitors who have fled from the heat of the plain come here to be cool.

The ancient monastery is now little more than a pleasant feature in the landscape, but parts of the building have been transformed into an hotel and there are a number of inns and pensions.

The views over the Valley of the Arno are magnificent, and so a leisurely traveller may well find it profitable to leave the highroad and spend the night in the coolness of Vallombrosa.

At Pontassieve, a road branches off northwards to Forli and Ravenna, and then, a little way outside the picturesque old town, there is a choice of two different routes. The first entails a three-thousand-feet climb up the steep Consumma Pass, and down into a charming but fairly desolate region known as the Casentino, and through Poppi and Bibbiena, two ancient little cities with remnants of fortifications, castles, towers and small primitive palaces built in the early Middle Ages. I was snowed up in Poppi many years ago, and I have seldom been colder, for at that time the only available form of heating was from huge copper charcoal braziers which gave out fearful fumes and little or no warmth.

The second and shorter road has fewer attractions, for it passes through a district where there are many small coalmines and factories which do, in fact, little to spoil the aspect of the country-side.

Shortly after leaving Pontassieve, the road rises and passes through a woodland of mountain oaks whose bright green leaves are a wel-come change from the dull silvery-green foliage of the olive trees that does, after a while, tend to become monotonous.

To the west, stretches the long low line of Chianti Hills which are rarely more than seven or eight hundred feet above the level of the river valley. Their slopes are patched with different shades of green and grey, the greens of the vines, the olives and the chestnut trees, the grey of the earth, the rocks and the dusty olive leaves.

In the remote districts of the Chianti the peasants still use the ancient names of Roman mythology for their hills and valleys, and refuse to accept the new styles imposed by the ordnance maps. Subtle in speech, like their Latin ancestors, they swear by the gods who were swept away by the rise of Christianity.

After leaving behind the medieval market square of San Giovanni Valdarno and the industrial buildings of Montevarchi, the grey towers and houses of Arezzo can be discerned across a broad flat plain.

Like Florence, this town was known to the Etruscans and the Romans, and then, in the Middle Ages, it became a small republic waging war against its neighbours, and rent from within by constant dissension between political factions and families greedy for power. In the fourteenth century, Arezzo was annexed by Florence.

Nevertheless, in spite of violence, pestilence and invasions, this place has had a fine tradition of art and of learning.

In the tenth century Guido Monaco elaborated the general principles of modern musical notation. In the fourteenth and fifteenth centuries many of the greatest Florentine painters and sculptors came to decorate the palaces, religious houses and churches of the city. Vasari, a native of Arezzo, wrote the famous *Lives of the Painters*, which is still read in the present day.

Only a mediocre painter, he distinguished himself as an architect by designing the Palace of the Uffizi in Florence, and was also responsible for the graceful colonnade which gives such character to the south side of the Piazza Signoria.

Arezzo is now merely the chief town of the agricultural province, and it has in no sense the atmosphere of a small capital, like so many of the provincial cities of Italy such as, for instance, Lucca, Parma or Modena.

A half day is quite sufficient to visit the sights, the two or three charming old squares, and in particular, Piero della Francesca's paintings in the church of San Francesco.

Piero della Francesca, being born in northern Umbria and very much influenced by the painters of Florence, combines the inquiring mind of the Florentine with the passion for air and light and space of the Umbrians who reflect the calm soft radiance of their countryside in the backgrounds of their paintings.

His genius as a fresco painter can be appreciated in his noble compositions on the walls of the church of San Francesco in the great series of *The Legend of the Cross*, and his indebtedness to both Masaccio and Ucello is obvious—to Masaccio for the nobility of his figures and to Ucello for his mastery of perspective. The beautiful white horses, petrified for ever, their hooves rooted to the ground; the austere figures, hardly human beings, their feet firmly planted in the earth, all have an architectural quality of permanence which makes Francesca's painting so extraordinarily restful and satisfying. Flooded with the tranquil silver light of Umbria, they are imbued with a certain mysticism and the solid forms contrast well with the delicately traced landscape background. Like Fra Angelico, Francesca is one of the greatest masters of colour, making use of the most wonderful tones of blue, violet and grey strengthened by a touch of vermilion and luminous white. In the fresco showing the Queen of Sheba adoring the Holy Cross, her headdress and the magnificent

Rome: the Church of Santa Maria Maggiore

The Appian
Way

The ruined aqueducts of the Roman Campagna

Panorama of
Naples

sweep of her attendant's cloak are focal points in a monumentally conceived design, and the delicate tracery of leaves against a pale glowing sky is full of variety.

Francesca has brought tremendous power and dignity into illustrating this lovely legend from the thirteenth century. To see these alone it is worth making the journey to Arezzo.

Only a few hundred yards away is the thirteenth-century Romanesque church of Santa Maria della Pieve. The central doorway has a vigorous frieze in relief, representing the months, and over the doorway on the right is a thirteenth-century *Baptism of Christ*, archaic in style, though touches of realism are evident in the leafy branches of the tree, in the descent of the dove and in the rather monotonous ripple of the water. The marble bas-reliefs in the interior are also thirteenth-century, the *Nativity* being particularly lovely.

In the polyptych over the High Altar we see the delicate glowing colours and the gilded richness of the Sienese, Pietro Lorenzetti.

The cathedral itself was started at the end of the thirteenth century, but not completed until the sixteenth. Its present façade was added in the beginning of our own century. Although it contains some interesting works of art, carvings and paintings, and has a beautiful figure of the Magdalene by Piero della Francesca, it must take second place to the Church of San Francesco for anyone making a short visit to the town.

On the second Sunday in June, on the 7th of August, and sometimes on other Sundays during the summer, Arezzo becomes very much animated when a medieval tournament is held in which representatives from the different wards of the city tilt against the figure of a Saracen which swings round and buffets the attacker with a kind of flail, unless his aim is true. The knights and their attendants and local magnates are dressed in brightly coloured fifteenth-century costumes and the excitement at the result of the contest is as great as in any football match in America.

This joust takes place in the Piazza Grande (Piazza Vasari), the principal square whose ancient towers, palaces and churches make a picturesque setting for this beautiful ceremony.

Beyond Arezzo, the countryside remains open, the colours of the landscape are duller than in the neighbourhood of Florence. High up on a ridge that extends to the east of the road, the fortified towns and villages succeed each other, for in the past this was disputed territory, and the population did not dare to dwell unprotected on the plain.

The grey ramparts of the grey city of Cortona reach up the slope to enclose the huge ruined fortress on the heights. There are well-preserved Etruscan walls here, and Etruscan tombs in the vicinity. In spite of its grimness, Cortona is worth a visit, not only because of the beautiful *Annunciation* by Fra Angelico, and the Signorellis in the Pinacoteca Signorelliana, but also because it is one of the best preserved medieval towns in Italy, and at present, quite neglected by tourists.

A few miles beyond Cortona, the smooth leaden surface of Lake Trasimene appears in its setting of wooded slopes. From the hills on the east bank Hannibal swooped down on a Roman army and destroyed it so completely that, according to legend, the muddy waters were tinged with the blood of the slaughtered soldiers.

On the western shore a promontory, crowned with a battlemented palace, juts out into the lake, and beyond, in the far distance, the rugged hills of Montepulciano stand out against the sky.

On one of the three small islands that stud the calm waters of Trasimene, St Francis fasted for forty days and forty nights in solitude, save for the company of a small friendly rabbit.

On the eastern shore the two small villages of Passignano and Magione are being developed into modest bathing resorts now that the scourge of malaria has been eliminated by D.D.T.

At the northern extremity of Lake Trasimene the traveller crosses the invisible boundary between Tuscany and the Province of Umbria which was formerly part of the Papal States. Even though the frontier is no longer marked by barriers and customs officials, it is still possible to note a subtle change in the aspect of the architecture, the slower speech of the population, and the more leisurely gait of the peasants on the highway. The scenery too is different, for here the valleys are wider, the slopes of the hills are gentler, and the grey tints of the landscape have a strange luminosity which the Umbrian painters reproduced so well.

In Perugia, however, the palaces and other buildings are peculiarly reminiscent of Florence because of the close political and artistic links that existed between the two cities in the Middle Ages.

On approaching the town by the long climb up from the station, the impression is a different one, for the shell of an Etruscan gate has survived over a score of centuries to the present day and stands just below a wide stone terrace on which Paul III built a huge fortress to dominate the turbulent citizens. An Etruscan Citadel stood on this site, but this structure was replaced by the Palace of the tyrants Baglioni, who in their turn were removed from power by the armies of the Church.

After the unification of Italy, gardens were laid out on the space formerly occupied by the fortress.

The view from the stone terrace is fine at all times, but at its best perhaps when the setting sun envelops the broad valley of the Tiber below in a golden radiance, and then its flaming red circle sinks slowly behind the tall ridges on the far horizon. Even in the hottest of summers cool breezes usually fan this spot, for Perugia is a thousand feet above the level of the sea, and can, in fact, be piercingly cold in winter.

The Corso Vanucci, the principal street of the town, gives the impression of the dignity and soberness of this Capital of Umbria which has so ancient a tradition of culture and erudition.

In the huge Palazzo del Cambio, Perugino's frescoes of Christian and pagan themes have the softness of colouring and the gentle blandness that were to distinguish his great pupil Raphael.

This Umbrian master, Pietro Vanucci, or Perugino as he was called, is too gentle, too softly pensive and sweet for our modern taste; his heads are for the most part without character and his people drift about in a languid dream, but despite these obvious deficiencies, he was a great painter of landscape. The Umbrian countryside stretches away for ever into the distance; sundrenched hills and valleys, feathery trees quiver slightly in a soft breeze. He spreads a magical country in front of us and peoples it with characters who are little more than wan shadows.

Although the Pinacoteca Vanucci is named after him, it only shows a few of his best works; the serene and charming *Madonna and Child* and the *Adoration of the Shepherds* being the finest. The rest are, for the most part, late paintings in which he was aided by his pupils.

Housed in the top storey of the Palazzo Pubblico, the Gallery is a complete collection of the works of the Umbrian masters, some early Sienese panels, a magnificent altarpiece by Fra Angelico and another great treasure—the polyptych of the *Madonna and Child with Saints* by Piero della Francesca.

The Palazzo Pubblico is in the Cathedral Square and its battle-

mented roof surmounts elaborately carved Gothic windows. A fine
outside staircase encloses a graceful loggia.

I have always found Perugia convenient and pleasant for a night's
stay on my way from Florence to Rome. On every side there are
magnificent views of the Umbrian countryside. I like to wander
through the streets and squares of the centre to pick out for myself
the splendid old palaces, the churches, and the narrow medieval
lanes that have remained more or less untouched.

Though the University is small, the presence of the students enlivens the ancient city, and in the summer the courses for foreigners
attract young men and women from all parts of the world.

Generally speaking, the food in the restaurants is excellent, and
there are also a number of cheaper *trattorie* and *pensions* that cater
for the undergraduates and the faculties of the University and the
schools.

The Etruscan Museum and the well-preserved tombs of the Etruscan cemetery nearby are of some interest, but since the best remains
of pre-Roman times are to be seen in Rome and Florence, it is better
for the hurried traveller to husband his time and to go on to Assisi.

Clearly visible from some distance away, the churches and towers
of Assisi stretch out along the dark hillside, shining almost white
in the brilliant sun. To the west stands the great Church of San
Francesco—three churches in one—where St Francis lies buried.
It was this saint, with his love of animals and birds and all living
things, who inspired Giotto to paint his moving series of frescoes
which are not only lovely in themselves, but play such an important
part in the history of Italian painting. So the church, set on a hill
above the smiling Umbrian countryside, is not only a monument to
St Francis, the most human of all the saints, it is a living testament to the greatness of the early Italian painters who illustrated the
Bible stories and the lives of the saints. They set them, not against a
majestic golden background, but used familiar forms in a countryside of trees and flowers and birds with a blue sky overhead and
rocks and grass and stones underfoot.

We enter through the great fourteenth-century doorway into the
lower church—dim and mysterious with only a little glowing light
seeping through the stained-glass windows, faintly illuminating the
vaulted roof, painted deep blue. It brings out the rich colours of the
frescoes—frescoes painted by the early Italians, by Cimabue, by the
Sienese and by followers of Giotto himself.

It takes some time to get accustomed to the gloom, but gradually we find miracle after miracle presented to us on the walls. There is such a wealth of painting to choose from that it seems best to spend time over one or two only—the small altarpiece by Lorenzetti with a gracious Madonna holding the Child with one arm and pointing with the thumb of her other hand towards St Francis. It is a picture which is timeless and of which I can never tire. Another by the same painter is the most moving of any in the church: *The Descent from the Cross* illustrated with an intensity of feeling which has never been surpassed. In complete contrast we have the imposing *Madonna* by Cimabue—the Virgin majestically enthroned surrounded by winged angels: St Francis stands gently to one side a little apart from this glorious golden company.

In the crypt below this storehouse of early Italian art is the Sarcophagus of St Francis chained to the rock. It is a most moving experience to pass into the little chapel led by one of the monks who tells a few simple facts about the saint's life, and offers up a prayer at the small altar.

If the lower church is dim and shadowy, the upper church is a wonder of light and space. The frescoes, or all that remains of them, in the Nave, Choir and Transepts are by Cimabue, still powerful and impressive, especially the great and tragic Crucifixion. But it is to see the famous series illustrating the life of St Francis that most travellers come—the series, painted soon after the death of the saint, by Giotto or his assistants. Pilgrims inevitably find their way through the colour and drama of the saint's life to the fading tones of *St Francis Preaching to the Birds*, the picture that never palls, however many times we see it. Just beside this most human of all Giotto's paintings is the portal of the upper church, and through it can be seen the sandy track to the village, the open country, the waving cypresses and the vineyards. Though travellers from all over the world surge into the church throughout the day, this little town regains its peaceful character in the tranquillity of the evening and in the faint mist of the early morning. Those who must speed on to Rome will probably leave it at sunset when the buildings glow warm, pale pink against the sombre velvet hills.

I have usually hurried through the hundred miles of country that lie between Assisi and Rome, and yet there is plenty to make one inclined to linger. On a warm spring day I should be tempted to wander for a while through the little walled town of Spello, which has some fine old monuments.

The road does indeed by-pass the historic and ancient city of Foligno, but this place was subjected to so many bombardments that much of its former charm has disappeared.

The ancient little city of Trevi, five miles further on, was more fortunate and escaped unharmed, doubtless because it had no strategic importance, and is built on an eminence away from the highway, and surrounded by olive groves. Though not as picturesque as Spello, it is also pleasant enough to be worth exploring.

Three miles further on the fountain of Clitumnus consists of a series of sheets of clear smooth blue waters in which are reflected the surrounding trees, and a small white temple. Poets, including Virgil and Carducci, have celebrated the beauty of this enchanting spot which is visible from the road, and Byron refers to it in the fourth canto of *Childe Harold*.

Soon the rose-coloured houses of Spoleto can be seen set out in tiers on the side of a hill that slopes steeply up to an immense castle which was inhabited for a while by Lucrezia Borgia.

This town was captured by Victor Emmanuel's troops in 1860, in spite of the papal garrison that was commanded by a courageous Irishman named O'Reilly.

An Etruscan stronghold, Spoleto later became a Roman colony. In the tenth century a Duke of Spoleto was for a while Holy Roman Emperor since he was descended from a daughter of Charlemagne. The husband of this lady, a Breton general, had been given the fief of the city, and had established himself permanently in Italy.

After passing through some wild and rather mountainous country, the road descends to the industrial town of Terni, which has nothing to interest the traveller.

The approach to Rome by the Via Flaminia is a strange one. After leaving a zone of barren hills and valleys, the traveller enters the rolling grey plain of the Campagna, which is mournful even in the springtime when the sun is shining brightly, and yet this region has a mysterious quality of its own. The vestiges of the past are slight, though they appear on all sides: near the road we can still perceive strips of narrow paved track which was the Via Flaminia more than two thousand years ago.

Small, nameless and shapeless fragments of grey stone appear in the sparse tufted grass or even in the gardens of the farmsteads.

Everything, in fact, is pervaded by the aura of antiquity, despite the hideous posters and the suburban villas that are springing up rapidly in the outskirts of the capital.

Soon, in the far distance, the dome of St Peter's rises up among the rooftops, the towers and the belfries.

A huge bridge on the left hand spans the valley of the Tiber, and on the far side there is already the bustle and movement and clamour of the city.

CHAPTER SEVEN

ROME: GENERAL FEATURES AND LIFE

I suppose that I have been to Rome perhaps thirty or forty times in the course of my life, besides living there for a period of several months some years ago.

On each of my visits I have been struck by different aspects of this astonishing city, and on each occasion I have had to refresh my memory of its two thousand seven hundred years of history.

It is now generally accepted that the first settlement on the Palatine Hill was made in the year 754 b.c., but that the legend of Romulus and Remus was evolved many years later and has little or no foundation.

The Sabines occupied the Quirinal Mount some time later and so the Romans had only six or seven hundred yards to go when they set out to abduct the women of their neighbours.

No one has established clearly who were the first inhabitants of the Eternal City, and whether in fact they had come to Italy as fugitives from Asia Minor after the capture of Troy.

The kings who ruled over Rome for two centuries were undoubtedly of Etruscan stock, and it is conceivable that they were driven out, not only because they were tyrants, but because they were aliens who had imposed themselves on their subjects.

Certainly the city prospered under the domination of these monarchs who constructed an immense wall around the town, and extensive portions of this rampart can still be seen in the neighbourhood of the Central Station.

The Tarquins were also responsible for the Cloaca Maxima, the huge drain that kept ancient Rome clean.

In the early years of the fourth century Rome was nearly overwhelmed by the Gauls, who destroyed the whole of the town, but were unable to break into the Capitol, which was saved, perhaps, by the cackling of the geese, as the legend relates.

The Etruscan states of Central Italy were conquered and annexed; the Carthaginians were driven out of the Peninsula after years of

Vesuvius and the
Bay of Naples

Pompei:
the Amphi-
theatre with
Vesuvius in
the back-
ground

war, but the real expansion of Rome began in the first century before Christ, and so most of the principal buildings of the city were constructed under the early emperors. Augustus restored many temples and monuments, and erected many more to celebrate the glory of his rule.

It was said that when he came to power he found a city of plaster, but he left behind him a city of marble.

At the height of its prosperity, according to Gregorovius, Rome had three million inhabitants, and the suburbs stretched right down to the sea. Ships from all parts of the western world sailed up the Tiber to unload their rich cargoes in the very centre of the city.

Aqueducts brought pure water from the distant hills, and an elaborate system of drainage ensured the health of the inhabitants.

Though the streets were narrow the palaces of the rich were immense, and there were houses of twenty storeys or more. The great glory of Rome, however, lay in her monuments: the huge baths, the circuses, the temples and the public places where the citizens could congregate. Tens of thousands of statues decorated the city, the gardens, the religious and civic buildings and the different forums, but most of these works of art have vanished, destroyed to make cement or taken away by invading armies.

When the capital of the Empire was transferred to Constantinople in the year A.D. 330, the splendour of Rome was diminished, and few great monuments were built after this date. Plagues and civil dissensions had already reduced the population, and many of the inhabitants left because of the high cost of living.

Nevertheless, in spite of the invasions and sieges that accompanied the Barbarian invasions, a number of churches were constructed, and some of the basilicas or district halls were taken over for Christian worship.

In the ninth century the countryside in the neighbourhood of the city was occupied for many years by the Saracens, and Rome was only saved from capture by the strong fortifications erected by Pope Leo IV.

After warding off the attacks of the Moslems, there was a period of internal anarchy when the nobles built strongholds in which their adherents could seek refuge when they were defeated by their rivals from other parts of the town.

In the fourteenth century, Pope Clement V fled from Rome and

F

established himself in Avignon so as to be as far away as possible from the constant strife that rendered life intolerable.

During the absence of the Pontiffs the confusion and rivalry between the various factions increased, so that only a small part of the population remained in the city.

In 1418 the Great Schism came to an end, and Rome began to prosper once more with the return of the Holy See. The Popes undertook the restoration of the ruined town and they assisted greatly in the revival of the arts and of learning by their direct patronage and by their personal influence.

The capture and sack of Rome by the troops of the Emperor Charles V in the year 1527, has often been said to mark the end of the Age of Humanism and the full flowering of the Renaissance in the Holy City, but it is only fair to note that many of the great artists who had contributed to its embellishment were already dead. Bramante and Raphael had passed away, though Michelangelo survived and executed many of his greatest masterpieces after that date, including the frescoes of the Sistine Chapel.

Towards the end of the sixteenth century, Pope Sixtus V restored many of the ancient monuments and rebuilt the greater part of the Palace of the Vatican.

During this century and the one that succeeded it, the Baroque churches and palaces of the centre of Rome were constructed, and to this day they are the principal architectural features of the city.

Some of the lovely fountains were also erected in this period, but others were created in the eighteenth century when the constant flow of tourists and pilgrims brought enough wealth to finance further expenditure.

After the Napoleonic wars Rome became one of the fashionable centres of the civilized world. Many English and some Americans came there to enjoy the mild winter climate and to participate in the active social life of the aristocracy.

The Piazza di Spagna with its neighbouring streets was the hub of the foreign colony whose members rented apartments and palaces and drove in the parks in their own *équipages*.

In this quarter there were foreign doctors, libraries, bakers, and chemists to cater to the needs of the visitors. The British brought their own horses and made foxhunting fashionable. The Roman aristocrats still follow the hounds across the bare plains of the Campagna in spite of the high cost of this form of sport.

In 1849 Pope Pius IX was driven out by a popular rising, and for a brief period there was a republican administration.

A year later, in spite of the gallant defence by Garibaldi's troops, the Papacy was re-established by French troops, who remained to protect the Holy See.

Twenty years later, at the outbreak of the Franco-Prussian war, Napoleon III was forced to recall the garrison. In September 1870 the small papal army had to surrender to the advancing forces of King Victor Emmanuel, the States of the Church were incorporated into Italy, and Rome became the capital, though the Pope showed his disapproval of the new régime by refusing to leave the precincts of the Vatican.

Many of the older Roman families did not accept the new dispensation and would have nothing to do with the monarchy until at last, during the Fascist régime, the rift was more or less healed by the Lateran Treaty of 1929 whereby the small area of territory round the Vatican was conceded to the Pope as a sovereign state where he could freely exercise his spiritual authority. This little state has its own railway station, broadcasting system, post office and police, and during the Second World War its neutrality was strictly respected.

Although the Pope is no longer held to be the prisoner of the Vatican, he does, in fact, seldom leave the precincts of the Palace and St Peter's, and so far, no Pontiff has ventured to go further than to the Alban Hills in the immediate vicinity of the capital.

The most striking feature of modern Rome is the rapid growth of its population from 420,000 at the beginning of the century, to something over two millions in 1956.

In 1900 the open country stretched to the gates of the city. Now the great majority of the Romans live in the vast new suburbs which have sprung up outside the walls, and many of them seldom penetrate into the old quarters.

The problem of dealing with the traffic in the centre of Rome seems to be almost insoluble, in spite of the tunnels that have been cut through the hills, the one-way streets, and the broadening of many thoroughfares. Nevertheless, Rome is still one of the most beautiful cities in the world, the view from the terrace of the Pincio gardens remains more or less unchanged.

I like this place in the early morning, but I like it best of all at sunset when there is a glow of red and orange in the western sky and the colours that tinge the city take on a deeper hue.

Just below extends the circular Piazza del Popolo with an obelisk in the centre surrounded by four stone lions with water gushing from their jaws. Bernini's large Baroque gateway was formerly the principal entrance to the city.

Two domed churches mark the beginning of the Corso, the narrow street lined by palaces that cuts across the centre of the old city to the monstrous white monument to Victor Emmanuel.

A little further away from the terrace, a curving line of rooftops marks the course of the hidden Tiber. Just beyond it the massive round Castel Sant' Angelo is surmounted by a bronze angel perched perilously on a small turret. Then comes the graceful outline of St Peter's, and to the left of it, the long green ridge of the Janiculum hill that serves as a pendant to the tall Monte Mario far away to the right.

There are so many landmarks that it would be impossible to enumerate them all, but one of them at least strikes a strange note here, and that is the little Victorian Gothic Church of England in the Via del Babuino. Incongruous as it looks, it has at least the merit of being designed by Street, a talented nineteenth-century architect who did not attempt to compete with the more imaginative work at hand, and paid no attention at all to the setting. The result is as defiantly English as a policeman's uniform.

There is so much to see that it is hard to know where to begin, but I would give priority to Christian Rome rather than to the Rome of Antiquity, for a surfeit of ruins tends to be monotonous, and the buildings of the Classical age were much of a pattern and lose their essential virtue of harmony when in a state of decay.

The Castel Sant' Angelo was indeed built by the Emperor as a tomb for himself and his successors, but historically it belongs as much to the Renaissance as to the Empire. Benvenuto Cellini was imprisoned here by Clement VII, and the same Pope took refuge in this stronghold when the Imperial troops occupied Rome in 1527.

During the siege, Cellini claimed to have fired the shot that killed the enemy general, the Constable of Bourbon, and his death certainly brought about the withdrawal of the attackers.

The terraced battlements will seem familiar to opera lovers, for the setting is used by Puccini in *La Tosca*, and serves as a background to a dramatic scene.

The Mausoleum was transformed into a fortress in the early

Middle Ages, and the statues that adorned it were removed, as well as all the marble facings.

In the thirteenth century the Popes left the Lateran Palace and took up their residence in the Vatican because of its proximity to the Castel Sant' Angelo which could be used as a place of refuge in case of danger.

A statue of this saint set on a pinnacle to commemorate the miracle by which he warded off a plague in the sixth century was replaced by a larger one in the eighteenth century.

In the early years of the nineteenth century, a fashionably dressed young Englishman arrived at the Castle. Having mounted to the battlements he climbed up the central turret, pulled himself up the flanks of the statue, and after balancing himself upside down with his feet in the air on the head of the angel for the space of two minutes, he came down again. On leaving the building, he jumped into a waiting carriage and drove away at full speed after having spent no more than half an hour in Rome, to which he had journeyed from England for the sole purpose of accomplishing this singular feat.

The apartments of various Popes, the chapel and the small museum in the Castle are of some interest, but the greatest attraction is the view of St Peter's from the battlements.

From this point of vantage there is the finest prospect of Bernini's semi-circular colonnade enclosing the huge piazza in front of the church. The three hundred and sixty-six pillars are spaced so as to allow for the movement of carriages, but in the present day pedestrians alone can avail themselves of the shade provided by this passage which is roofed and surmounted by countless statues of saints with flowing draperies in strongly defined attitudes.

The general effect is one of great harmony, for the two gracefully curved arms of the colonnade seem to be an essential part of the architectural composition of the church and of its classical façade.

The plumed jets of two large fountains sparkle and flutter in the sun, and in the centre of the square rises up a tall obelisk brought to Rome nearly twenty centuries ago by the Emperor Caligula.

His kinsman, Nero, burnt and crucified Christians near this spot. The tradition is that St Peter was one of the victims and was buried nearby.

In the fourth century Constantine founded the Church of St Peter's, but only part of the crypt of this structure remains.

Julius II commissioned Bramante to design the present basilica, but he died within a few years of undertaking this gigantic task.

Other architects started to continue his work, and each of them attempted to modify the original plan, but it was not until thirty-two years later that real progress was made when the aged Michelangelo undertook to clear up the confusion of direction.

After his death, Michelangelo was succeeded by Maderna, and Maderna in his turn was followed by Bernini, who did virtually supervise the completion of the world's largest and most important church.

If Bramante was responsible for the planning of the interior, Michelangelo must have the credit for the superb design of the huge dome, and Bernini for the exuberant decoration which contrasts with the rather ponderous disposition of the masses.

Maderna's façade and portico possess architectural unity, but they do partly screen the view of the splendid dome for anyone standing in the Piazza and, since they are out of scale with the rest of the structure, they diminish the impression of size.

The building of St Peter's was not only a great artistic achievement, it was also an engineering feat of unusual merit, for the huge size of the building presented all sorts of technical difficulties. When Michelangelo designed the dome, he set out to surpass all the achievements of the ancients, and in particular the Pantheon whose dome had been admired so much by the architects of the Renaissance.

The area covered by the church is more than twice as great as that of Cologne Cathedral, and its height is such that the whole of St Paul's Cathedral could stand in the interior without touching any part of the structure—in fact St Peter's can hold a congregation of 60,000 people.

I am tempted to give these guidebook statistics because, as I have just explained, the square façade gives a false impression of the size of St Peter's, and its immenseness is only apparent inside the church or from a distance.

As you approach from the Piazza, the Dome seems to disappear, and nothing is left but the columns, pediments and statues of the façade.

Above the central entrance is the balcony where the newly elected Pontiffs make their first appearance as Popes to give their blessing to the expectant crowd.

The bronze door below is only opened on great occasions. It was designed by Antonio Filarete, a pupil of Donatello's, and it is decorated with panels in bas-relief representing Our Lord, the Virgin Mary, St Peter and St Paul, as well as some scenes in the history of the Papacy.

The surrounding frieze has motifs taken from Roman mythology, such as *Leda and the Swan*, the *Rape of Ganymede* and figures of different gods.

The mosaic of a ship with Christ walking on the sea to draw Peter from the waves is known as "La Navicella". It is a seventeenth-century copy of the original by Giotto in the Vatican Museum.

The "Holy Door" on the right remains closed, for it is only opened every twenty-five years on the occasion of the Papal Jubilee, which is attended by thousands of pilgrims from all over the world, who are granted plenary dispensation of their sins.

The first impression of the interior is an unforgettable one, for the proportions of the structure are such that the wonder of its size can only become apparent gradually. The huge arches, the ponderous pillars, the immense vault of the dome do combine to give an effect of heaviness which is diminished however by the voluptuousness of Bernini's flowing Baroque *décors*.

Over the High Altar, at which the Pope alone may celebrate Mass, Bernini erected the black and gold canopy supported on four tall twisted columns. This monument is perhaps too big even for this setting, and does indeed dwarf the statues and tombs in its immediate vicinity, and yet it seems fitting in this place, where there are so many masterpieces by the same artist, or by a member of his school.

After many visits to St Peter's, I still find it impossible to describe in detail the countless memorials, tombs and decorations. I can only content myself by indicating those which seem to me to be most worthy of attention.

First of all there is the bronze statue of St Peter, executed in the fifth century, and revered by all the Catholic pilgrims who flock to this church to kiss his foot.

This heavily draped figure sits erect in his chair, holding in one hand the keys of the Church, and the other is raised with the first and second fingers stretched upwards in benediction. The face is bearded: over the strong curling hairs a wheel-shaped halo confers an air of dignity and solemnity to the saint.

One foot is hidden by the robes, the other projects beyond the pedestal, and is worn and polished by the touch of thousands of visitors throughout the centuries.

One of the interesting features about this statue is that it is believed to be a real likeness of the apostle whose features have been handed down through the generations by successive artists.

In the centre of the church and almost under the vault of the dome, is the confessional, surrounded by marble balustrades and with steps leading down to the gold casket placed on a stone that is held by many believers to be the tomb of St Peter.

However, of all the monuments here, the most inspiring artistically is the *Pieta* by Michelangelo in a chapel on the right-hand side near the entrance. Executed in 1499 whilst he was still a young man, it can nevertheless be counted as one of his greatest masterpieces, though it appeals to the emotions and to the heart, whereas many of his later works have an intellectual quality which is lacking here.

The slight figure of the Virgin, with her strong youthful face bowed over the recumbent figure of Christ, expresses love, reverence and pity, as well as the eternal spirit of motherhood. With her right hand she supports the limp body of her Son, on whose features are revealed all the agony and suffering of a sorrowing world. The folds of heavy draperies flowing down to the ground skilfully complete the lines of this composition which combines tenderness, strength and harmony.

The stiff, formal monument to the Stuarts by Canova is of such purely historical interest that it cannot provide any possible comparison with Michelangelo's genius and inspiration, yet I usually go to see it before leaving St Peter's.

Two winged angels mourn before a doorway in a tall marble sepulchre on which have been carved the royal arms of Great Britain. Below a line of wreaths and swags are the portraits in bas-relief of James the Old Pretender, Charles the Young Pretender, and the Cardinal of York his brother.

All three of them lived for many years in Rome, the father in an austere manner, Bonnie Prince Charlie in a continued state of debauchery after the gallant failure of the '45.

It is interesting to note that the expenses for this memorial were paid for by George IV, who could scarcely be accused of undue sentimentality in his personal relationships.

Nearby is a monument to Maria Clementina Sobieska, wife of the

Old Pretender, a lady who was brought to meet her future husband after a series of extraordinary adventures and escapes, for the agents of the House of Hanover were determined to prevent her marriage.

Unfortunately, her subsequent life was far from happy, and she had her share of the ill luck which dogged the last of the Stuarts.

CHAPTER EIGHT

ROME : VATICAN : TRASTEVERE : BATHS OF DIOCLETIAN : VILLA BORGHESE

A TOUR of the Vatican can be exasperating and exhausting, especially during the tourist season, unless a good deal of thought is given to it beforehand. There can be nothing more disappointing than a first sight of the miraculous frescoes in the Sistine Chapel when the floor is crowded and the babel of voices completely destroys the atmosphere of a church.

Better by far to make two or even three short visits seeing one section at a time at a period when the coachloads of sightseers are in St Peter's or the Colosseum.

Most organized tours are busy seeing St Peter's early in the morning, so it is a good idea to go to the Vatican immediately it opens. The Sistine Chapel is often more or less deserted until about ten o'clock. After seeing it, go back to the Raphaels, the Angelico Chapel and the Borghese apartments. The next morning, in the same way, you will find the Pinacoteca uncrowded, and a third visit will allow you to see the Vatican Museum and the sculptures. As most people spend at least three days in Rome this should be perfectly possible, and there will still be a good deal of time left each day to see some of the churches and other monuments. For those who are only making a very short visit, a conducted tour though crowded, rushed and uncomfortable, does give an opportunity to see the more important art treasures without wasting time over things of secondary importance.

The Sistine Chapel was built towards the end of the fifteenth century during the reign of Pope Sixtus IV from whom it takes its name. He called together the foremost painters of the day to take part in its decoration. In the space of this one chapel we can see the work of most of the more important Renaissance artists. Signorelli, Ghirlandaio, Pinturicchio, Roselli and Perugino decorated the walls, illustrating scenes from the Bible. Michelangelo's outstanding achievement is the ceiling where he depicts the creation of the world, and the destruction and subsequent regeneration of mankind. On the west wall is the enormous *Last Judgment* which he painted in the middle of the sixteenth century in place of the paintings by Perugino. Although Raphael's paintings are not seen here, but in the loggia and stanze, he did take part in the scheme of decoration by designing the famous series of tapestries.

Although all these frescoes are part of a complete decorative scheme, each painting is a separate unit and calls for individual attention. Even the magnificent ceiling, conceived as an architectural whole, has its series of panels, each a complete composition of inestimable value, a powerful expression of Michelangelo's entire control of his medium, his wide knowledge of the human mind and body. The great force of his conceptions is seldom relieved by the decorative landscape backgrounds so dear to his contemporaries. His painting is the work of a man who was before anything else an architect and a sculptor. He painted architectural features in the ceiling in such a way that, from below, they seem to be part of the building, and the painted figures at the corners simulate carvings in stone.

It is strange that, when this sort of thing is done superbly well, it ceases to strike us as bad taste. Most of us despise the habit of painting beams on the cement-fronted semi-detached house to make it look like half-timber. We criticize the shopkeeper who has the wooden front of his shop painted to look like marble. Perhaps it is because these things are usually done badly or applied to buildings which are already hideous. Certainly no one in his senses criticizes the Italians of the Renaissance or of any other period for painting in architectural details to unite the frescoes with their architectural setting. Just as the Primitives often merged their frame with the painting, so later painters overcame the problem of an awkwardly placed door or window by continuing its architectural features into the design.

Certainly the whole effect of the Sistine ceiling is of a remarkable architectural unity and the immense size of the rectangle is comfortably broken up by the nine separate panels.

Everyone is familiar with the magnificent series of the Creation and Fall of Man, with the flowing movement across the width of the ceiling and with Michelangelo's extraordinary genius in expressing power and vitality contrasted with inertia and death. Adam is lifeless, but only temporarily, for we know that when the immensely powerful Creator continues his forward movement and touches his drooping hand, he will spring to life. In the *Expulsion from the Garden of Eden* and the *Temptation* we have, on the one hand, the vital bodies of Adam and Eve stretching out to take the fruit and, on the other, the dejected drooping bodies as they leave the garden. How like in composition they are to Masaccio's *Adam and Eve* in the Carmine in Florence, yet they do not move me nearly so deeply as the simpler, less sophisticated figures by the earlier painter.

Incredibly powerful and brilliantly executed as is the *Last Judgment* on the end wall, I find it confused, terrifying and crushing as a whole, but intensely interesting in detail. Some of the groups of figures are astonishingly lifelike and dramatic.

After the tremendous impact of Michelangelo's genius, which becomes almost too much to bear at times, it is a rest to linger lovingly over the paintings on the walls and enjoy the enchanting landscape backgrounds and the restful poses of the dignified figures as painted by the less dynamic contemporaries of the sculptor.

Raphael's wonderful paintings in the loggia and stanze show another aspect of late Renaissance painting as manifested by the sophisticated, polished Umbrian master. He owed so much to the great names of the Renaissance—to Boticelli, Leonardo, Michelangelo and Perugino—yet, in combining some of the characteristics of these masters' work, he manages to infuse much of his own personality and to show a mastery of composition which though derivative is unequalled. I am always a little repelled by Raphael, as I feel the slightly smug gaze of his women following me, but no one can deny that, at his most irritating, he is a very great and accomplished artist and, at his most captivating, a charming gentle painter, warming everything he touches with the soft Umbrian light and presenting his interpretation of the Bible with a perfection and humanity that cannot fail to draw one.

Raphael was called in to help in the decoration of the apartments of Pope Julius II. Other painters were already working there, but, when the Pope saw Raphael's painting of the *Dispute of the Sacrament* he was so much impressed by it that he commissioned him to complete the whole decoration and had the other paintings destroyed. Raphael kept the ceiling decoration out of deference to his master Perugino.

Probably the most famous of Raphael's frescoes is the magnificent

School of Athens which is a masterpiece of design, although some of the attitudes are a little strained.

The enchanting little series of paintings decorating the loggias and illustrating stories from the Bible were painted, or at any rate designed, by Raphael.

After the tremendous experience of seeing the Sistine Chapel and the Raphaels the little Fra Angelico chapel is like another world divided by centuries from the restless spirit of the late Renaissance. It is a calm, beautiful world, looked at through the eyes of a saint with a delicate and original sense of colour and a wonderful ability to enhance the atmosphere of a church.

The Gallery of Maps is not only richly decorated by sixteenth-century painters, but has a series of maps of considerable interest to anyone with the leisure to study them.

But perhaps of more importance to the footsore sightseer, it has the most lovely views of the Vatican Gardens. The Gallery of Tapestries has the famous tapestries carried out from the cartoons by Raphael now in the Victoria and Albert Museum, London.

Unless you have time for repeated visits it is absolutely essential to pass by all but the very best of the exhibits in the sculpture rooms, for the actual distance to be covered is considerable and, if you spend time on looking at everything you pass, you may be too tired to reach the world-famous sculptures.

In the Gallery of the Candelabra you will find a beautiful fifth-century Greek carving of a running girl, and in the Hall of the Biga the Roman Chariot at one time used as an episcopal chair.

The Hall of the Animals has a strangely assorted collection of animal sculpture, badly displayed and for the most part of secondary interest. But the real object of most visitors to these galleries is the Court of the Belvedere where the magnificent Greek Apollo of the fourth century B.C., gloriously godlike, seems to be stepping down from Mount Olympus before our eyes, and the *Torso Belvedere*, so greatly admired by Michelangelo, whose sculpture shows its influence over and over again.

The group of the *Laocoön* of the first century B.C. is too tortured a work to give me any satisfaction, but the composition of the snakes and the twisted limbs is so skilfully carried out that the whole has a flowing unity and is perfectly balanced.

The Pinacoteca possesses an excellent collection of Italian paintings and a few from foreign schools. The early works are particularly interesting and there is a triptych painted by Giotto, or at any rate designed by him. Apart from the fresco in St John Lateran, this is the only painting in Rome which can give us an idea of Giotto's work. Against a golden background, Christ sits surrounded by angels. On either side is the Martyrdom of St Peter and St Paul. On the reverse of the panel stands the Apostle Peter in a glorious scarlet pontifical robe with figures of angels on either side. In the Hall of Melezzo da Forli is the fresco which was originally painted on the walls of the Vatican Library, but which was transferred to canvas.

It shows Sixtus IV appointing Platina as Prefect of the Vatican Library and has many excellent portraits. It is particularly lovely in colour; venetian red, soft magenta, dull blue, brilliant blue, green and gold are so distributed as to give a scintillating effect of light. The fragments of a larger composition by Melezzo da Forli designed for the cupola of a church, show us the most delightful heads of angels, tilted in graceful attitudes and encircled with starry haloes.

Through the room of Pinturicchios and Peruginos, we come to some of the finest of Raphael's paintings: the *Coronation of the Madonna*, painted when he was only nineteen, is still very much in the style of his master, Perugino, and contains a portrait of the youthful artist. The *Madonna di Foligno* with the Madonna as a gentle, warm, Queen of Heaven enthroned in clouds, was commissioned by Sigismondo Conti as a thank-offering for his escape from a bomb explosion. In the background the city of Foligno is represented with the bomb dropping.

The *Transfiguration* is one of Raphael's loveliest pictures and was the last thing he painted before his death at the age of thirty-seven. It expresses perfectly the effect of Christ soaring up into Heaven and is a triumph of balanced composition. The lower part of the picture was finished by his pupil, Giulio Romano. Vasari tells us that the painting was hung above Raphael's bier as he lay in state, and it was later carried in the elaborate funeral procession held in honour of Italy's most highly esteemed painter.

Comparatively few of the people that visit the Vatican City continue to explore the region that lies to the west of the river and is known as the Trastevere, and yet it is in this district that you can see the real Romans at work and at play. The suburbs are inhabited by newcomers from the provinces, and in particular from the Abruzzi and the deep south, which are at present depressed areas. The centre tends to be cosmopolitan, but the inhabitants of the

Trastevere are real Romans whose ancestors have lived in this quarter for generations, and some may, for all I know, be directly descended from the citizens who dwelt here in the days of the Empire.

The real Trastevere consists of a network of old streets that lie to the south of a line drawn between the Ponte Sisto and the Ponte Palatino. A wide brash avenue called the Viale Trastevere cuts through one end of this district, and its cafés, bars and shops are patronized by a working-class clientele. On summer evenings the pavements are crowded with men in shirt-sleeves, women in light dresses and children in scanty garments who come out to avoid the heat and stuffiness of their crowded dwellings, and it is here that you are sure to hear the soft Roman dialect. Unlike the Tuscans they do not swear by the gods of old but use a wealth of religious expletives. They also gesticulate in an astonishing manner.

However, most visitors will find greater entertainment in the narrow streets where those who can afford it indulge in gargantuan meals eaten very slowly at tables set out on the pavement.

The food is excellent, though rather rich and heavy, but the fish in particular is fresh and of good quality. I can recommend the *fritto misto del mar*, the scampi, the cuttlefish. All these dishes are usually fried and so, for those who like something less greasy, I would suggest veal cooked in marsala, the steaks, or the baby lamb which is a speciality in Rome.

The *pizza*, tarts made with cheese and flavoured in different ways, are very popular with the locals, and there are an infinite variety of *pizze*; some are decorated with tomatoes and anchovy, others with different kinds of olives, and so on. Most restaurants pride themselves on having a special recipe of their own, and the people who are having a gala night often have a *pizza* between each course, for the service is unhurried, and the Italian customers like to make a very leisurely meal.

Some of the *trattorie* have become fashionable with smart Romans, and prices have risen accordingly, others are frequented by writers, painters and poets. In one that I know of, a cobbler extemporizes his own verse in dialect, but he has been taken up by one of the literary cliques of the Via Margutta.

I cannot venture to recommend any particular one of these places for their character changes with lightning rapidity.

Within a few months of being discovered, a humble tavern may develop into a smart restaurant, with an orchestra, shaded lights and well-trained waiters who expect to be suitably rewarded for their urbane service.

The best plan is to explore all the romantic little streets and to find for yourself the ideal place for a pleasant evening.

If you are lucky and get a magnificent meal for a minimum price, take my advice: don't boast about your success, or you may discover that by the time you return to Rome your quiet and essentially Italian *trattoria* is now patronized almost exclusively by conducted parties, that the fish tastes like flannel fried in machine oil, and that the pinkish vinegar given to you as wine costs almost as much as champagne. It is an experience that I have had in other countries, but never, so far, in Rome . . .

I sometimes wander through the medieval streets of the Trastevere by day, for even when the sun is shining they do not lose their enchantment, and though certain slum features are revealed, there is also plenty of colour. If there are no really notable monuments, there are ancient doorways, picturesque old courtyards, and sometimes stone coats of arms half effaced by time.

In the Convent of Santa Cecilia there is a wonderful recumbent statue of this saint made in the sixteenth century when her tomb was opened and her body was found to be in a perfect state of preservation although eleven hundred years had elapsed since her death.

A few hundred yards away from here is the Isola Tiberina, an island best seen from the other bank, for it is on this side that it has kept its medieval aspect. At the northern end the Hospital of St John was built on the site of a temple to Æsculapius, but I still prefer the little street of picturesque houses, and I have sometimes sat in the simple tavern overlooking the river.

The bridge is the only one that has survived from the time of the Roman Empire to the present day.

A short way to the north the Corso Vittorio Emmanuele is a broad and busy street that cuts straight through from the Tiber to the Piazza Venezia. It is an ugly street, but it was cut in only sixty days, in order that the Emperor Charles V should have an impressive approach to the Palace of the Vatican.

On the far side of this thoroughfare stretches one of the most interesting districts of old Rome, and it is one through which I like to wander at venture, looking at the huge patrician palaces, examin-

The ancient city of Amalfi from the sea

View from a balcony in Ravello (near Amalfi)

Capri: the Faraglione

Ischia: the Aragonese Castle

ing the windows of junk shops, or merely dropping into a little tavern for a coffee or a glass of wine.

As a rule I finish my stroll at the Piazza Navona, a huge eliptical open space, laid out on the site of the Circus of Domitian which could accommodate 30,000 spectators.

In the centre there are two fountains by Bernini, the first consisting of a massive rock surrounded by figures symbolizing the world's four largest rivers: the second is adorned with tritons and the figure of a Moor.

There are two churches in this square: the first, Sant' Agnese, has a Baroque façade by Borromini, and the other, San Giacomo, is the place of worship for Spaniards.

I have sometimes lunched at one of the restaurants in this square in order to enjoy the view of the Baroque composition formed of churches, palaces and fountains, whilst listening to the soothing splashing of water nearby.

If you have time and a taste for statuary do not fail to visit the museum in the monumental ruins of the Baths of Diocletian, which are almost opposite the Central Station.

The museum has been completely redecorated and rearranged so that all the pieces of sculpture are well lighted and displayed to the best advantage against soft grey and brown velvet hangings. Here you will find some of the loveliest carvings in Rome: the *Birth of Venus* executed in the fifth century B.C. by a Greek sculptor with a magical sense of rhythm, suggests the flow and transparency of water in the lines of the draperies. The *Maiden of Anzio*, so beautifully posed and perfectly proportioned, belongs probably to the third century B.C.

It was discovered late in the nineteenth century after a tidal wave had carried away the earth which had buried it for hundreds of years. The very life-like, but rather brutal figure of a boxer is the work of the sculptor of the beautiful Belvedere torso in the Vatican. It is possible that it is a portrait of Clitomachus of Thebes, winner in the Olympic Games in 200 B.C.

Perhaps the most glorious carving of the whole museum is the small equestrian statue of a child. A charming little boy carved partly in marble, partly in alabaster, flings up one arm to urge on the toy-like alabaster horse which leaps upwards, his forequarters supported by a tree trunk.

From the Baths of Diocletian it is not far to the Palazzo Barbarini

G

which houses an important collection of paintings and is spacious enough never to be crowded.

A portrait of Philip II by Titian is here as well as Tintoretto's St Jerome, and the famous painting of Narcissus by the seventeenth-century Caravaggio, noted for his brilliant effect of chiaroscuro.

A few minutes' walk along the Via Sistina will take you to the top of the Spanish Steps and the Pincio. In a previous chapter I described the wonderful view from the terrace of the Pincio, a place which no one who comes to Rome ever fails to visit, and yet the gardens were laid out only during the French occupation of Italy in 1811 by a skilful architect named Valadier.

The terrace can be reached easily enough by a short steep road from the Piazza del Popolo, but I have always preferred the approach from the top of the Spanish Steps because there is a lovely prospect of the city the whole of the way.

On one side there is a balustrade overlooking small orchards and the studios at the back of the Via Margutta. Beyond the red roof-tops, palaces and towers stretch all the way to St Peter's, and a hum of traffic rises from the busy town below.

The Villa Medici is a splendid Baroque residence built in the seventeenth century for Cardinal Alessandro de' Medici, but it was taken over by Napoleon to become the French Academy of Art. The splendid formal gardens can be visited by applying to the porter, who will also guide you to the Belvedere from which there is a still better view than from the terrace below.

Beyond the Villa Medici, and on a small eminence on the same side of the road, the Casino Valadier is one of the most attractive restaurants in Rome, but certainly not one of the cheapest, for the food here is of the best, and guests are served at tables outside, or indoors by a window from which you can gaze at most of the principal monuments in Rome whilst eating.

Finally we reach the gardens of the Pincio where children play in the alleys, young lovers lean on the balustrade of the terrace and the thirsty drink Coca-Cola sitting round the tin tables of the lemonade booths.

In the Borghese Gardens, on the far side of the town wall and adjacent to the Pincio, the scene is a different one, for in this case the immense private park of the Borghese family was only opened officially about fifty years ago, though in fact the public was admitted on certain days of the week.

Here there are broad avenues, groves of pines and of ilex, and gallops for equestrians. Not far from the Porta Pinciana, the gate at the top of the Via Vittorio Veneto, is the Casino delle Rose, a first-class restaurant with tables in the open air, dancing and music.

A little further away the Giardino del Lago, the former private garden of Prince Borghese, is by far the most enchanting spot in this park, for here the vegetation is denser, and the tall trees are grouped round a small lake. Statues, columns and grottoes gleam against the dark foliage which casts mysterious deep shadows on the sandy paths.

The Borghese Gallery was the private gallery of the Borghese family until it was bought by the government at the beginning of this century. It was one of the best private collections in Europe.

The famous reclining statue of Pauline Bonaparte by Canova shows an astonishing skill in modelling and in rendering texture, but apart from the gracefulness of the pose I find little to recommend it; the faithful reproduction of flesh, draperies and bedding shows great dexterity on the part of the sculptor, but little creative ability.

Among outstanding paintings of the Italian schools are Raphael's *Entombment*, and the vigorous *Boy with a Bunch of Grapes* by Caravaggio which, although it does not have the appeal of the *Narcissus* in the Barbarini, has warmth and richness. The greatest treasure of the collection is Titian's *Sacred and Profane Love*. This curious title was given to it in the eighteenth century, before which time it was usually called *Two Women at the Fountain*. In any case the title is of little importance; the painting of a nude woman and a heavily draped figure seated at a fountain in a warm glowing land-scape is a miracle of light and colour in which the figures and draperies and landscape are in perfect harmony.

In complete contrast to the Borghese Gallery, the Villa Giulia has a really superb collection of Etruscan Art. The gallery has been completely rearranged and is, to my mind, one of the best displayed collections in Europe. Quite apart from its great interest to the Etruscan-minded, its layout and decoration are outstanding.

CHAPTER NINE

THE STREET SCENE : THE VIA VITTORIO
VENETO : THE PIAZZA DI SPAGNA : THE
OLD QUARTERS OF ROME : THE
AVENTINE : THE JANICULUM :
THE FORUM : THE APPIAN WAY

I F the Piazza di Spagna was the hub of Rome in the nineteenth
century, to-day fashionable life centres round the Via Vittorio
Veneto, which winds its way up a slope to the Porta Pinciana
from the Piazza Barberini.

This district is known as the Ludovisi quarter, and it was laid out in
the late nineteenth century in the gardens belonging to the princely
family of that name. There are broad streets and avenues of modern
houses. The Central Station is near and, by passing through the old
walls at the Porta Pinciana, one finds at the other side, the splendid
gardens of the Villa Borghese and the Pincio.

Since it is on a height, the Ludovisi quarter is healthy, sunny in
the winter, and cooler than the old town in summer, and yet I find
this region rather lacking in character.

However, the Via Vittorio Veneto is pleasant enough, for trees
shade the pavements, there are smart shops, and fashionable and
beautifully dressed people sit at the tables set out on the broad pavements and, in particular, at Doney's, where the members of Rome's
smart set congregate.

There are few private houses in this street where Ministries alternate with luxury hotels and the windows of the big travel agencies
display alluring posters.

Half-way up the hill on the right-hand side United States marines
stand outside the former palace of the Queen Mother, now the
American Embassy. A little further on, on the same side, Rolls-
Royces, Hispano-Suizas, and Isottas draw up in front of the neo-
baroque Hotel Excelsior, and mink-clad ladies, and business tycoons,
pass through the swing doors into the crowded lounge.

There is movement in the Via Veneto throughout the day, but in the evening the pavements are thronged with tourists and Romans strolling up and down for the parade which is so essential a part of life in a southern town.

In the Piazza Barberini at the lower end of the street, everything is in striking contrast to this urbane scene, for here there is the quick movement and incessant bustle of a business quarter, and indeed many of the chief newspaper offices and commercial houses of Rome line the Via del Tritone which leads down to the Corso.

Nevertheless, in the centre of the Square amid the surge of buses and cars, Bernini's Triton throws up a cool jet of water into his huge stone shell.

A turning to the left a few yards down the Via del Tritone leads to the most monumental and celebrated of Roman statues, the *Fontana di Trevi.*

In the niche of something like a Baroque triumphal arch stands an immense statue of Neptune in a conch-shaped chariot drawn by sea-horses whose tossing heads are held by tritons. The clear foaming water flows into three superimposed stone basins into a large pool. Rills and miniature water-falls splash from a disorder of large rocks on either side. On hot evenings the Roman populace comes to sit on the parapet or on the stone benches set out in an amphitheatre. The people gossip and enjoy the freshness of the spray, the rustling, whispering, dripping murmur of the fountain. If you cast your coin into the Fontana di Trevi you will surely return to Rome, is the legend, but who reaps this rich harvest I do not know.

The Via Sistina that leads out of the Piazza Barberini, is a narrow street, but here the atmosphere is an aristocratic one, as opposed to the smartness of the Via Veneto. Indeed, the small bars and restaurants of this street are more discreet and the good taste of the displays in the shops more natural, and yet more calculated.

The hotels here are perhaps less modern, but more in keeping with the traditional fastidiousness of the Romans—of the two best, one, the Hotel de la Ville, has preserved lovely decorations of the early nineteenth century, and from the other, the Hassler, there are superb views over Rome.

The Church of Santa Trinita dei Monti was built by Charles VIII of France in 1495, when he was setting out to dominate the whole of Italy. Restored since that time, it is known to the whole world because it stands at the top of the Spanish Steps and is, in a sense, part of that admirable conception which looks like the gigantic stair-case of a Baroque palace.

From the terrace in front of the church there is one of the finest views of Rome, at its best perhaps on a warm night when the lovers sit on each level whispering to each other in the cool breeze that blows in from the sea. The steps curve in a horseshoe round a second ballustraded terrace and then broaden out in their descent to the Square and the Barcaccia, a boat-shaped fountain by Bernini, built to commemorate the stranding of a barge on this spot during some extensive floods. Keats, Shelley and, perhaps, Byron lived in one of the colour-washed houses half-way up the steps where the peasant women from the country used to offer their services as models to the painters of this artists' quarter.

At night too, a glance into the dark courtyard of the Spanish Embassy to the Vatican reveals a fountain charmingly lit up with coloured lamps.

The Via Condotta was, and is still to a certain extent, the Bond Street of Rome, with fashion shops, shirtmakers and boutiques selling fancy goods and coloured silk scarves.

The Café Greco, quite near the Square, was founded in the eighteenth century, and has changed little in aspect save for the souvenirs and portraits of eminent men of letters, painters and musicians who congregated there for good conversation.

The narrow lanes that branch off from the Via Condotta have survived the impact of many discerning tourists and are still essenti-ally Roman in character. There are small wineshops and bars, and pleasant little *trattorie* with tables on the pavement or in shady courtyards.

As a rule the food in these places is good and not expensive, and the white Frascati on draught is excellent and refreshing.

Sometimes wandering musicians come to play or sing to the guests and, generally speaking, the atmosphere is a friendly and cheerful one.

The Via del Babuino and the Via Margutta, the street parallel to it, are the main thoroughfares of the artists' quarter, though the arrival of rich amateurs from different parts of the world has tended to put up prices and spoil conditions for the genuine professional.

The Piazza del Popolo, which I have already described when viewed from the terrace of the Pincio, seen from any angle is one of the most beautiful of Roman squares. On one side is the Porto del

Popolo with seventeenth-century decorations, on the other, the two little domed churches which guard the entrance to the Corso.

In the centre, a tall and slender Egyptian obelisk rises up from between four sphinxes. To the north, the tiered terraces and gardens of the Pincio, to the south, a curved line of trees behind a low wall complete the full circle of the plan.

In most Italian towns there is a main street called the Corso, because on certain days in the year riderless horses were raced down these thoroughfares in the presence of excited crowds who betted hard and freely. In Rome these races continued until about 1880 when they had to be abandoned because of the growing traffic.

I like the Roman Corso, with its huge palaces and narrow pavements, and its Baroque churches, but it is best seen late at night or in the very early morning, when the surging noisy traffic is relatively quiet.

A few hundred yards from the Piazza del Popolo on the left-hand side, a short street leads to the Augusteo, the Mausoleum where the Emperor Augustus was buried, a large round building by the riverside, and surrounded by trees. His tomb has recently been opened up, but it is of little interest save to archæologists.

The Piazza Colonna is in a sense the real hub of Rome, for it is right in the centre of the city, and it is certainly one of the noisiest and busiest places in any capital.

The huge column in the centre was erected in honour of the victories of Marcus Aurelius, and it is adorned from top to bottom with bas-relief depicting the battles in which his soldiers took part.

The beautiful Palazzo Chigi is now the Italian Foreign Office, and the Chamber of Deputies is installed in the Piazza di Monte Citorio.

A large café named Aragno in the Piazza Colonna is frequented by journalists, civil servants and members of Parliament. It is, in fact, an essentially Italian place with little in common with the bars and teashops of the Via Vittorio Veneto.

Although I do not like to spend too much time inspecting Roman ruins, I never fail to visit the Pantheon whenever I am in Rome, partly I think because it has decayed so little, but mainly because, as a building, it is perfect of its kind. Originally a pagan temple of the fourth century, it was shortly afterwards converted into a church, and then later it served as a burial place of great Italians.

The beauty and attraction of this building lie in the fine simplicity of the huge dome and its perfect proportions. A round hole in the centre of the vault casts a strange and brilliant light from above. The exterior is rather bare, since the marble facings and the copper roof were removed by vandals many years ago.

To return to the Corso through a maze of little streets is difficult though the distance is short, and I have always had to use a map though my sense of direction is good.

The Piazza Venezia is dominated by the immense white colon-naded Victor Emmanuel monument which serves as a background to a wealth of gilded statues and friezes in the Victorian manner. In the harsh light of noon the whole structure glitters and is almost unbearable to look at, and yet it is designed on the lines of other buildings that stood here centuries ago, and must have looked very much like one of the temples of the Augustan age when they were new. Only too often we forget that many of the ruins in Greece and Rome have only acquired a certain dignity through the patina of age and the romantic aura that is attached to them.

This Piazza takes its name from the battlemented Palazza Venezia which was formerly the Embassy of the Venetian Republic and now belongs to the Italian State. Under Fascism it was one of the official residences of the Duce, who often addressed his followers from a balcony facing the Square.

Mussolini left his mark on this district when he pulled down some rather picturesque old houses and built the Via dei Fori Romani, a broad and impressive avenue which passes between Trajan's Forum with its tall column and the Roman Forum to connect the Piazza Venezia with the Colosseum and the Arch of Constantine.

This piece of town development was much criticized at the time, for this district that was cleared had the nostalgia and charm that Piranesi conveys so well in his prints and etchings of Rome. Now many of the ruins that were embedded in other buildings, or stand-ing haphazardly at a street corner, are tidied up and neatly labelled, and the result is something like an outdoor museum.

The Colosseum is too well known to require description—suffice it to note that only a third of the original structure remains, the rest was taken away as building material at different times throughout the centuries. Faced with coloured marble and shaded by a huge canvas awning, the amphitheatre must have looked far larger than it does now, and of course infinitely more cheerful.

By day the towering mass of grey stone is gloomy and rather

depressing, but in the soft silvery light of a full moon, the vast ruins have a romantic aspect, though they are not the place for romance since the police are apt to arrest anyone indulging in excessive love-making in public.

The Church of Santa Maria in Aracoelli at the top of a long steep stone stairway just a little way behind the right wing of the Victor Emmanuel monument, was built in the eighth century and subse-qently restored. It is on the site of a temple to Juno, where, according to the legend, the Sybil announced the birth of Christ to the Emperor Augustus, who immediately founded a shrine to the unknown God.

This church is a place of pilgrimage because of a wonder-working image of the Child Jesus covered with jewels. In one of the chapels there is a fresco depicting the life of St Anthony by Benozzo Gozzoli.

A little higher up on the crest of the same hill, the Piazza del Campidoglio is on the exact spot where stood the Capitol, the citadel of ancient Rome.

In the sixteenth century, Pope Paul III decided to dignify the aspect of the Campidoglio and entrusted Michelangelo with the task. The gilded bronze statue of Marcus Aurelius was brought from the Lateran to the centre of the square. Only traces of the gilding remain, but there is a legend that at times the traces of gold increase and will go on doing so until, at the end of the world, the statue has become all golden again. The imposing Senatorial Palace was erected in the twelfth century, but its present façade was carried out from the designs by Michelangelo after his death. Its towers, its pedimented windows, its monumental sweeping stairway, its foun-tains and its statue of Rome, face us as we climb up to the square. Added dignity is given by the two lateral palaces, almost like side-wings, which house the famous Capitoline museums of sculpture and paintings.

Here you can see the famous *Dying Gaul* carved in the second century B.C.—a most moving and life-like naked figure of a man struggling to rise, then drooping down exhausted.

There are busts of famous poets, generals and philosophers of the Greek and the Roman periods, of Demosthenes, Cicero and Socrates, of the Roman Emperors and their wives.

In the Room of the Doves you will find the beautiful little *Mosaic of the Doves*. Made of minute marble pieces it is extraordinarily delicate in workmanship. Three of the doves seem to be turning to look at us, the fourth stretches to the basin, says Pliny, and "darkens it with her shadow".

The bronze *Boy with the Thorn* is familiar to everyone as it is perhaps one of the most often copied of all the ancient pieces of sculpture, but the impact of the original Greek statue cannot fail to move us by its perfection.

In this museum, too, is the *She Wolf of the Capitol* feeding Romulus and Remus. Of Etruscan origin, it is magnificently conceived, the simple, strong lines of the great beast contrasting with the soft rounded forms of the plump twins.

From behind the Capitoline Museum in the Via del Campidoglio, there is the most impressive view of the ruins of the Roman Forum. First of all, in the foreground, the three columns that are left of the Temple of Castor and Pollux, and then, a little further on, the beautifully designed arch of Septimus, and in the background the huge mass of the Colosseum and the triumphal arch of Titus. On the right-hand side rises the Palatine Hill, also covered with a mass of ruins, but planted with evergreen trees.

In the valley on the far side of it, but unseen from the Capitoline, the outlines of the immense oblong Circus Maximus are clearly discernible.

There are so many remains of ancient Rome in this area that it would be impossible, and in fact rather tedious, to enumerate them all. For me, these remains create a strange and rather melancholy landscape of great charm. Despite my studies of history and of the classics, I cannot find the patience to examine in detail these fragments of the long centuries of existence of a nation, and I am sure that most intelligent people cannot favour pedantic sightseeing. Surely it is a waste of time and energy to look at buildings that have little or no æsthetic appeal when seen individually and without a prolonged study of their history and of their functions.

I do find pleasure in looking at the small circular Temple of Vesta and the little square Temple of Fortune that are to be found near the southern extremity of the Circus Maximus near the Tiber, for both these buildings are more or less intact, and their perfect proportions are made more apparent by a beautiful setting.

The Church of Santa Maria in Cosmedin nearby, is claimed to be one of the oldest churches in existence, and it certainly preserves most of the essential features of the early Roman basilicas. Built on the site of a temple, it embodies many of the features of the original structure, including the twelve columns of the aisle.

There is a tradition that if a liar inserts his hand into the open mouth of the stone head in the porch of Santa Maria, it will be snapped off . . .

By continuing a few yards down the riverside it is possible to go up to the top of the Aventine Hill by a steep and almost countrified lane. There are convents and churches on the crest of this hill, and shaded public gardens with a terrace overlooking the Tiber and some regions of central Rome. The best view of all is to be had by peeping through a round keyhole in a garden gate opposite the Palace of the Knights of Malta which offers a vista of a lovely avenue of trees that forms a framework to the Dome of St Peter's in the far distance.

Rome, even more than Florence, is a city of lovely walks. The summit of the Esquiline Hill, immediately to the north of the Colosseum, has also preserved a delightfully rural aspect.

No one should fail to go to the park on the Janiculum, the high ridge on the far side of the Tiber, and the time to choose is the late afternoon. Then the red roofs and the ancient buildings of Rome are bathed in a golden light, and the blue Alban Hills in the distance are turned to deep purple in the rays of the setting sun.

I also like to wander through the little narrow streets at the base of the Quirinal, and then to climb up to the fine square in front of the former Royal Palace. An obelisk and two huge groups of statuary representing horse-tamers, were brought here from the Baths of Constantine.

The Palace was built as a summer residence by Pope Gregory XIII in the sixteenth century. It was taken over by the House of Savoy in 1870, and it is now used as the residence of the President of the Republic.

After a few hundred yards the Via del Quirinale becomes the Via XX Settembre, a street that runs along a ridge to the Porta Pia, one of the Baroque gateways in the city wall.

This thoroughfare is lined with large palaces, government offices and ministries, but at night, the section furthest away from the Quirinal is thronged with middle-class Romans who frequent the numerous cafés and *espresso* bars, and even do some shopping, for many shops remain open until a late hour.

A turning to the right leads past the lovely fountains of the

Piazza Esedra to the admirably-designed Central Railway station. This building, the new University, and Mussolini's immense sports stadium, are modern architectural achievements of real merit and are worth examining.

The Piazza dei Cinquecento in front of the station is the point of departure for suburban and country-bound buses, though some long-distance buses leave from other parts of the city.

The splendid underground railway is a perpetual source of amusement to the Romans, for it passes through the least populated districts of the capital, but it does connect the main station to the Colosseum, the station for the neighbouring seaside suburb of Ostia, and the beautiful church of St Paul's without the Walls. (San Paolo fuori le mure.)

I do not care for Ostia, with its black sands, gimcrack villas and seething crowds, but I often visit the Protestant Cemetery, which is within two or three minutes' walk of the Ostia station in Rome. Keats and Shelley are buried here among the cypress trees, the urns, and classical monuments to the British, Germans and Americans, who so often died in their early manhood as the result of the unhealthy climate. In the early spring the gardens are full of violets and snow-drops, and the roses frequently bloom here until close on Christmas.

In the Middle Ages the Pyramid of Caius Cestius, which over-shadows the cemetery, was believed to be the tomb of Remus.

The Church of San Paolo was first founded in the fourth century, then rebuilt, enlarged and altered throughout the ages until it was half destroyed in the beginning of the nineteenth century, though subsequently restored.

Nevertheless, in spite of these vicissitudes, St Paul's retains much of its ancient splendour, and the structure has kept its original form and much of its ornamentation. Immense in size, and of noble pro-portions, with a richly ornamented ceiling supported on small Roman arches that rest on Corinthian pillars, the principal feature is the choir whose thirteenth-century mosaics represent Our Lord with St Peter, St Andrew, St Paul and St Luke.

Since this Basilica was under the protection of the Crown of Britain before the Reformation, the emblem of the Garter can be seen carved in different parts of the building.

The thirteenth-century cloisters escaped both decay and restora-tion, and are the finest in Rome, except perhaps those of the Church of St John Lateran.

This Basilica was founded in the fourth century, and next to St Peter's it is the largest church of the Holy City, and in fact, the Cathedral of Rome.

The adjoining palace was the residence of the Popes until the transfer of the Holy See to Avignon. When the Great Schism came to an end, the Pontiffs took up their abode in the Vatican, and they have remained there ever since.

The Lateran Church was repeatedly destroyed and rebuilt, but the greater part of the present structure dates from the restorations in the seventeenth century.

The fine eighteenth-century façade with its columns is surmounted by a stone balustrade on which stand St John the Baptist, St John the Evangelist and a number of ecclesiastically dressed figures and, upon a pedestal above the central pediment, a triumphant effigy of Christ holding the Cross.

Beneath Him, and between two sets of double pillars, is the balcony from which the Blessing is given on certain feasts of the Church.

The chillness of the immense white marble nave is relieved by the brilliantly decorated ceiling designed perhaps by Michelangelo, but more probably by Giacomo della Porta, and also by the richly adorned organ, and the thirteenth-century mosaics of the apse.

There is such a wealth of monuments, pictures and mosaics in St John's that I would advise the hurried visitor to seek out only the fresco by Giotto on the first pillar to the right of the main entrance, the cloisters and, lastly, the fifth-century Baptistry. This building is one of the oldest Christian buildings in Rome, and there is even a legend that it was constructed expressly for the baptism of Constantine the Great. The bronze doors with their prolonged musical echo were brought here from the Baths of Caracalla.

The Scala Santa in the Lateran Square, a flight of twenty-eight marble steps reputed to have been brought from Jerusalem, is venerated by Catholics because of the tradition that it was used by Our Lord after He had been crowned with thorns.

At the top of the Scala Santa, the Sancta Sanctorum was a chapel of the original Lateran Palace which is so sacred that only the Pope may officiate, save on Palm Sundays when the Canons of St John's come here in procession. The painting of Christ above the silver tabernacle is one of the earliest of the kind in existence.

A walk of a quarter of an hour down the Via Merulana leads

from the Lateran Square to the Basilica of Santa Maria Maggiore; it was founded, it is said, in the fourth century by St Liberius to whom the Virgin appeared in a vision with directions to build a church wherever he would find fresh snow in the morning.

This legend is commemorated on the fifth of August each year, when showers of white rose leaves are thrown down from the ceiling on to the worshippers.

The tall bell tower was erected in the fourteenth century and the lovely Baroque façade dates from the mid-eighteenth century, but the interior has kept its original shape, for the ceiling, decorated in the fifteenth century, is in harmony with the rest of the building.

The chief treasure of this church is a reliquary behind the High Altar containing the Cradle of Our Lord that is said to have been brought to Rome in the seventh century.

Early on Christmas morning there is a procession in honour of this most prized relic of the Basilica, which contains among other things the brains of St Thomas à Becket carefully preserved in two little bags.

On entering Santa Maria Maggiore, the first impression is of the richness of the decoration. Forty-two columns of Greek marble line the huge nave which is paved with mosaics in brilliant colours to contrast with the white and gold of the walls, and of the ceilings gilded with the first gold brought back from America. This radiance is continued by the mosaics above the chancel arch, and in particular those of the apse which depict the *Coronation of the Virgin Mary*.

Besides these three Basilicas which I have described, there are fifty or sixty churches of great architectural interest, or that contain important works of art.

CHAPTER TEN

THE VIA APPIA : TIVOLI : BRACCIANO : THE CASTELLI ROMANI : THE PONTINE MARSHES : THE COAST ROAD TO NAPLES

WHEN I first saw the Appian Way many years ago it still possessed all the nostalgic charm of the seventeenth or eighteenth century when eager travellers drove over the cobbles to examine the tombs and monuments that line this most ancient of roads. In the present day much of the enchantment is lost because lorries, buses and cars speed along this historic highway which has become as busy as an *autostrada*.

Thirty years ago the bare rolling plain of the Campagna stretched out towards the blue Alban Hills, unbroken save for the derelict arches of the aqueduct, and the odd fragments of ruins scattered about everywhere.

In the intervening period the tentacles of the city have reached out towards the countryside, and untidy groups of buildings are springing up on all sides, some even in the vicinity of the Via Appia itself.

This oldest of Roman roads was constructed three hundred years before the birth of Christ, and eventually linked up the capital with the town now known as Brindisi. During the first century of its existence it was little more than a kind of cemetery for people of distinction for whom were erected monuments and tombs on either side of the thoroughfare.

Then by a strange twist in the evolution of history this most pagan of highways became closely associated with the rise of Christianity, and the survival of the early Christians throughout their intense persecution.

So, on the surface, there are mounds of ruins, tombs, fragments of all kinds with half-effaced inscriptions and bas-reliefs of the time of the Republic and of the Empire, whilst, in the catacombs below ground, there are countless evidences of the burning faith of the members of the new religion who could only worship in hiding, or had to seek refuge under the earth.

When at last Constantine proclaimed religious toleration, the catacombs continued to be used as cemeteries, and so many of the sepulchres were made in the fourth and fifth centuries.

I have visited most of the catacombs, some of them repeatedly. Sometimes I am filled with awe, and deeply moved by the visible signs of so much fortitude. At other times, particularly if I am forced to accompany a large party of people, I am overcome by claustrophobia and make a dash for the surface.

Between ten o'clock in the morning and five o'clock in the afternoon the ceaseless flow of traffic and the constant movement of tourists does really mar the enjoyment of what is left of the melancholy charm of the Via Appia. Here again, in the height of the summer season, it is better to rise early and see this strange and unique landscape in the soft light of morning when the only people astir are the peasants and a few workers cycling to their jobs.

The same tactics are also advisable for those making an excursion to Tivoli, and for the same reasons, for the beautiful gardens of the Villa d'Este are also apt to be crowded in the daytime. Then the tour of Hadrian's Villa can be very tiring when the sun is at its hottest, for there is a great deal of walking to be done.

Although the Roman Emperor's country residence was stripped of many of its treasures to adorn the great house at Tivoli and the palaces of Rome, there still remain mosaic floors and extensive ruins of temples, baths and porticoes.

However, I feel that this place is only of moderate interest except to keen archæologists and students of Roman history.

The Renaissance Villa at Tivoli is another matter, or to be more precise, the monumental water gardens that have made it so famous, for the interior of the Villa has been deprived of nearly all its furnishings.

To form the gardens the side of a hill was terraced and planted with trees, adorned with statues and flower beds. Between them flows and sparkles clear water that trickles in small rills, murmurs in little waterfalls, and foams like snow in larger cascades, or rushes through stone channels to pause in smooth basins and pools at each level.

Clouds of iridescent spray hover between the tall ilexes and cypresses and over the flowering bushes and orange blossom, and most sounds are drowned by the music of the splashing, dripping and whispering coming from every side.

Royal Park of Caserta: Diana's Pool

Bird's eye view
of Orvieto

From the topmost terrace one looks down on the contrasting greens of the vegetation below, and beyond, at the vast greyish expanse of the Campagna to the distant towers and domes of Rome.

There are frequent bus services to the capital, and as the journey takes little over an hour, it is quite practical to stay at Tivoli and do sightseeing in Rome by day and enjoy the coolness of the country at night.

Incidentally I have been sometimes asked whether it would be agreeable to commute from one of the seaside resorts in the vicinity of Rome—my answer is definitely in the negative—the morning and evening trains are always crowded, the coast here is not attractive, and the beaches are far too popular.

If I had a car I would think of staying at Bracciano, an ancient little town on the shores of a beautiful lake. The accommodation is very limited, and not over luxurious, but the bathing is good of its kind. The surrounding country is still unspoilt, and there are pleasant walks over the wooded hills to rustic country villages and fishing hamlets.

The immense Castle of the Orsini dominates the rather featureless little town and gives it character, but fortunately the built-up area is away from the lake, and so its shores have remained pleasingly rural. The water is usually a smooth leaden blue, there are low wooded hills on the opposite side seven miles away. At intervals on the beaches and cliffs, there are small white villages, castles and strange nameless ruins of no particular attribution. There is a local legend that when the sun is particularly strong the vanished city of Sabate can be seen in the depths of the lake.

Another story which I believe to be better founded, is that the trout caught here sometimes attain a weight of nearly thirty pounds, and this only twenty-five miles from Rome.

A second excursion that may be made fairly easily from Rome by car or by bus, is to go to Tarquinia where the mural paintings of the Etruscan tombs are singularly well preserved and of great beauty, but most of these frescoes can also be seen in excellent reproduction in the Archæological Museum of Florence.

Tarquinia itself is an ancient and picturesque little town with medieval fortifications, quaint streets, and tall towers.

It is situated on the edge of a low hill overlooking the reclaimed marshes of the Maremma that stretch for six or seven miles to the shores of the Tyrrhenian Sea. Since I have described the Etruscan

H

cities more fully in my books entitled *By Italian Shores* and *Summer at San Martino*, I will content myself by making this very brief allusion to an enchanting and highly interesting region.

If you should wish to continue your journey southwards by road, there is a choice of two routes of about the same length but presenting different attractions. The first, which I will describe in a subsequent chapter, goes inland and passes through Cassino and Caserta. The second crosses the Pontine Marshes and keeps close to the coast a good part of the way.

From the scenic point of view it is the one that I prefer, and since there are fewer hills to be negotiated, the journey should take rather less time, but there are temptations to stop at different places on the way.

It is possible, though reprehensible, to start off on the journey by using the Appian Way, and undoubtedly many people do so. Then, personally I should prefer to deviate through the Frascati, the nearest town on the Alban Hills, and also one of the most charming.

The vineyards on these slopes produce the wine which is so popular in Rome, and yet almost undrinkable anywhere else. It is at its best within two or three hundred yards of where it was grown, and the further it travels the more it tends to deteriorate. It is unfortunate, for it is refreshing, inexpensive and palatable.

Frascati, however, has other attractions, for it is situated on the very edge of a ridge overlooking the Campagna, and I can think of few pleasanter ways of spending a summer evening than by dining on the terrace of one of the restaurants here and watching the sun sink behind the dome of St Peter's. At such times the whole landscape is enveloped in a violet light that gradually grows deeper as the red glow fades in the western sky, and the lights in the distance begin to twinkle through the faint haze.

In the sixteenth century many Cardinals and members of the princely families built huge villas to which they withdrew in the summertime.

The finest of these are the Villa Aldobrandini, built by Della Porta, Boromini's Villa Falconieri, and Vasanzio's Villa Mondragone. The gardens of each of these residences are open to the public, and are adorned with grottoes, cascades and statuary.

The road to Albano passes through wooded hilly country and leaves Grottaferrata on the right. This village is noted for its ancient monastery containing a Byzantine picture of the Virgin. In spite of the proximity to Rome, country fairs are held here on the twenty-fifth of March and on the ninth of September every year, and these festivities attract peasants from the whole of the surrounding neighbourhood.

After leaving the ancient little town of Marino, the sombre lake of Albano can be seen at the bottom of an extinct crater. It is surrounded on all sides by wooded slopes, covered with violets in the early spring.

Rocca di Papa, three or four miles away to the left, is a small summer resort perched up on a rock nearly 2,400 feet above the level of the sea. There are delightful walks through the woods to the villages and lakes of the region.

At Castel Gandolfo, situated on an eminence above the lake, there is a large sixteenth-century villa built for Clement VIII, and it is still used as a summer residence by the Pope. In 1931, after the Lateran Treaty, it was completely renovated and the beautiful grounds of the Villa Barberini added to the estate.

At Albano the road joins up with the No. 7 highway to Naples which follows approximately the same course as the Roman Via Appia.

At this point the road to Anzio branches off to the left.

The fighting that occurred when the Anglo-American forces landed here did little permanent damage to the town, which is an ancient one, for it was the birthplace of Caligula and of Nero. Under the Roman Empire, this was a popular summer resort as well as a commercial port of some importance.

Anzio is a place to avoid in July and August, for the beach is always crowded with day trippers and visitors staying at the little boarding houses and cheap lodgings.

Genzano, the next and last of the "Castelli Romani", stands on heights dominating the Lake of Nemi, a small circular sheet of water, surrounded by densely wooded slopes, and in a hollow which was in all probability the crater of an extinct volcano.

In the past, as in the present, it was noted for its beauty, especially by the Romans who staged aquatic festivals here.

Under the Fascist régime, the lake was drained in order to see what relics of the past were hidden in its depths. No treasures were found, but two galleys in a good state of preservation were salvaged and placed in the small local museum, which was destroyed by the Germans in 1944.

A little further on, the Appian Way descends to the Pontine Marshes which have been completely reclaimed during the last sixty years. Naturally enough the ground is as level as a billiards table, and deep channels have been dug to drain away the water, but the moisture is such that the vegetation is always a brilliant green.

The little white farms scattered all over the countryside are modern, for most of them were built when the land finally became available for cultivation some thirty years ago.

In 1933 Mussolini laid the foundation stone of Littoria and Sabaudia, both constructed to serve as market towns to the newly developed regions reclaimed from the marshes.

The Duce tried to take all the credit for the splendid work done in this region, but it had been begun long before his entry into politics, though in all fairness, it must be said that he was responsible for the completion of this large-scale scheme of drainage and rehabilitation. The planning and architecture of the new towns is good, and the same is true of the agricultural buildings.

As usual, Mussolini was intent on impressing the peoples of the world as well as those of his own country and, being an ex-journalist, he was expert at publicity.

Many of the achievements attributed to him were in fact merely completions of plans interrupted by the First World War, but the fact remains that most of the Pontine folk are still Fascists and revere the memory of the man who did so much harm to Italy.

The drive through the marshes is not an unpleasant one, for the light here is particularly clear and lends unusual brilliance to every feature of the landscape. A short way inland, a low ridge of hills follows the course of the Via Appia to the south.

Unseen from the main road, the village of Ninfa at the foot of these hills is worth visiting in the springtime. In the early Middle Ages Ninfa was a flourishing city, but in the sixteenth century the inhabitants were driven away by the dread scourge of malaria, and the place was submerged by the rising tide of the undrained marshes, only to reappear again years later. Now the mellowed ruins of the ramparts, the castle, the palaces and the church are mirrored in a small lake, and in the months of April and of May the ground is carpeted with wild flowers.

Not far away on the heights, the immense Castle of Sermoneta is one of the best preserved medieval fortresses in the country, and it is still occupied by the Caetani family, who received their estates in southern Italy from the Byzantine Emperors in the eleventh century.

In the sixteenth century the Castle belonged for a while to the Borgias, and the infamous Lucrezia stayed in it repeatedly.

From the battlements there is a view across the width of the Pontine Marshes to Monte Circeo, a hill that rises abruptly out of the surrounding flatness and juts out into the sea.

Centuries ago this promontory was an island; according to an old tradition, the island where the witch Circe kept Ulysses in thrall. The cup from which his companions drank and were turned into swine was greatly prized by the Emperor Claudius, but nothing is known of its subsequent history.

Circe's Hill is eighteen hundred feet high, and is worth the rather arduous climb from the village of San Felice Circeo, a little way up the southern slope.

From the summit there is one of the most extensive and beautiful prospects in the whole of Italy. Looking northwards, if the day is fine and clear, it is possible to discern the Dome of St Peter's in the far distance. In between lie the lagoons and towns of the Pontine Marshes. On the seaward side, the deep blue outlines of the Ponza Islands rise mistily out of the sparkling waters.

To the east there is a fine vista of hills and of the taller mountains beyond. Then finally, turning towards the south, the eye can follow the coast to the promontory of Gaeta, and sometimes, far away, the white plumes of smoke rising from the cone of Vesuvius can be discerned.

Wandering across the slopes and heights of Circe's Hill, the climber encounters ruins of temples, Etruscan walls, and strange unaccountable remains of prehistory.

Monte Circeo has been turned into a national park because of its natural beauty, and also because of the unusual character of the vegetation on its slopes, each of which has a different climate according to its particular aspect.

On the northern side, the trees, flowers and plants are alpine, but on the southern side, which is sheltered from the wind, the flora is subtropical.

At the foot of the hill a small and altogether delightful little resort has been developed recently, and it is one that I frequently visit for a bathe and a dish of lobster eaten to the accompaniment of the really excellent local white wine.

San Felice Circeo is four or five miles from the highway, but from there you can take an adequate subsidiary road along the coast and rejoin the Via Appia at Terracina, an ancient town with monuments of only secondary interest. The beach here is a good one, and the bathing facilities are adequate, and so after all you may find yourself disposed to stop here for an hour or two.

About a mile outside the town a ruined gateway marks the former frontier post between the Papal States and the Kingdom of Naples, and though the boundary has ceased to exist, the deep South begins here.

Unfortunately the road swerves inland, away from the mountainous coast that stretches as far as Gaeta where the Via Appia rejoins the sea.

From Terracina onwards an acute observer would notice subtle differences of architecture and manners which are due to a different tradition, and to different administrations in the past. One is constantly reminded of the fact that United Italy has not yet been in existence for a century.

Fondi, the first town of any importance, was badly battered and bombed during the Second World War, and the consequent rebuilding has taken away much of its former character.

However, this town was repeatedly attacked and plundered by invading armies because of its strategic position commanding the access by road to Naples. It was also taken and sacked by the famous corsair, Barbarossa, when he attempted to kidnap the beautiful Julia Gonzaga from the massive and well-fortified castle.

She escaped just in time, but the disappointed pirate avenged himself by slaughtering many of the unfortunate citizens of the town.

A secondary road from Fondi covers the eight miles to the little seaside town of Sperlonga which has a lovely beach, but few amenities for the tourist.

Itri, on the Via Appia, is remembered as the home and birthplace of "Fra Diavolo", the hero of Auber's opera. Far from being a brigand, he was leader of a partisan movement against the occupying forces of Napoleon I. He also acted as an intelligence agent for the British and for the exiled King of Naples. In spite of his great courage, his many disguises and the help that he received from the local population, he was eventually caught and executed by the French.

A few miles further on, the road passes the suburbs of Gaeta, and reaches the sea at Formia, an attractive seaside resort that appears to have completely recovered from the devastations of the last war.

I recommend a halt here for a drink or a meal on the terrace of one of the hotels in order to enjoy the view of the really lovely bay.

To the south the coast is flat and straight, but inland rise the hills of the Minturno which faced the British troops for a long time when they were halted at the Garigliano River in their advance on Rome in 1944.

At the extremity of the northern arm of the bay is Gaeta, formerly one of the fortress towns that guarded the approaches of Naples. It was fated to be attacked and captured many times during the course of its long and eventful history. Byzantines, Saracens, Normans, Angevins, Spaniards and French fought in turn for the possession of this citadel.

During the Napoleonic wars it was courageously defended by the Neapolitan troops and the British sailors of Admiral Sir Sidney Smith, a specialist in what we should call to-day, sea and land operations.

In 1848 during the Roman Republic, Pope Pio Nono took refuge here and was joined by many of his cardinals at the Royal Palace lent to him by the King of Naples.

In 1860 Francis II, the last King of Naples, was besieged here for nearly four months by the troops of United Italy after they had captured Naples—he was, of course, forced to surrender eventually, and after his abdication he retired into private life.

I have never stayed for long at Gaeta, but I have always had the impression that it would be quite an agreeable place for a summer holiday. The town is ancient and in a beautiful situation—on the far side of the headland there is a long stretch of beach far from motor traffic, and the population is noted for good looks.

In this region one encounters blue eyes and fair hair frequently, doubtless because of a Norman or Viking strain in the race, and this colouring combined with the warm southern complexion can be very attractive.

Beyond Formia, the Via Appia cuts inland once more and passes through scenery of only moderate interest. The hilly region behind Minturno has remained very primitive. In the remoter villages, peasant costumes are still worn, and the inhabitants seldom come down to the more sophisticated atmosphere of the plains.

Veterans of the Second World War may wish to linger at the Garigliano and Volturno rivers to revisit the battlefields where they fought, but ordinary tourists will do well to go on as quickly as possible to Naples.

After crossing twenty miles or so of dull flat plain, it is possible to get back to the sea just before Pozzuoli where there is a prospect of the Bay of Naples with the Miseno Peninsula to the north, and of the distant headland of Sorrento to the south.

Pozzuoli, with its slums, its beaches covered with shabby bathing establishments, has never attracted me, despite its temples, its amphi-theatres and other sights so beloved of the eighteenth-century and nineteenth-century travellers. They revelled in the volcanic exhala-tions of the Solfatara, where clouds of steam rise from the warm sand. They delighted more understandably in the Lago Averno, the Avernus of the ancients, a round lake two miles across, supposed to be one of the chief gates of Hell.

For a consideration guides will show you the grotto by which one could enter the infernal regions, but few people are prepared to pay for this privilege nowadays.

The shortest road to the centre cuts inland once more, and, after passing through some industrial suburbs, it plunges suddenly into a long tunnel which leads right into the city of Naples.

CHAPTER ELEVEN

NAPLES

I HAVE been to Naples many times during the past twenty-five years, and I also lived there for six memorable months, but on my last visit I was impressed more than ever by the Greek attributes of the population. There have been many invasions, occupations and incursions here; countless people of countless races have sojourned in these regions, but the strong Hellenic strain has survived all these vicissitudes and is still predominant at least among the true Neapolitans, those who live in the crowded streets of the Centre.

Little or nothing is known of the prehistoric inhabitants of southern Italy because there are so few visible remains of the peoples who lived in these regions before the ninth century B.C. The first concrete fact of which we are assured is that some Greeks from the Island of Rhodes settled in Naples in the eighth or ninth century B.C., and that they established themselves on the Pizzofalcone, a kind of rocky crag that dominates the Piazza San Ferdinando, the square on which the San Carlo Theatre is situated.

The small fortress city was called Parthenope, a name which was given to the Republic created by Napoleon out of the former Kingdom of Naples, though Parthenope was merely a siren who had practised her wiles on passing seamen. Unlike most demigods, she succeeded in dying and was buried, so the story goes, somewhere on the rock where the citadel was built.

Later, other Greeks came to found colonies on the shores of the bay where the climate and vegetation were so much like those of their own land, and one of these settlements, Neapolis, was situated on the site of the present city.

In due course all the Greek territories in southern Italy were annexed by the Romans, though the inhabitants continued to use their own language, and clung to their traditions, for they were not completely latinized until the first or second century B.C.

Under the Empire, Naples became very popular with the wealthy

Romans, who built large villas on the shores of the bay, and Tiberius spent the last years of his life on the Island of Capri.

The Barbarian invaders swept over southern Italy, but they were driven out by Belisarius. Byzantine rule was contested later on by the Lombards from the north and the Saracens from the south. However, the influence of Constantinople continued to be exercised over Naples itself until the city was formally annexed by the Norman Kings of Sicily in the first half of the twelfth century.

When the Holy Roman Emperor, Henry VI, married a Norman princess, both Sicily and southern Italy passed to the Hohenstaufens. The greatest, Frederick II, founded the University of Naples and fostered the arts and learning throughout his Italian domains.

In 1268, Charles of Anjou, brother of St Louis of France, dispossessed the youthful Conradin of Hohenstaufen and became King of Naples in his place.

Within a few years of their arrival the French made themselves so unpopular that the revolt known as the Sicilian Vespers broke out at Palermo. Thousands of the Angevin troops were massacred, and the island was annexed by the King of Aragon.

In 1442 the descendants of this monarch succeeded in adding the mainland of the Kingdom of Naples to their possessions. By the end of the century both Naples and Sicily were united to Spain and remained under the domination of that country until 1748, when the two states were separated once more, though each of them was ruled by a king of the house of Bourbon.

Towards the end of the same century, Sir William Hamilton became British Ambassador, and he exercised great influence on the policy of King Ferdinand IV. Lady Hamilton, an ex-housemaid, became a close friend of Queen Maria Carolina, the daughter of Maria Theresa, and the sister of Marie Antoinette of France.

It was in Naples that Admiral Nelson met Emma Hamilton and fell under her spell. It has often been suggested that she induced him to shoot Admiral Caracciolo, the pro-French sailor, although an amnesty had been promised to all those who had taken part in the revolt that led to the short-lived Parthenopean Republic.

When the French returned they were welcomed by the bulk of the population, and Joseph Bonaparte became King of Naples, to be succeeded shortly afterwards by Joachim Murat, the husband of Napoleon's sister Caroline.

In 1814 Murat abandoned his brother-in-law and was allowed

to retain his kingdom. In 1815 Murat returned to his allegiance to the Emperor and was driven out of Naples by the Allies.

In October of the same year, the ex-king landed in Calabria, hoping that he would be restored with the help of the Liberals who disliked the rule of the Bourbons. He was immediately arrested, court-martialled and shot, but his numerous descendants are leaders of fashionable society in Paris to-day.

The reactionary measures of the Neapolitan monarchy were continued until 1860, when Garibaldi and his "Thousand" conquered Sicily with the greatest of ease, and with the adherents that he acquired there he crossed the Straits of Messina and was welcomed as a liberator by the population of Naples. A plebiscite held the same year resulted in the uniting of southern Italy to the north.

It may be tedious to enumerate these historical events, but the atmosphere of Naples and the character of its inhabitants have been created by over two thousand years of foreign domination. Even now the people of southern Italy assert that they have been starved economically by the Government in Rome, and that they have not had their share of the public expenditure—like the Irish, they are and always have been against the government, and that attitude is maintained irrespective of the party in power. Like the Irish too, the southerners go in for politics, and they usually have more than their fair share of the seats in the cabinet. Then, but this may be due to regional unemployment, the *Meridionali*, as they are called, tend to become policemen, carabinieri or civil servants, jobs which are not really suited to their restless nature and inquiring minds.

The *lazzaroni*, the gay, carefree, idle slum-dwellers of the city, were traditionally attached to the Bourbon monarchs who prided themselves on using the popular dialect of the port quarter in their ordinary conversation.

Foreigners are apt to imagine that the bulk of Neapolitans are *lazzaroni*, whereas in fact they are a small but very noticeable minority. Naples has one of the biggest universities in Europe, a large and highly cultured middle class, vast industrial suburbs, and a very prosperous business community. Admittedly, the casual tourist does not encounter people belonging to these categories, nor are they of any particular interest to him unless he happens to talk Italian.

The best way to approach Naples is from the sea, and if possible on a large liner so as to be able to get a fine prospect from the height of the top deck. As the ship glides forward, the huge cone of Vesuvius slowly rises up in the distance, and from the crater an immense plume of white smoke drifts lazily up into the deep blue sky. In the foreground, the cliffs of Capri glisten in the sun, and its rays fall also on the white houses scattered on the green slopes of the uplands.

To the north, the tall Monte Epomeo, the extinct volcano of the Island of Ischia, is outlined against a violet and misty horizon.

Suddenly, just as one passes the first shores of the rugged Sorrento Peninsula, Naples itself begins to take shape: the headlands of Miseno and Posilippo to the left, and then the tiered houses of the city set out on a vast natural amphitheatre topped by a grim fortress. At water level, the Castel dell' Ovo and the Angevin Castle are on either side of the red façade and terraces of the Royal Palace.

When you land, you land in the heart of the city, and tumble straight away into the laughter, song, noise and unending poverty that characterizes Naples. Sunburnt, ragged men slumber on the quayside as they have slumbered for the past three thousand years, drawing life from the sun, and a glass of wine and a plate of spaghetti if they can get it. Since the south is over-populated and under-developed economically, work is hard to get, but the true Neapolitan lives for the moment, and cares little for the morrow, though the bare necessities he requires are scarcer than in the past.

In the eighteenth century many of these beachcombers had no clothes and were prevented from leaving the dockside because of their nakedness, but even in the first years of this century the younger children in the slums seldom wore any garments in the summer.

One of the principal gateways of the dockyards faces the gardens of the Piazza Municipio, which is the hub of the city for the foreign visitors.

To the left is the Maschi Angioino, the five-towered castle of the Angevin Kings, distinguished by the superb ornamental gateway which is in fact a triumphal arch erected to commemorate the accession of Alfonso I of Aragon. Ornamented with bas-relief, pediments and classical columns it follows the tradition of Rome rather than of the Gothic Age, and it certainly does not harmonize with the massive medieval towers that flank it.

The interior is rather nondescript, but the courtyard does form a magnificent background for the plays presented there during the summer months.

The Royal Palace is also little more than a fairly pleasing architectural feature in the landscape, for the state apartments are furnished in what to me is not a pleasing style. Nor do I particularly care for the work on the walls and ceilings.

Naples, of course, is endowed with so much natural beauty that there is little temptation for conventional sightseeing, especially as the genius of the place has always been concentrated on music or the theatre.

There are, of course, churches and monasteries of some splendour, but it is a really unforgettable experience to see the opera in the fine auditorium of the San Carlo Theatre, for even if the performers are not always of the first rank, the audience is the most appreciative and sensitive to music in all Italy.

The circular Piazza del Plebiscito, facing the west wing of the Royal Palace, is a fine piece of urban designing, aptly completed by the domed church of San Francesco di Paola which is planned more or less like the Pantheon.

Two or three streets lead out of the right-hand side of the Piazza del Municipio. The first of these, the Via de Pretis, a broad ugly commercial street, is continued by the Corso Umberto, an even more hideous and featureless street that comes to an abrupt end at the Central Railway Station.

The real artery of Naples, the Via Roma, divides the central part of the city from the maze of narrow little streets on the lower slopes of Vomero Hill.

Locally the Via Roma is still called the Toledo, after the Spanish Viceroy who was responsible for its construction. If the foreign rulers were disliked, the domination of the Government in Rome is still resented, and this resentment is increased by the wisecracks of the northerners such as "Naples is an African city without a European quarter", remarks which do not endear them to the people of the south.

From early morning until late at night the narrow pavements of the Toledo are astir with a seething bustling crowd, some walking slowly and stopping to gesticulate more freely in order to emphasize a point, others rushing to a job, and the remainder window-shopping, gazing at the cameos, the brilliant coloured ties, the delicate lingerie, and the ready-made suits on display. The *espresso* bars also do continuous business, selling not only diminutive cups of black coffee, but also Coca-Cola and the multicoloured Neapolitan ices which originated in this town.

In the small side streets on the slope, there are the signboards of innumerable *pizzerie*, for in this land of *pizza*, they rarely talk of *trattorie*, though both terms refer to popular taverns.

If you have not been innoculated against typhoid you will take your life in your hands if you try out dishes containing the local shellfish, such as Spaghetti con *vonvole* (mussels) or cockles.

It is possible that I may be maligning the Neapolitan, for the laws about food hygiene are strict, and they are rigorously enforced by the severe penalties imposed on those who disobey them. I have neglected to take these precautions myself, yet I have never suffered from the food poisoning that Oscar Wilde contracted here, and that probably contributed to his death some months later.

Of the regional dishes I can recommend the small swordfish, and still more the red mullet—the meat here is not so good as in Florence or Rome, and I do not care for dishes prepared with tomato. Of the local wines, the Vesuvio is the cheapest, and the Capri if it is authentic is excellent, but Capri would have to be a very large island to produce all the vintages that bear its name.

If you are prepared to pay a slightly higher price, the Corvo of Sicily is agreeable in very hot weather as it can stand icing without deteriorating, but of course it cannot be obtained on draught.

Italian beer has vastly improved of recent years, and the Peroni on draught is light and thirst-quenching, but in bottle it is just as expensive as wine.

I like these little back streets off the Toledo, with their long strings of washing flapping in the breeze, the little purple swordfish on the slabs, the brilliant displays of tomatoes, red peppers and fresh fruit.

The people are colourful too, and friendly enough to the courteous foreigner, and if he reciprocates their friendliness, they will rarely take advantage of him to cheat him—if he is surly, why then he deserves anything that is coming to him. Life here is a perpetual comedy with more than a hint of tragedy in the background. If you sit for a while in any of the back streets of Naples all the characters of the traditional theatre will walk past you in the space of a few minutes—the lithe, mischievous Harlequin, the beautiful wayward Columbine, the mournful Pierrot, and the jealous, sardonic hunchbacked Punchinello. Punch really existed; he was a cobbler who joined a company of strolling players and became a stock character in the *Comedia del Arte*, and the immortal hero of puppet shows in every corner of the civilized world.

The laughter and joyousness of Neapolitan life is seen at its best in the month of September, when a mammoth procession makes its way down the Toledo and along the Riviera di Chiaia to the shrine of Piedigrotta with its miraculous Virgin.

Float after float passes slowly down the narrow street, bearing elaborate set pieces that appear to have little to do with religious life, for they are usually representations of some aspect of the history or legends of Naples. Goddesses, tritons, monsters in costume wave to the crowds, but the goddesses or nymphs win the greatest applause.

Young men and young women in tall cardboard hats run about on all sides blowing on paper trumpets and buffeting everyone with bladders. Others crown the unsuspecting with immense boxes from which there is no escape, there are skirmishes on all sides and occasionally when tempers are frayed, white-uniformed policemen intervene, whilst the onlookers jeer at the disputants. On the whole the people are good humoured and gay, even though they do not forget to bring their babies, who usually fall asleep in spite of the din of the celebration.

Processions of this kind, and of course illuminations, are frequent events, but the Neapolitans never lose their Carnival spirit, even though they may be ragged and have empty stomachs—food they feel is good, but laughter and song are better.

To the south of the Toledo, or if you insist on being pedantic, the Via Roma, are some of the oldest quarters of the city. You must go as far as the Piazza Dante before turning off into the narrow streets and squares which are so well worth exploring without too much conscientious method. Sooner or later you are bound to come across the crumbling palaces, the Baroque churches with glittering interiors that will reward your persistence.

Strangest of all are the *guglie*, immense columns to commemorate a saint and covered with Baroque or Rococo ornamentations of southern exuberance. In this climate and setting they possess real beauty, for they harmonize with the rich colouring of the exotic fish and fruit and vegetables displayed in the shops and on the stalls, the dazzling white of the flapping laundry, the brilliance of the blue sky.

The same exuberance and lavishness of decoration can be found in the cathedral, and in particular in the shrine and chapel of St Januarius San Gennaro, the patron saint of the city, who is reputed to have saved the Neapolitans so often from plagues, famine, fire and, most of all, from the destructive eruptions of Vesuvius.

A phial containing the blood of this holy man is brought out on the first Saturday in May and on the nineteenth of September. If the blood should become liquid, as it often does, then the succeeding months will be fortunate ones for the people of Naples.

This ceremony takes place in the Church of Santa Chiara in the spring, and in the cathedral in the autumn, but on each occasion it is followed by a gigantic procession in which the statue of San Gennaro and those of twenty others are borne through the streets in the presence of immense crowds.

This *Festa* is certainly the most impressive of all the manifestations that take place every year in Naples because of the tremendous faith of the Neapolitans in their "miracle" and the tense atmosphere of emotion that prevails whilst they are waiting for it to take place.

Before leaving the city for Pompeii everyone should visit the National Museum, where the finest statuary from the excavations from Pompeii and Herculaneum have been placed.

Amidst numbers of mediocre and a few very fine copies, are some great treasures of Greek art, interesting antiquities from Pompeii and a good collection of Italian paintings including some masterpieces.

The famous Farnese Bull, however well-modelled it may be, means absolutely nothing to me. It is restless and overcharged. The dramatic effect is spoiled by being diffused over a multitude of details and I cannot find anywhere a subtle touch to bring relief.

You will have to pass by a great many things of secondary interest to find the beautiful relief of Orpheus, Eurydice and Hermes of the fourth century B.C. The three figures are linked together with a subtle rhythm of movement and a gentleness of expression which saves their dignified, upright bearing from any feeling of remoteness.

Through rooms of Greek and Roman portraits you will come to the bronzes, mostly found in the ruins of Pompeii. Here lies the chief glory of the museum.

A delightful dancing, bearded faun, a jovial little Silenus crowned with ivy, and a young satyr and the misnamed Narcissus from the school of Praxiteles, make the first room unforgettable.

Autumn on the
Lake of Bolsena

The rooftops of Montepulciano

In the second room a wonderful archaic statue of Apollo playing a lyre is a masterpiece of the fifth century B.C. It was found at Pompeii, but was originally placed in the market square at Sparta.

In the next few rooms are bronzes from Herculaneum. Especially lovely are the *Head of a Boy* and the *Hermes in Repose*, his long slim legs so perfectly proportioned and his god-like body relaxed in rest.

Some ten rooms are devoted to the gay, decorative wall paintings from Pompeii, Herculaneum and Stabae; lovely colourful pictures which must have made the houses of these ancient cities a joy to live in. They were not painted by great artists of the day, but by decorators who took a delight in showing the everyday life of the time and in painting the trees and flowers and birds they saw around them.

Having few native-born artists of repute, Naples borrowed "foreigners" from the rest of Italy and her great families collected works of art from many European countries with the result that she has in the Pinacoteca not only some lovely Sienese work and good examples from most of the other great Italian schools, but also some paintings from the Netherlands and Spain—there is a delicious El Greco portrait of a boy, his face lighted by the fitful flicker of a candle flame.

Do not miss Masaccio's famous *Crucifixion* with the despairing figure in the foreground dramatically expressing unbearable grief.

The Transfiguration by Giovanni Bellini is a very fine example of this Venetian artist's work. It has a lovely landscape background and a sky full of racing clouds contrasting with the solemn upright figures and the stupefied men on the ground. Indeed, the Venetian school is very well represented and the museum has five Titians, including a magnificent full-length portrait of Paul III.

The beautiful little *Zingarella* by Correggio of the school of Parma never fails to delight me. Bathed in a golden light, the Virgin bends lovingly over the Child and a little rabbit pushes his nose through flowering shrubs to gaze at Him.

Besides the National Museum there are, of course, many other museums in Naples, but none of them of such outstanding interest that they merit a visit by anyone making a short stay. However, I do like the Palace of Capodimonte up on the hill on the inland road to Rome, for it is a superb eighteenth-century residence with a fine park, and the collection of *Capodimonte* china is really beautiful.

I

The Museo Nazionale di San Martino in the Baroque Carthusian Monastery on the hill of the Vomero contains exhibits illustrating the history of Naples throughout the ages and also the immense Rococo *Presepe* by Cuciniello. The Holy Family is represented here against a background of high mountains and, in the foreground, vivid scenes of Neapolitan life.

Another section is given up to pictures and mementoes of the popular theatre, the later phases of the *Comedia del Arte*, and the picturesque puppet shows.

A belvedere on the top of the museum buildings offers a comprehensive view of the Bay from the Sorrento Peninsula to the islands of Capri, Procida and Ischia.

The Vomero is a prosperous middle-class and upper middle-class suburb with modern streets, large blocks of comfortable flats, and a number of restaurants and cafés with terraces where one may sit at night and watch the glittering lights of the city below, and the reflections in the dark inky depths of the sea nearby.

CHAPTER TWELVE

NAPLES (*Continued*)
SANTA LUCIA : THE RIVIERA DI CHIAIA :
POSILLIPO : PROCIDA : ISCHIA : POMPEII :
AMALFI : RAVELLO

THE small headland of Santa Lucia juts out into the blue waters almost immediately to the north of the Royal Palace, and it is here on the front that you will find many of the smartest hotels and restaurants of Naples.

Having heard the songs and legends concerning this romanticized spot you may well have imagined a picturesque fishermen's quarter with white arcaded cottages and waterside terraces overgrown with vines. Nothing could be further from the realities of the present day. Such a quarter did exist, but it was swept away when a handsome front was built, and the modern hotels and apartment houses were constructed at the same time. Yet I must admit that if I like to wander through the narrow streets of the old town, I do not object to staying in luxury at Santa Lucia.

The one remaining feature of the past, the Castel del' Ovo, is a fortress built in 1154 by the Norman king, William I, on a tiny island connected with the mainland by a breakwater that forms a harbour for fishing boats and yachts.

On the terrace facing the island there are the tables of several restaurants patronized by nearly every visitor to Naples.

The situation is a charming one; the food and service at these places are of the best, and musicians entertain the guests with Neapolitan songs to the accompaniment of tinkling guitars. Prices unfortunately are rather high, but who can grudge the money spent on a really delightful and leisurely evening's entertainment?

Behind the small headland of Santa Lucia, the Via Chiaia begins at the Piazza Trieste in front of the San Carlo theatre and passes behind the steep hill known as the Pizzofalcone to link up with the lovely gardens of the Riviera di Chiaia. The Via Chiaia is short and rather narrow, but it is the best shopping street in Naples, and it is here that you may see smart and well-dressed people taking their morning stroll.

The Riviera di Chiaia is a broad avenue, divided from the equally broad Via Caracciolo by the gardens of the Villa Communale. The Via Caracciolo runs along the sea for nearly two miles—altogether a successful piece of planning, appreciated to the full by the Neapolitans, especially on warm summer evenings.

The aquarium, in the centre of the gardens, is one of the largest and most comprehensive in the world, for the Mediterranean contains an infinite variety of fish, and many of them are beautiful in shape and colour.

At the far end of the Via Caracciolo there is another small harbour for smacks and yachts. I would hesitate to patronize the bathing beach, for the absence of tides here and the proximity of a large town can scarcely tend to keep the water free from pollution.

A funicular near the harbour makes frequent ascents to the suburb on the heights known as the Rione Flegreo.

The Via Mergellina is a continuation of the Via Caracciolo along the water's edge, and here also there is a delightful prospect of the Bay of Naples, of Vesuvius, and of Capri, a landscape which seems to change in shape and colour at all times of the day.

Beyond the small Church of Sanazzoro, the road to Posillipo gradually rises up the slope of the high ridge that runs the full length of the small peninsula, and the prospect of the bay widens. On the water's edge, and with its foundations actually standing in the sea, is the strange unfinished Palazzo di Donn' Anna that looks like one of the majestic Roman palaces that Claude and Poussin loved to paint.

Then as one goes onwards there are magnificent villas and gardens resplendent with flowers, flowering shrubs, trees laden with lemons or oranges. Here and there colour-washed cottages have survived from a more primitive age. Sometimes the sea is screened by the vegetation, at others it reappears between a framework of dark green leaves or black cypresses.

At intervals small paths or lanes lead down to the sea. One of them, I forget which, is broad enough for a car to descend to a small harbour with two or three restaurants on the quayside.

Just before the village of Posillipo the Discesa di Marechiaro goes down to the small fishing village where the Neapolitans come to bathe and eat gargantuan meals on the terrace of one of the rustic *trattorie* near the waterside. On Sundays the place is crowded; large family parties work their way through immense mounds of spaghetti and tomatoes, fried cuttlefish, veal cutlets and fruit washed down by gallons of wine, whilst stout musicians bawl out interminably the popular songs of the region. Their voices are good, and the guitars tinkle agreeably enough, but I am getting a little tired of the tune of *Santa Lucia*, the *Return to Sorrento*, and *Funiculi Funicula*, but then I suppose that I have been to Marechiaro fifty or sixty times at least.

When I lived in Naples I used to hire a small boat and row round the headland of Marechiaro to a pleasant little cove where the water was cleaner and there was less noise and bustle. Sometimes if the sea was really calm it was still more agreeable to go further out into the bay and to drift about whilst the yachts laden with sunburnt girls and men glided past us.

The hours passed quickly enough in the brilliant light of the sea and the sky, which lends enchantment to the hills, the white villas, the green vineyards, and to a landscape that is fashioned by nature to such perfection. Distant islands seemed to float on the surface of the deep blue water, and occasionally dolphins would dive and frolic and curve near by and give gaiety and movement to the placid scene.

In the evening a soft breeze would drive us reluctantly back to the shore, where the land still held the warmth of the day.

.   .   .

Since I have already described the Bay of Pozzuoli, I will content myself by repeating that, romantic as it must have seemed in the past, its shores are spoilt for me by the unsightly iron works, ship-yards and rather sordid bathing establishments that succeed each other along the coastal road, and yet I have often enjoyed driving swiftly from Posillipo to the far end of Cape Miseno, which reaches far out in the sea in the direction of the Island of Procida.

The Cumana Railway has frequent trains to Miseno from the centre of Naples, and a ferry plies from the far end of the Cape to Procida, so with good timing it is possible to catch a steamer that goes on to Ischia.

However, it is easier and infinitely more pleasant to go directly from Naples by the steamer that leaves the landing stage near the Piazza del Municipio. The journey takes about two hours and is worth making if only because of the views of the harbour, the Bay of Naples and the coast of the Peninsula of Posillipo.

Most of the steamers call at Procida, an enchanting island about two and a half miles long and little more than a mile broad. The houses facing the harbour are painted in brilliant colours and their reflections in the smooth green water mingle with those of the schooners moored at the quayside.

The south of the town is dominated by a large castle on an eminence, but since the place is now used as a reformatory the Neapolitans tend to shun the island, for like most Italians they hate to go anywhere near a prison.

There are two good bathing beaches on Procida, but they are rarely crowded, probably because there is such a complete lack of hygiene on the island that it has not been developed in any way for tourists.

The inhabitants are quite friendly, but completely unlike their neighbours in other parts of the region, for they claim to be of pure Greek descent, and until recently they wore costumes of a Greek pattern on feasts and holidays.

In spite of this racial strain many of the islanders have fair hair, blue eyes and Nordic complexions, and so it is conceivable that they are also descended from the Normans.

The long main street of the town straggles inland for nearly a mile and a half, and then, as soon as the houses begin to grow thinner, the ground slopes down to a small fishing harbour and to a beach with bathing huts and a small restaurant. On this side Procida looks out over the small wild islet of Vivara and on to the eastern shores of Ischia.

Vivara is uninhabited, though years ago it belonged to an eccentric priest who populated it with all sorts of exotic wild beasts which have since disappeared.

The approach to Ischia is impressive because Monte Epomeo, in the centre, is over 2,500 feet high, and from nearby at sea level it appears to fill up the whole horizon.

It is in fact an extinct volcano which has not been in eruption for many centuries, but earthquakes have been frequent. The last important one occurred seventy years ago and blotted out half the population and destroyed most of the houses on the northern side of the island, so that little of architectural interest remains.

The town of Porto d'Ischia is on one side of the little harbour, which is completely circular, for it is formed out of the crater of a small volcano. The white sandy beach extends as far as the castle built on a small islet to the south, and connected with the mainland by a causeway.

A fortress was first constructed on this site by some Greeks from Syracuse, who established several colonies on the shores of the Bay of Naples. They were succeeded in turn by the Romans, the Byzantines, the Normans, the Germans, and lastly, by the kings of the House of Aragon, who transformed the castle into a luxurious palace. In the early years of the sixteenth century the beautiful Vittoria Colonna lived here and entertained painters, writers and poets, including her close friends Michelangelo and Raphael.

A service of motor buses covers the twenty-mile road round the island, passing first of all through Casamicciola and Lacco Ameno, villages with thermal springs and baths for the treatment of an incredible number of diseases, including, so one of the publicity folders declares, senility and impotence.

Fishing smacks and coastal schooners berth at Forio, on the west side of the island, and the excellent white wine of Ischia is shipped off from here to Naples and other places on the mainland.

The little town is an ancient one and some fragments of the old fortifications remain to give it an air of picturesqueness.

The south coast of Ischia is rugged and hard of access because the road swerves inland to serve the needs of villages situated several hundred feet up the slopes of Monte Epomeo, but two tracks descend to the hamlet of Sant Angelo, a charming little place with excellent bathing.

The water here is so clear that there are unlimited opportunities for underwater fishing.

At Fontana, the highest point on the southern section of the highway, a path leads up to the summit of Epomeo from which there is one of the most comprehensive views in the whole of Italy, for it is claimed that on a clear day it is possible to see nearly three hundred miles of coast.

The climate of Ischia is mild in winter and there are certainly fewer mists than at Capri, but the rainfall is quite heavy. The sea is seldom warm enough for bathing before the middle of May, and quite frequently it is too cold to continue swimming after the end of September.

The excursion to Pompeii need not take more than a morning or an afternoon, for the means of transport are unlimited—you can go by the electric train of the Circumvesuviana in forty minutes, or by one of the regular bus services, or alternatively you can avail yourself of one of the coach trips organized by the travel agencies.

Few tourists take the trouble to visit Herculaneum, which is only four miles from Naples and can be reached by train in exactly a quarter of an hour, and yet the ruins excavated here are in a better state of preservation than those at Pompeii. However, since the setting is less beautiful and the remains uncovered are far less extensive, the layman may reasonably by-pass Herculaneum and content himself with what there is to be seen at Pompeii. If you are going by car it is just as well to take the *autostrada*, for the old road passes through the slums of Portici and is terribly encumbered with pedestrians and horse traffic.

Fortunately the fourteen miles to Pompeii can be covered quickly, for the spreading suburbs of Naples have marred what used to be quite an attractive landscape, and the wayside posters are at their ugliest here.

On the left there are frequent glimpses of the sea, and to the right the jerry-built villas are scattered among the vineyards of the lower slopes of Vesuvius.

I have to confess that I have never troubled to make the ascent of this, or of any other volcano, for I abhor what our eighteenth-century ancestors called the "more hideous manifestations of nature". There is a motor road to within a few hundred feet of the summit, and as there is a funicular up the rest of the way, you can have the pleasure of looking down into the crater.

Years ago I did see a minor eruption of Vesuvius that lasted for several days. The inland road from Pompeii to Salerno was covered with a two or three foot layer of ashes, and from my terrace at Naples I could see columns of black smoke issuing from the cone-shaped top of the mountain. At night a deep fiery glow filled the sky, and it seemed as if huge flames were belching out of the crater.

Everyone is familiar with the tragic history of Pompeii, with the terrible story of earthquakes which destroyed many of her treasures and, when the town had been partly rebuilt, the terrific eruption of A.D. 79 which completely overwhelmed it.

Here was a little town, popular as a pleasure resort, surrounded by luxurious villas. Her small and rather mean houses were gaily painted with colourful scenes—her streets were narrow and all but her public buildings small. We know something of the life of her people from the paintings found in the houses and transferred to the museum in Naples and also from the few that remain in the ruins.

It is better to go with a guide round the site, and indeed it would be utterly wearisome to wander around without someone to find the points of interest for you, for the ground to be covered is vast and the way difficult to follow.

I believe that all the guides are excellent, but the last time I went we had an exceptionally witty and erudite man who made the whole visit most interesting and brought the mournful, desolate town to life, reconstructing it for us in a most vivid way. So much so that after a short while the site lost its depressing, forlorn aspect and took on a strange beauty in the brilliant white light. Lines of broken columns flank the paved roads, ending here in a rounded arch, there in a broken façade of a temple. Between the columns tall umbrella pines are silhouetted against the sky—the incredibly blue sky. Dark cypresses rise up along the Road of the Sepulchres; grasses and flowers grow out of the crumbling stone, and always, in the background, is the purple, terrifying splendour of Vesuvius.

Then, rather unexpectedly, one is reminded of the everyday life that people led here so long ago—you can see the wheel ruts left on the cobbled pavements of the narrow streets, the remarks scrawled on a wall during a municipal election, the ovens where bread was baked, and in the museum, a loaf coated in lava but with the outlines of its shape intact.

In the museum also there is the recumbent figure of a girl, suffocated evidently by the eruption, for her face is buried in one arm, and the other arm is thrown forward in a gesture of despair. The body, petrified at the time of the disaster, is graceful and slim, the feet and hands small and well formed, the legs perfectly shaped. Although nearly two thousand years have passed since she died, I have always been profoundly moved on looking at her, though doubtless she suffered far less than many of the victims of the violence of our modern wars.

This feeling is soon dispelled on going out into the bright sunshine that fills the ruins of the forum with light and radiance, so that one quickly forgets the tragic and sudden annihilation of the population of a town where everything must have contributed to joy and happiness—beauty, prosperity and ease, though perhaps a certain amount of corruption. This is not mere conjecture, for Petronius left a fairly complete record of the sophisticated pleasures of a rich man in Pompeii just before the eruption, but then the picture that he presents may be one-sided.

In recent years the ruins of Pompeii have been floodlit during the summer season. In the darkness only the finest features of the old town are illuminated, and this imparts to the lines of columns, the individual statues, a mysterious dignity which is absent in the glare of the day. Sometimes performances of classical dancing are given in what must assuredly be the most perfect of settings.

You would be well advised to hurry through modern Pompeii, a featureless, ugly town with a huge dusty square, and nothing of historical interest. However, this dreary place has to be passed on the road southwards to follow the classical circuit of the lovely Sorrento Peninsula.

The coaches run by the tourist agencies usually go straight on along the plain to the outskirts of Salerno and then off to the right at Vietri so as to follow the whole of the south coast of the Penin-sula. I have always found it preferable to take the short cut across the hills to Maiori. This route does not save any time, for the road is a steep and winding one, but it passes through wild and lovely country, and the descent from the rough shrub and forest of the highlands to the groves of orange and lemon trees is unusually attractive.

Maiori itself is an enchanting little town at the mouth of a torrent, with an ancient church and a small arcaded square. Here as else-where on this rugged coast, the hills descend steeply to the sea, and the soil on the slopes is terraced for vineyards and orchards. At intervals there are watchtowers, built centuries ago to warn the population of the coming of pirates, and to serve as refuges in the case of a swift raid.

The coastal road winds in and out to follow the endless small bays and promontories. In each village the little white houses are built in tiers down to small shingly beaches where red fishing nets are drying between the brightly coloured boats.

Next to Maiori comes, aptly enough, Minori, and, two miles further on, Atrani, which is separated from Amalfi by a high rocky crag. Over a thousand years ago Amalfi was a city state with a powerful navy, and a fleet of merchant ships that traded with all parts of the Mediterranean.

For a while the small republic was under the protection of Byzantium. Later, after defying the Normans for a while, she was forced to become a tributary of their ruler, King Roger. The decline began when the Amalfitans were defeated at sea by the Pisans, and it was accelerated when the Genoese and the Venetians became the dominant powers of the Inland Sea.

In the ninth, tenth and eleventh centuries Amalfi was very prosperous, and the inhabitants were Greek in language and culture. One of her citizens, Flavio Gioia, is believed to have invented the compass, and her navigators were among the first to draw up a code regulating trade at sea.

In the present day the town, greatly diminished in size and population, still bears the signs of having been the seat of a great civilization. Two ancient monasteries on the hillside have been transformed into hotels without losing any of their original architectural attributes.

Whilst the sea-front has the aspect of a pleasing little bathing resort, the market square and the narrow streets of whitewashed houses inland have kept something of the atmosphere of a Greek town. Many of the shop-fronts are open like those of the Middle Ages, and the fruits, vegetables and flowers displayed have the colour and fullness that only a southern climate can produce.

The cathedral at Amalfi is certainly magnificent, with its steps sweeping up to the painted and gilded façade and its strange, oriental-looking tower, its cupola supported by columns rising up against the dark rocky hillside.

At night when it is illuminated it is a wonderful sight and, as there are several cafés in the small square, one that can be enjoyed in comfort.

But you must climb the steps by day to see the great bronze doors to advantage; the doors wrought in the year 1000 and inscribed in silver.

In the crypt lies the body of St Andrew; the head was removed and is in a silver reliquary in St Peter's, Rome. The adjoining cloisters are built in Arab style with narrow pointed arches, coupled columns and brightly-painted decorations.

Up an extremely steep hill winds the road to Ravello. It is well worth the extra time needed to go by horse-cab rather than by car, for a leisurely approach is the best one, as the views on all sides are incredibly lovely with the clear, wide sky above and the brilliant blue-green sea below.

After a mile or so of climbing, at the turn of the hairpin bends, you will see twin churches clinging to the precipitous crags; one is the monastery of San Lorenzo and the other Ravello Cathedral, founded in 1087 by Nicolo Rufolo, Duke of Dora. Though restored in the eighteenth century, it still remains one of the loveliest churches in the Amalfi peninsula.

The great bronze doors with fifty-four reliefs depicting the story of the Passion were given to the church at the end of the twelfth century and are the work of Barisano da Trani. More splendid than anything else in Ravello, and for that matter, in the whole of this part of Italy, is the glorious thirteenth-century pulpit commissioned by Nicolo Rufolo to please his beautiful wife. Twisted columns with glittering coloured mosaics rise from the backs of archaic lions to support the pulpit decorated with geometric patterns in mosaic and gold. A great golden eagle guards the central panel: the ambone is decorated with delightful mosaic panels of birds and strange beasts. There is a fine elegance combined with the brilliant, almost oriental, splendour of this pulpit, one of the many treasures given to the city by Rufolo.

It was for the Rufolo family that the eleventh-century Palazzo Rufolo was originally built in the Arab style. It has recently been restored and the elaborately designed gardens are open to the public. From the flowered terraces there are suberb views of the coast. It was the garden here that brought to life Wagner's imagined garden of Klingsor in *Parsifal*. Indeed he wrote in the guest book in the spring of 1880 "Richard Wagner, wife and family: the enchanted garden of Klingsor is found".

If you look straight down you see almost at your feet the vineyards on the steep slopes above Amalfi, the orchards and, a little below them, the white houses surrounding the majestic cathedral seemingly on the very edge of the dazzlingly blue sea.

CHAPTER THIRTEEN

POSITANO : SORRENTO : CAPRI : CASERTA : CAPUA : CASSINO : ROME

THE road to Sorrento continues to wind along the rocky coast as far as Positano through the same enchanting scenery as before—on one side are the terraced vineyards and orchards on the steep, stony hills, and on the other the sea frothing against the rocks and the small beaches two or three hundred feet below. Occasionally there are white villas covered with creeping rose trees, and gardens full of flowers and oleanders.

First comes the village of Praiano, and then Positano, beloved of painters and writers, a small town on the side of a steep slope that curves round a little bay.

Centuries ago it was a busy port and the white cubic houses are a sign of prosperity in the days when the Greek influence was still strong.

The local inhabitants are determined that the character of this place shall not be changed by coach parties and day trippers, and so there are no road houses, no catch-penny amenities. Nevertheless, Positano is no longer cheap, and it has become very popular recently. In order to obtain accommodation during the summer season it is necessary to reserve rooms many weeks beforehand, but then it is an ideal spot for a holiday.

The road continues along the coast for two or three miles inland to cut across the narrow neck of the peninsula and down through orange and lemon groves into Sorrento, for there is no highway round the end of the headland.

Since Sorrento faces due north, it has always been a popular bathing resort in the summer, for a cool wind usually blows across the Bay of Naples, and the heat is seldom unbearable. Then, since the climate is mild in winter, the vegetation is luxuriant, and flowers bloom throughout the greater part of the year.

As there are frequent services by bus and rail to Naples and some of the steamers call here on their way to and from Capri, the population has grown rapidly, and Sorrento is no longer a small town.

There are a great many hotels here, and the best of them are situated on the edge of the cliff, and have lifts going down to their own private beaches.

The bathing is quite good, and the temperature of the water is high considering the relative coolness of the atmosphere.

The greatest attraction of the place is the view across the Bay to Vesuvius, Naples and the headlands beyond Naples.

At night the whole sweep of the coast is illuminated by the lights of the towns and villages that gleam like jewels in the darkness, and sometimes when the sea is particularly calm, both the lights and the stars are reflected on its smooth silky surface.

Although a part of the town was rebuilt in the nineteenth century, there still remain some picturesque old streets, and a few fine palaces and villas. Some of the villas in particular are attractive because Sorrento has been visited by people of distinction for the past two centuries, including Mrs Beecher Stowe, Nietzche, Maxim Gorki and, more recently, Benedetto Croce and Norman Douglas, both of whom lived here for many years.

The shops are of interest to women because the local needlework and embroidery are excellent and not too expensive. There is also a local industry for making inlaid wood boxes and small pieces of furniture. Unfortunately the designs are elaborate and hideous though the craftsmanship is good.

On summer evenings there are often performances of the Tarantella, the strange dance of southern Italy whose movements are supposed to have been copied from those of the large spider of that name.

Another theory is that it originated in Arabia, and that it was brought here by the Spaniards who had learned it during the Moorish occupation of their country.

On the Sorrento peninsula it has not died out, mainly because of its entertainment value to the summer visitors, for the local inhabitants infinitely prefer the American dances and hot music.

Here, as in many other parts of the world, the travel industry has helped to perpetuate folk lore and even induced municipal authorities to do something about the preservation of ancient monuments.

If you have a car, one of the pleasantest excursions to be made from Sorrento is to drive to Termini on the extreme point of the peninsula, and almost opposite Capri. Here there are two or three rustic-looking restaurants with terraces overlooking the sea. Prices are not particularly moderate, but the food and wine served are of the best.

The coast road back to Naples and along the northern face of the peninsula has been rather spoilt by ribbon development, but at intervals there are fine views of the whole of the Bay of Naples.

The villages on the way to the terminal of the *autostrada* at Pompeii are picturesque of aspect but tend to be far too crowded for comfort. The first of these places, Seiano, is almost a suburb of Sorrento, but Vico Equenses, three miles further on, has a tree-lined square overlooking the small fishing port. The houses here are brightly painted, and there are one or two reasonably good restaurants.

Castellamare di Stabia is a large spa and seaside resort frequented mainly by Italians of the South who come here to treat their digestive troubles.

The two beaches of sand attract families with small children, and so these visitors, together with the local inhabitants, tend to make this town very difficult for motorists.

.   .   .

I suppose that few tourists come to Naples without going to Capri, and yet each time I go there I swear that nothing will induce me to return to a place that has become as commercialized as Blackpool, Atlantic City or Margate.

Nevertheless, its basic attractions have not changed, for nothing can alter the brilliance of the light and colour, the strange and wonderful configuration of the hills and cliffs, and the clear luminosity of the sea.

It is just as well, for every morning during the summer season a fleet of ten or twelve steamers sails across the Bay of Naples and deposits from ten to twelve thousand frenzied excursionists on the Marina Grande, the little port of the island. These tourists of all nationalities surge along the stone pier to queue for the funicular up to the town, or cram into the coaches and large cars that are waiting on the quayside. Within a space of minutes more than half the members of this invading host have procured peaked straw caps with the word *Capri* embroidered in red, blue or gold, and are posing to be photographed by their friends.

Fortunately the crowds disperse quickly and there is soon room to move. Small as Capri is, it is still possible to find some corners where life is normal, by avoiding the more obvious targets for sightseers.

To be fair, the vogue for this island is not a new one. It began with the Emperor Tiberius who came in search of solitude and built himself no less than twelve villas.

Contemporary historians declare that he gave himself up to all sorts of fearful debauchery, and frequently threw people who displeased him over the side of a cliff or tortured them in a vile way.

Like Amalfi and Positano, Capri was repopulated by Greeks of Byzantium when southern Italy was reconquered by Belisarius, and the older buildings are almost identical to those on many of the Greek islands to-day.

In 1806 a French garrison was driven out and Sir Hudson Lowe, later Napoleon's gaoler at St Helena, was appointed Governor. Two years later the British were forced to surrender to Joachim Murat's troops after a gallant resistance in which many of the defenders were killed.

In the nineteenth century a number of travellers came to visit the Blue Grotto, which was discovered not more than a hundred and fifty years ago.

All through the summer, tourists are rowed into this marine cave in the side of a cliff, and its popularity remains undiminished, for the effect of the sunlight shining through the entrance into the darkness within produces a wonderful blue radiance in the water.

If the sky is overcast, the luminous colours are duller, and if the sea is rough, the trip can be a very unpleasant one.

Incidentally, I have seen the excursion steamers tossed about sufficiently to make the majority of their passengers really sick in the short journey across from Naples.

Doubtless my readers will accuse me of being embittered on the subject of Capri, but I knew the island long before it was submerged by the wave of popularity which has taken away so much of its pristine charm and simplicity—in those days the village of Anacapri could only be reached by walking up the famous steps on the hillside, or by driving slowly up the winding road in a carriage. There was no cable car to the summit of Monte Solaro, and the peasants did not spend the summer selling curios of all kinds to the tourists.

Axel Munthe, Norman Douglas, Compton Mackenzie have des-

Springtime in Siena

The ancient
towers of San
Gimignano

cribed Capri as it was before the fall, so I must leave it at that, and return to the present day.

Capri is, roughly speaking, shaped like the figure eight, and the town is situated high up on the narrow neck of land that connects the two parts of the island.

In the smaller and eastern section the hills rise to an altitude of just over a thousand feet, with Monte Tiberio rising up steeply from the furthest point of land.

The extensive ruins of one of the Emperor's villas can be visited on the slopes of this mountain. The real attraction of this place is the scenery, and the walk through the lovely countryside with varied prospects at every twist and turn of the path.

Below, in the rocky bays and inlets, the colour of the sea is always changing from the deepest emerald to the most brilliant blue. In places the water is so clear that one can see the waving seaweed, and the coral depths of different hues. At others, a shining surface reflects the white glancing rays of the sun.

When it is not too crowded the town also is full of enchantment. The small square is surrounded by dazzlingly white houses, and the gay parasols shade the terraces of the cafés—then there are strange and varied types to be seen. First of all the tourists of so many nations who tend increasingly to become standardized, irrespective of their place of origin, and then the eccentrics who have always gravitated towards Capri; the long-haired men in brilliant shirts, and the short-haired mannish women. Lastly, the people of fashion, the film stars, and from time to time, well-dressed and distinguished-looking visitors who stroll about unconcernedly through the seething mass of trippers.

A short walk by a path that winds through an all too urban-looking park leads to the small bathing beaches of the Marina Piccola, where there are shady trees, pleasant villas, and some quiet guesthouses, most of them run by Central Europeans.

On the eastern side of this bay the cliffs come to a sudden end, but they are continued by the beautiful lone rocks rising out of the sea that are called the Faraglioni.

From the square there is a frequent service of buses up to the heights of Anacapri, a village that has become rather too suburban-ized for my taste, but it is no good being discouraged by this circumstance.

Since the bulk of visitors converge on Axel Munthe's house, the

K

paths that radiate out through the countryside in all directions are comparatively deserted and so you may still recapture something of the Capri of the past, particularly if you go towards the lighthouse on the southwesterly point of the island.

Again, despite my carping, life improves considerably when all the steamers have departed with their loads of passengers, for then at last there is room to move. The seething mob in the square becomes an animated and lively crowd, and the strains of Neapolitan singing merge quite pleasantly with the hot music echoing from the night haunts. In the country lanes near by, the cicadas begin their incessant shrilling, and early in the summer, the nightingales throb passionately in nearly every tree. Fireflies flicker, and the stars shine brightly, though so high up in the sky.

At the water's edge the little waves lap gently, and froth with phosphorescent gleams as they swirl against the rocks. Down at the quayside the Marina Grande has reverted to the past and is once more a fishing village, where the white-clad local girls stroll up and down talking to the handsome sunburnt lads, and the older people sit and sip their wine at the tin tables outside the taverns.

So, in spite of too much brash commercialism, there is still some magic left in Capri, whether you stay at one of the luxury hotels or at one of the inexpensive pensions which can be found with a little diligent research. Incidentally, the blouses and needlework made locally are cheap and of first-class quality.

.   .   .

The inland route to Rome is only moderately attractive from the scenic point of view, but in compensation it does pass through Caserta, Capua and Cassino, all of them interesting places to visit. Also, by making a slight deviation, it is possible to visit Tivoli without too much loss of time or expenditure of petrol.

For the first twenty miles the country is flat and definitely ugly. At times, the hemp plants drying in the fields give out a really disagreeable smell of rotting vegetation. The villages and towns appear to be poverty-stricken, and are completely devoid of character, and one is led to wonder why this district was selected for the construction of a royal residence and a summer one at that, when there are so many really lovely sites in the neighbourhood of Naples. Why, for instance, did not the Bourbon monarchs build a palace on the point at Posillipo where there are lovely views and fresh breezes to cool the heat of the midday sun?

The answer is, I think, that hunting was considered to be the most attractive sport possible for a king, and that the seaside did not become fashionable until George IV went to Brighton in the late eighteenth century. Both he and his brothers took to sea bathing because it was believed to be a remedy for gout, and this treatment was only given in the autumn.

As I know from personal experience, Caserta is cold and damp in winter and stuffy and airless in summer.

The palace is immense, for it was intended to accommodate not only the king and his court but also the officials who composed the administrative staff of his government, and, of course, a host of civil servants as well.

Louis XIV is frequently criticized by historians for building Versailles, but there, as at Caserta, all the offices of the state were installed under one roof, a system which doubtless tended for greater efficiency, for it is copied by all the municipal authorities in Great Britain and elsewhere when they construct their costly civic centres.

Charles III, who commissioned Vanvitelli to design the palace at Caserta, was the most enlightened and able of the Bourbon monarchs who reigned over the Kingdom of Naples, and he was also a patron of the arts and a man of great taste.

Few people take the trouble to visit this splendid royal residence, mainly, I imagine, because the exterior is rather forbidding, and also because the majority of authors who compile guide-books seem to dislike Baroque architecture.

The approach to the rather heavy façade is laid out with the harmony and dignity characteristic of the age, and so the first vision is from a wide straight avenue that broadens out into an immense circular piazza in front of the principal entrance. Over the main gateway four columns support a small pediment, but the rest of the wall is unadorned save for groups of four pillars at each angle of the building.

The four huge courtyards are equally devoid of ornamentation, doubtless because the architect was instructed to husband his resources so as to be more lavish in planning the interior.

The royal staircase is divided by a round arch in the centre that affords a perspective of the nude statue of a god in a niche.

The two lines of shallow steps have elaborate marble ballustrades, and three tall round arches on the landing reveal the splendours of a domed hall. Here indeed we have a Baroque composition of great harmony and perfect balance, regal in design and execution.

The state apartments are singularly free from the garishness that characterizes the interior of so many royal palaces.

First of all the antechamber of the Guard with marble panels of bas-relief, surmounting graceful stone swags and set between flat Ionic pilasters. Magnificent lustres hang from the vaulted marble ceiling that is inset with coloured marbles and exuberant painting symbolizing the seasons and the glory of the Farnese family.

The chapel is a faithful copy of the one at Versailles and decorated with the same luxurious lavishness. Saloons, bedrooms, and boudoirs are hung with silk or damask, furnished in the ornate but harmonious style of the eighteenth century—even the bathroom is a splendid example of how swags and garlands of gilt or marble can be used with a riot of carved cupids, goddesses, and painted medallions to create enchanting compositions.

The small theatre is lined throughout with marble, and the five tiers of boxes are separated by pillars of alabaster, and an immense crystal lustre hangs in front of the royal balcony. The ceiling is decorated with figured plaster mouldings and an allegorical painting of Apollo killing the python.

Folding doors at the back of the stage open out on to a vista of trees, cascades and lawns that can be used as a natural background to pastoral plays.

Lastly, in one of the halls there is a magnificent *presepio* peopled with innumerable figures in the peasant costumes of the eighteenth century, and yet devoid of all stiffness because of their animation.

In my opinion the monumental gardens of Caserta are among the most beautiful of their kind in the world, though they are not laid out on the huge scale of those at Versailles, and they have not the individuality of the romantic and extravagant cascades of Tivoli.

Here we have the order and the logic of the Age of Reason applied to form a single composition with the palace, but ornamented with all the imagination that can be used in a Baroque design. So, between green velvet lawns bordered with double rows of thick hedges and trees, a succession of marble fountains and pools affords a vista from the palace apartments to a cascade and to the waterfall above it, whose foaming torrent pours out of the mountainside nearly two miles away.

A little way beyond the first of the fountains, the still waters of a marble basin mirror the surrounding landscape until they are broken by the vast jets that gush out of the mouths of immense stone dolphins.

At the next level, the cascade of Æolus tumbles into a semi-circular pool surrounded by statues symbolizing the winds. Behind them are stone arcades, and the terrace above has ballustrades surmounted, at intervals, by smaller groups of statues.

A second basin, broken up by seven small cascades, is again terminated by a waterfall whose stream is increased by the jets flowing from tritons and nymphs.

As the ground rises the cascades, basins and fountains succeed each other, and each of them is adorned with groups of marble gods and goddesses whose white limbs are reflected in the silver surface of the water and drip with the foam and the spray surging up around them.

The culminating point of this astonishing piece of landscape gardening is the last waterfall that splashes into a circular pool.

Looking back from this point we can see the same wonderful succession of pools, fountains and basins leading down to the distant palace.

Three or four miles away the old derelict town of Caserta Vecchia has kept its ancient character and atmosphere, for it is seldom visited by tourists though it has a fine twelfth-century Norman cathedral, a medieval castle, some fourteenth-century mansions, and the ruins of extensive fortifications.

The new town on the plain below was constructed at the same time as the royal palace, and is completely devoid of character.

I have always speeded on my way from Caserta to Capua, for the road is level and there is nothing about the scenery to induce one to linger.

Santa Maria Capua Vetere is built on the site of the ancient town of Capua which flourished under the Etruscans and the Romans. It was so prosperous that when Hannibal and his soldiers wintered here they lived in such luxury that they lost the toughness that had made them victorious in the past.

When this city was destroyed by the Saracens, the remaining inhabitants took refuge in the loop of the Volturno where the modern Capua now stands.

The Roman amphitheatre at Santa Maria Vetere is one of the

largest in Italy, but the ruins are only in a moderate state of preservation.

An underground temple is remarkable because of the vivid mural paintings of Mithra, and of the initiation ceremonies of this strange cult which was so popular in the latter years of the Roman Empire that at one time its adherents were more numerous than those of the Christian religion.

The new Capua is almost surrounded by the dark green swirling waters of the Volturno, and for this reason it was an important fortress before the Union of Italy in 1861.

So throughout the centuries this unfortunate city was besieged, captured and sacked by successive invaders. Cæsar Borgia, for instance, slaughtered no less than five thousand of the male inhabitants in 1501.

In the Second World War Capua was repeatedly bombed and many houses were destroyed.

In 1944 it looked a sad and desolate place, and it still has a mournful aspect now. In the eighteenth century, when a large garrison was stationed here, the social life was active and the atmosphere was gay, and indeed many of the buildings in the squares and streets were constructed during that period.

For a while the road continues to run across a flat and almost marshy plain, but soon a long range of mountains appears on the skyline. Low wooded hills rise up on either side of the highway.

Then to the north, the fortress-like monastery of Cassino appears to block the advance of any invading army towards Rome, and this actually did happen in 1944.

After making successive stands on different strategical positions, the German armies found a natural defence line behind the Garigliano river and on the range of mountains that begins on the edge of the Mediterranean a few miles to the south of Minturno. The monastery was occupied, for it was indeed the key of the No 6 road to Rome.

The Allies were reluctant to destroy a monument of such antiquity and religious standing, but eventually, after due warning, the monastery was blown up by aerial bombardment. The town also was flattened out; the result was a scene of devastation such as I have seldom beheld in the course of my extensive wanderings. On the lower levels there was a mass of greenish-yellow slime, and there were so many deadly mosquitoes that troops were forbidden to halt within the area. Now the Monastery has been completely rebuilt on exactly the same model as its predecessor, and the great library has been reopened. The valuable religious manuscripts and early printed books that it contained had been taken away to a place of safety during the war, and all of them are intact.

Cassino was founded in 529 by St Benedict and so it is the Parent House of the Benedictine Order. Repeatedly destroyed during the Barbarian invasions, it attained its greatest fame in the eleventh century, and was visited by prelates from all parts of Europe.

Visitors may lunch at the Monastery by applying to the father in charge of hospitality, but they are expected to make adequate contributions to the alms box. There is also accommodation for male visitors on the same conditions.

From the top of the building there are views of the valley below, and in particular of the rugged Abruzzi Mountains.

For the rest of the way to Rome, the landscape is hilly and not unattractive, but there is no place of real interest on this part of the route. Frosinone, badly battered during the last war, is situated on a high ridge. Alatri on the top of a high hill has some well-preserved fortifications including those of a massive castle, and Fiuggi is a spa with waters which are claimed to be beneficial to gout and bladder troubles.

CHAPTER FOURTEEN

ROME : FLORENCE : PASSING THROUGH
VITERBO, ORVIETO OR BOLSENA :
PIENZA : SIENA : SAN GIMIGNANO

THE Via Cassia, known also as the R.N.2, is the most direct
route from Florence to Rome, though there are a number of
possible deviations, each of them sufficiently interesting to be
worth considering. So, for instance, by taking the Via Claudia,
which branches off to the left about twelve miles out of Rome,
there is an opportunity of halting for a while on the shores of Lake
Bracciano.

Further on, the Via Cimina forks to the right and skirts the Lago
di Vico before rejoining the Via Cassia at Viterbo. This lake is in
the crater of an extinct volcano, and so it is surrounded on all sides
by a ridge of hills and set in a deep hollow. There are no villages on
its shores, presumably because they must have been malarial.

The tradition is that Hercules was asked to give a proof of his
great strength: he did so by plunging a huge bar into the earth, and
when he withdrew it, the lake formed in the hollow that was left.

Since few people pass this way, the scenery has not been spoilt and
there is still much charm to be found in this deserted region, and
more especially in the deep blue waters of the lake and the wooded
slopes of Monte Venere, the hill that rises up from its northern
shores.

If Venus was the tutelary goddess of the mountain, the Romans
believed that the nymphs Melissa and Almatea, two of Jove's nurses,
dwelt beneath the waters of the lake.

I must plead guilty of always having hurried my visits to Viterbo,
the next place of importance, because of the superior scenic attractions of Bolsena, Orvieto and Siena, and I am inclined to think that
most people would agree with me. Yet Viterbo is an ancient and
historic city with many fine monuments, a number of medieval
streets, and some large squares with fountains playing in the centre.

The cathedral is noteworthy only because it was the scene of a violent drama in the thirteenth century, when Prince Henry D'Almayne, nephew of Henry III, was murdered by Guy de Montfort, the son of Simon of the same name, who was killed at the Battle of Evesham.

Both these knights were returning from the Crusades, but the chance encounter at Viterbo furnished the opportunity for an act of vengeance which Dante condemns in the *Purgatorio*.

During the same century many of the Popes resided here in the palace, of which the great hall alone remains—within its walls no less than six Popes were elected by conclave.

After a period of great prosperity, the fortunes of Viterbo declined when the Holy See was transferred to Avignon, but there was a short revival in the sixteenth century when a native of the city, Alexander Farnese, became Pope under the name of Paul III.

A few miles on, Montefiascone is reached after a steep and winding climb, for it is situated on the crest of a hill two thousand feet above the level of the sea, and well over seven hundred feet above the plain.

It is a strange and rather forbidding place with dark gloomy houses clustered round the dome of the Renaissance cathedral. *Est*, as the local wine is called, is produced in three or four different kinds of vintage, of which the dry white variety is by far the best.

It is a mistake to hurry through Montefiascone without halting to take in the view from the public gardens. From here there is a wide and extensive prospect of the Etrurian countryside.

To the south-east, rolling plains and low hills extend towards the high ranges of the Apennines. To the north, one looks over the vast expanse of the Lake of Bolsena, which is over forty miles in circumference.

The shores are wooded, and wooded hills come down to the water's edge. In summer, the surface is a vast sheet of shimmering blue darkened by the reflections of the surrounding forest land.

By deviating to the left it is possible to encircle the lake and pass through the two fishing villages of Capodimonte and Marta. The first of these is situated on a small peninsula and is of great antiquity. A splendid Renaissance palace adjoins the castle that once belonged to the Farnese family.

From this place one can hire a boat to row out to the Isola Bisentina, on which there is a small village, another Renaissance palace belonging to the Farnese, a beautiful church—and five little chapels. One of these is decorated with frescoes by a pupil of Benozzo Gozzoli.

As far as I know there is nowhere to stay at Capolungo, but there are, or there were, one or two simple *trattorie*.

Marta, the second village, is built right on the edge of the lake, and some of the older houses have cellars constructed to serve as small covered harbours to the fishing boats. Marta is a picturesque place with narrow streets and the ruins of a castle on a hill nearby. A square opens out directly on to the lake, and from there one can look across at Bolsena on the opposite shore and at Montefiascone on its high ridge.

The main road runs along the eastern shore to the medieval town of Bolsena, which is dominated by the four tall towers of the castle on the slope above it.

It is a place of unusual interest, because of the ruins and relics of past ages, from the days of the Etruscans to the present time.

The first view of Orvieto in its Etruscan site is unforgettable. Beyond the crest of hills which shelter Bolsena, the wide valley is filled with peach, almond and fig trees and vines, surrounded by a sea of corn. Now from this valley rises an island of soft pink rock crowned with towers and old walls out of which is uplifted the great cathedral with its delicate golden, jewelled façade. Encircling the whole enchanted scene are mountains of blue, violet and rose, some snow-capped and disappearing into infinite distance.

To me there is nothing in the whole of Italy with just the sense of quiet grandeur that is felt before the thirteenth-century cathedral of Orvieta. Only the finest artists worked on its architecture, its sculpture and its paintings.

The pinnacled façade is taken straight from the glowing, gilded pages of an illuminated manuscript.

The great cathedral was erected at the end of the thirteenth century by order of Pope Urban IV to commemorate the Miracle of Bolsena when an unbelieving Bohemian priest witnessed the unexplained appearance of drops of blood on the host and was convinced of the doctrine of transubstantiation.

The beautiful bas-reliefs decorating the pillars represent incidents from the Old and New Testaments and, above the doors, mosaics on a golden ground depict scenes from the life of the Virgin.

The interior, like that of Siena Cathedral, is constructed of alternate layers of black and light stone. The gallery above the arcades is decorated with elaborate carving.

Among the many fine frescoes which enliven the walls the most interesting are those by Fra Angelico and Signorelli.

Fra Angelico entered into an agreement with the rulers of Orvieto on 14 June 1447 to employ his summer recess of three months every year in painting the chapel of St Brizzio in the cathedral, in fresco, for which he was to be paid 200 golden florins per annum.

He only worked for three months, probably because he was so distressed at the death of his assistant, who fell from the scaffold. For fifty years the ceiling alone was decorated, then Signorelli carried out his vigorous figure compositions of the *Last Judgment* on the walls. In *Sketches in Italy and Greece*, J. A. Symonds recreates the scene of the decorating of the chapel:

"Angelico came first, in monk's dress, kneeling before he climbed the scaffold to paint the angry Judge, the Virgin crowned, the white-robed army of the Martyrs, and the glorious company of the Apostles. These he placed upon the roof, expectant of the Judgment. Then he passed away, and Luca Signorelli, the rich man who 'lived splendidly and loved to dress himself in noble clothes', the liberal and courteous gentleman, took his place upon the scaffold. For all the worldliness of his attire and the delicacy of his living, his brain teemed with stern and terrible thoughts. He searched the secrets of sin and of the grave, of destruction and of resurrection, of heaven and hell. All these he has painted on the walls beneath the saints of Fra Angelico. First comes the Troubles of the Last Days, the preaching of Antichrist, and the Confusion of the Wicked. In the next compartment we see the Resurrection from the Tomb, and side by side with that is painted Hell. Paradise occupies another portion of the chapel."

There are several other interesting early churches well worth a visit for those staying more than a few hours in Orvieto. There is an extensive Etruscan necropolis, most of the tombs dating from the fifth century and some of them in a good state of preservation. Many painted vases were found in the tombs and are now in the local museum.

A walk round the ramparts gives one unforgettable views over the valley to the mountains, and brings one to the church of St Juvenalis with its fading frescoes of the Umbrian school.

The through road to Florence does not, of course, pass by Orvieto, but goes straight on over the high ridge of Radicofani, and then over some arid volcanic country to Siena.

As the deviation by Orvieto takes in more pastoral country, it is necessary to wind and turn through small green valleys and over low hills.

First of all there is a descent to Chiusi, one of the old Etruscan cities, with really remarkable tomb paintings that rival those of Tarquinia, and an archæological museum with outstanding exhibits of pre-Roman art.

Then high up on a hill, the spa of Chianciana is beautifully situated, but pervaded by the atmosphere of intense boredom characteristic of such places.

By now the frontier between Umbria and Tuscany has been crossed, and this fact is made more apparent by the alert gait and the cheerful but quarrelsome behaviour of the peasants by the wayside.

The road skirts the beautiful hill town of Montepulciano, famous because of its splendid palaces, its medieval town hall and well-planned streets.

From the castle there is a wide prospect of the lakes of Trasimene and of Chiusi, and of the hills and mountains behind Perugia. The clear light, the strong colours, the well-defined outlines, and the purples and violets of the distant horizons are those of the seventeenth-century painters, or still more those of the backgrounds of the earlier religious pictures. In the patchwork of vineyards, fields and olive groves, the black lines of cypresses stand out like soldiers on the march. Castles and battlemented villas crown the crests of hills, red-roofed villages nestle round tall steeples in the hollows. All the pageantry that makes up the basis of Italian art is there.

The three or four inns are sufficiently comfortable for an overnight stay in order to wander through the ancient town and enjoy the beauty of the sunset, the patchwork of shadow and light in the streets after the fall of night.

Pienza, the next little town, is virtually the creation of the Piccolomini Pope, who was born here in the beginning of the fifteenth century. The Piccolomini Palace, the Palazzo Municipale and the church were all built under the ægis of this pontiff who often made prolonged stays here.

A soft clear light spreads over the warm red earth of the ploughed land and the shimmering green and silver of the olives. The dark poplars decorate the hillside that sweeps down to the winding road to Siena. Precisely silhouetted against the sky, villages and castles crown the summits, and the pale warmth of pink-washed farm buildings is enhanced by the strong black lines of cypress.

The great attraction of Siena lies in the fact that it is still a medieval town in aspect and yet possesses all the movement and activity of a modern town.

In the centre most of the narrow stone paved streets have no footway for pedestrians, and cars have the greatest difficulty in advancing through the constant ebb and flow of people.

Here, as in most Italian towns, there are many palaces, but they are for the most part battlemented and have narrow Gothic windows, for the decline of Siena's power and prosperity began with the Black Death, which wiped out three-quarters of the population.

The thirteenth-century cathedral, built entirely of black and white marble, is one of the few really satisfactory pieces of Gothic architecture in Italy. Yet the present structure is only the transept of a church which was not completed because of the ravages of the Great Plague.

In the interior, the coloured stone gleams in the darkness and does not spoil the effect of the numerous shrines and pictures. The marble pavement is covered with "graffito" drawings representing scenes of Bible history.

This pavement is usually protected by wooden floorboards, which are removed for a few weeks during the summer months.

This, indeed, is the time to visit Siena, for it is one of the coldest towns in Italy in winter. In the hot months, it is true, the countryside is burnt to rich greys and browns that do, as a matter of fact, enhance the strange but beautiful configuration of the landscape.

The colours of the earth are repeated in the town itself with its semi-circular main Piazza dipping down to the town hall. Despite its formidable medieval strength, the tall slim tower gives it a feeling of lightness and prepares us for the delicate frescoes we find inside, and for the glowing jewel-like panels in a golden background in the picture gallery.

Here, in the town hall, Simone Martini painted the *Captain Guido Riccio da Fogliano*, baton in hand, seated on a magnificent horse which strides out purposefully over the hills against an azure sky broken by flowing pennants and the delicate outlines of castles

and towers. The powerful horse treads firmly on the ash-grey, dusty
battleground, his head proudly lifted; his lovely orange and cream
saddle-cloth with black geometric pattern which follows the flowing
line of the drapery, complements the curves of the hills.

It may be the astonishing vitality of the horse which makes this
fresco so impressive and attracts our attention before we see Simone
Martini's other lovely paintings.

With beautiful delicate majesty he depicts the Virgin and Child
surrounded by gold-haloed angels, all dressed in patterned brocades
and protected by a gorgeous canopy supported on frail slender
columns. The pose of the Mother and Child, though dignified and
majestic, is gracious and tender and has lost the awe-inspiring
remoteness of the Byzantine paintings from which the Sienese painting developed.

The tradition of decoration in mosaic remains with the Sienese
and is shown in their love of glowing, jewel-like colour and the air
of mystery which they keep so well. Though many of these pictures
were contemporary with Giotto, they show very little of his interest
in solid form; they prefer to concentrate on delicious detail, flowing
rhythm of line, and to set their paintings in a wonderful paradise
suggested by the Tuscan landscape.

Ambrogio Lorenzetti gives us an entertaining picture of life in
town and country in his remarkable frescoes of *Good and Bad
Government*, as well as magnificent portraits of the more distinguished citizens of Siena. Although the frescoes are somewhat lacking in architectural unity, individual figures and details are
sensitively handled. In showing the effects of good government he
gives us a wonderful picture of Siena itself; warm pink and brown
houses, grey and white palaces, turrets and towers, streets and
squares all throbbing with the happy busy life of a prosperous community working and playing. The fresco showing the effects of good
government in the country is a most delightful landscape; one of the
rare early landscapes, for here Lorenzetti had the excuse to let himself go with the background. Prosperous country folk go along the
winding roads taking produce to market, driving healthy-looking
animals; hunting, sowing, tending the land, fishing by the beautiful
deep blue lake. All is set against a pattern of hills, trees and
meadows and mountain peaks, with an odd tower or village to vary
the line.

But it is not so much in the frescoes that the characteristics of the

Sienese school are typified, for frescoes by nature of their technique have a pastel quality of muted colours, and must also be broad in design, as they have to be painted swiftly and surely with little opportunity for correcting any lack of decision. It is in altarpieces and smaller panel paintings that the exquisite colouring and attention to detail are most apparent, and it is significant that Duccio, the unquestioned leader of the Sienese school, should never, as far as we know, have painted any frescoes.

It is strange that he and Giotto should have been painting at the same time, both in Tuscany, in towns only about fifty miles apart. They were both pioneers, and rebelled against the rigidity of Byzantine art in its decadence. Both show the beginnings of Gothic gracefulness in their work, and yet each is the founder of a completely different school.

Duccio and the Sienese clung to much of the Byzantine tradition, and that they never broke their traditional link with the East is apparent in their love of gold and jewels, richness of texture and the "miniature style", although they brought tenderness and grace, a melodious flowing line and a charm which breaks away from oriental stiffness.

Giotto departed from the Byzantine conception of a remote and majestic art, and brought his Bible stories down to earth, identifying them with the life of the times and setting them in the Tuscan landscape; making his figures solid forms rather than symbols, and delighting, not only in the patterns of nature, but in the mass of foliage, in the depth of the sky and in the subtlety of the varied horizon.

The Sienese delighted in giving intense pleasure in their paintings, in producing a glowing miniature, and they were not greatly concerned with discoveries in technique or in experimenting. Duccio was one of those outstanding personalities who was greater than the movement he led. His painting can hold its own with any of the great Italians, and has that monumental quality which gives it a timeless appeal.

His most impressive painting can be seen in the museum of the Opera del Duomo, the glorious *Majesty* with the Virgin and Child in the centre, posed, according to Byzantine tradition, in a dignified way but with a feeling of movement and a gentle expression in the almond-shaped eyes. The golden background and the pattern of haloes keep the tradition of a golden paradise, but there is variety in the kneeling figures and in the tilt of the faces which relieves the painting from any feeling of monotonous repetition. He has kept the Virgin in the glory of heaven, but has forged a human link which enlivens the whole design and saves it from the remote and rather wearisome symbolism of late Byzantine art.

Still more lovely Sienese paintings are to be found in the Pinacoteca. It is quite unlike the galleries of the capital cities of Europe, for to most of us the names of the painters are unknown, and we go on a visit of discovery like looking through a collection of precious stones and finding some wonderful new settings of deep glowing colours. Perhaps one of the loveliest of all is the *Annunciation* by Ambrogio Lorenzetti, where the Virgin in deep blue with a glowing red lining to her cloak, is seated on a little throne, her slender hands crossed on her breast and her gentle face in profile against the gold background. Kneeling on the pink and grey and black tiled floor is the winged angel in soft pink and gold and grey, a delicate and subtle contribution to the swelling tide of Italian achievement.

Twenty miles away, in the many-towered city of San Gimignano, Memmi, Simone Martini's brother-in-law, painted another *Majesty*, using the same composition and types of figures as Martini employed in the Town Hall, but ranging them in a more formal manner with less fluidity of line and variety of detail.

San Gimignano, though enjoying a flourishing independence for some centuries prior to the internal strife of the fourteenth century, had a Sienese Mayor. Mino de Tolemei da Siena depicted him kneeling before the Virgin Mary in the Council Chamber where, in 1300, Dante himself spoke for the Guelfs. Although San Gimignano was not lacking in native talent, painters came here from Siena and, in the fourteenth and fifteenth centuries, when San Gimignano came under the rule of Florence, Florentines also came.

Here in the Palazzo Pubblico is a lovely collection of paintings, many of them, such as Ghirlandaios and Benozzo Gozzolis, brought in the late nineteenth century from the suppressed convents. Most lovely of all is Pinturicchio's *Madonna Enthroned*. Though this Umbrian painter cannot be classed with the greatest of the Italians, he drew inspiration from such painters as Perugino, Pollaiuollo and Verocchio. He took very little interest in mastering the subtle movements of the human figure, in rendering atmosphere or distances. He does not seem to have had the sophisticated enquiring mind of

Ravenna: the Byzantine mosaics of Sant' Apollinare in Classe

Venice: the splendid façade of St. Mark's Cathedral

the fifteenth-century Tuscan and Umbrian masters, but he delighted in painting the delicate Umbrian landscape, the feathery trees, the castles and towers folded in the soft green hills, and he recreates them to make a drop curtain behind his stiff, flat figures dressed in most wonderful clothes. In the *Madonna Enthroned*, the saint on the right is dressed in a wonderfully painted white robe of a brilliance and substance that make it much more interesting than the characterless figure it clothes.

To look from the windows of the Palazzo Pubblico is to look straight into an early Sienese painting, especially in the evening light when the little trees and towers and villages scattered over the hillsides are tipped with gold. The dark masses of the great towers of San Gimignano, like huge factory chimneys, cut across the delicate pattern of the countryside and a multitude of bells peal out and echo in the narrow streets.

In these fortified hill towns it is often the Palazzo Pubblico that is more important as a centre than the cathedral. It usually occupies the best position in the main square and is the first large building to attract the visitor's attention, yet the cathedral here in San Gimignano is full of interest with its twelfth-century façade and Romanesque interior decorated with frescoes by Benozzo Gozzoli, Ghirlandaio and Pollaiuolo. Indeed the walls are completely covered with paintings, and only someone making a very leisurely tour of the town has time for more than a general impression, especially as at every gap in the buildings one is inclined to stand and gaze at the magnificent views of this lovely unspoilt countryside, which, though it may be grim and forbidding in the winter, is an absolute delight from May to October.

L

ROUTES FROM FLORENCE TO VENICE : FORLI, RIMINI, SAN MARINO, RAVENNA, FERRARA, PADUA

THERE are three possible routes from Florence to Venice, each of them interesting and agreeable in its own way, as I know well, for I have used them all repeatedly at different times.

The first of these routes passes through Bologna, a town of arcaded streets and ancient palaces, and the seat of one of the oldest and best universities in the whole of Italy, with a school of medicine of world-wide fame. This city also claims to be the gastronomic capital of Italy, and most impartial gourmets would be ready to support this claim.

Between Florence and Bologna the scenery is varied, for the road crosses first of all through typical Tuscan country with picturesque villages, patrician villas and castles, monasteries and convents on every side. Then there are two high passes to be negotiated, each of them over three thousand feet high. The second of these, the Passo di Radicosa, is on the frontier between Tuscany and the Romagna, and from then onwards there is a noticeable change in the character of the people and the architecture—the Romagnole are a tough, dour people, and their rustic dwellings have neither the grace nor the charm of the Tuscan cottages.

The road gradually descends a bleak bare valley in the stony barren Apennines, until suddenly the vast plain of northern Italy opens out in front.

In spite of its pleasant little taverns, its tall strange towers, and its infinite variety of monuments, I do not like Bologna, for it is bitterly cold in winter, and stiflingly hot in summer. Then the rest of this route is over the flat and unvaried country which does have a strange attraction, because of the wide expanse of sky and the strange effects of light, but the long journey tends to become monotonous and uninteresting after a while.

The second route to Venice passes through Ravenna, and for this reason alone it is the best to take, though it has the added advantage that it is short and also affords a glimpse of the Adriatic coast.

The road follows the course of the Upper Arno for a few miles and then, at Pontassieve, it forks to the left up the wooded valley of the Sieve. I like to stop for a coffee at San Godenzo, a little medieval town on a spur, surrounded by olive groves and dense woods of chestnut trees.

The highway climbs steeply another two thousand feet to the top of the Muraglione Pass where the air is usually fresh after the heat of the lower levels.

There is an inn here with terraces overlooking the valley of the Sieve with its lovely gradations of green foliage, beginning with the sombre oaks near the top of the Pass, continuing with the lighter shades of the chestnuts down to the olives and the vineyards on the lower slopes.

On the far side of the Muraglione, the road follows the windings of the Montone river towards the great northern plain. In places the graceful arches of old stone bridges span the stream as it surges and bubbles through brilliant green meadows.

After the parching heat of Florence, the freshness of the foliage and the clear water rippling over the stones through this Arcadian landscape are pleasing to the eye, as Dante noted on his way north-wards into exile with his heart full of bitterness.

At San Rocca San Casciano, the ruins of a castle and fortifications are a reminder that in the past this was a frontier zone, and that the approaches to Florence were carefully guarded.

At Terra del Sole on the former boundary, the ancient ramparts still enclose a picturesque little town.

Soon the tall Venetian steeple of Forli looms up on the horizon. It is a prosperous city with broad squares and splendid Renaissance palaces. On Mondays the market attracts many peasants from the surrounding countryside, and even on other days there is plenty of movement, for this agricultural centre has over eighty thousand inhabitants. The tall, dark red brick campanile of the Duomo dominates the wide expanse of the piazza. Torrigiani, the architect of the Henry VII Chapel of Westminster Abbey, is buried here in the cathedral, for he returned to Italy after having inspired the English and taught them something of the meaning of Renaissance art.

Incidentally, Forli has its own school of painters, and the best works of Melozzo and Andrea Palmezzani are only to be seen in the museum, and Melozzo was one of the best pupils of Piero della Francesca.

Indeed there is much to be seen in this town, but for most people any time spent here means less time spent in Ravenna, not more than forty minutes away by a broad flat road that lends itself to speeding.

The third of the routes to Venice is the longest and in many ways the most attractive, but it entails some steep hill-climbing and careful driving.

In this case also it is necessary to follow the valley of the Upper Arno as far as Pontassieve, but instead of branching off to the left the road goes straight on and climbs up over the northern arm of Vallombrosa at the Consuma Pass and down into the delightful region known as the Casentino.

At the little old town of Poppi the highway branches off to the left and passes through the immense forest of Camaldoli and near the ancient convent where Lorenzo the Magnificent established his celebrated academy. This religious house was founded as a hospice for travellers; in the Middle Ages it became a centre of learning, and it was here that some of the first books in Italy were printed.

The cloisters are medieval, and the chapel is Baroque, but the chief attraction of this place is the wonderful sylvan setting, and the hermitage, higher up on the hillside.

At Badia a Pratiglia, a little way further on the main road, is a small mountain resort in the forest with a number of modest hotels and pensions. In the height of summer accommodation here would be scarce.

The four-thousand-foot-high Passo dei Mandrioli is often closed in winter and the early spring because of snow. The descent on the far side is very steep and needs to be negotiated with great caution.

A little way beyond Mercato Saraceno, a secondary road on the left-hand side leads to Rimini, one of the most popular resorts on the Adriatic. On this coast prices tend to be far lower than on the west coast; the water is clean, the beaches of white smooth sand are well adapted for sunbathing.

During the Second World War the old town of Rimini was seriously damaged, but the beautiful Temple of Malatesta has been carefully and successfully restored, and the Roman bridge built by Tiberius escaped destruction.

The small mountain Republic of San Marino, a few miles inland, is perched high up on the pinnacle of a rocky hill. The town, the fortifications and the castle are well preserved, the view is magnificent, but in the height of the summer season the place is crowded with excursionists.

From Rimini to Ravenna the road follows the line of the coast, but the sea is out of sight most of the way. The scenery, on the whole, is dull, but at Cesenatico the harbour is full of fishing smacks with wonderfully coloured sails, and the scene on the quayside is picturesque and full of movement. A little before reaching this town the traffic passes over a small muddy stream that looks like a dike in the marshland: it is the famous Rubicon that Cæsar crossed on his triumphant progress to Rome.

Not many years before the Second World War, Ravenna was a desolate city set in unhealthy marshland some miles from the Adriatic coast. Only a few adventurous tourists penetrated her melancholy, damp streets to find in the plain, almost barn-like brick buildings a wealth of early Christian and Byzantine art. Her treasures were hidden almost to the same extent as ancient civilizations were buried under the earth, and as communications were indifferent and she did not lie on the route to anywhere of importance, she slept and decayed for centuries.

The nineteenth-century travellers, in their conscientious pursuit of everything of artistic interest, stayed in one of the two hotels described as "tolerable as very rough Italian inns", and enjoyed the strange desolation of the countryside and the damp, decaying churches, the grass-grown streets and the misty, swampy plain stretching to Classis and the sea.

Until you enter into the buildings of Ravenna and gaze on the splendour of the mosaics, it is difficult to visualize her as a great city which was, at one time, more important than Rome.

It was from Ravenna that Julius Cæsar set out on his famous Crossing of the Rubicon: the Emperor Augustus chose it as a naval base to protect the East Mediterranean sea routes and, in the fifth century, Honorius transferred the seat of the Western Empire here from Milan.

Gibbon, in the *Decline and Fall of the Roman Empire*, tells us that Augustus prepared a harbour three miles from the old town capable of taking two hundred and fifty warships, and that the harbour was soon linked to Ravenna itself by the populous quarters of Cesarea and Classis. A series of canals passed through the midst of the city dividing it up into islands, and communications were maintained by boats and bridges as in Venice. The surrounding country for miles was a great impassable morass, but the regular tides of the Adriatic which swept the canal saved the water from stagnation and floated the vessels into the heart of Ravenna.

In 404 Honorius developed the town into an Imperial residence and during his reign and that of his sister, Galla Placidia, it attained its greatest glory. In 493 Ravenna came under the rule of the Goths for half a century and during the reign of Theodoric there was great building activity.

In 539 Belisarius, General to Justinian, conquered the city and it became dependent on Constantinople.

In almost every case these fifth and sixth-century churches are very plain outside—of pink brick with round campaniles, sometimes leaning and usually seeming to totter, with small rounded windows, tiled roofs and no decoration at all. They form a kind of rough outer husk protecting incredible richness within. Dimly lit and mysterious, the very dust in the interiors seems to hold the glitter and magic of the thousands of coloured stones that make up the mosaic decorations. The faint light seems to travel lovingly over the uneven surface of the walls and reveals a background of shining gold behind majestic figures draped in glowing colours; the folds seem to move and fall in front of our eyes as the separate stones catch the light and throw back coloured fire. The details are simply designed, the figures austere and somewhat stiff, but this effect is admirably offset by the moving and flickering of the brilliant colours.

You need an entire day to be able to visit the chief buildings of interest in Ravenna, but if you are only making a short halt, it is best to go into the Basilica of San Vitale and the Mausoleum of Galla Placidia which is close by.

This mausoleum is one of the oldest and most complete monuments of the fifth century in Ravenna. The walls of the interior are completely covered with mosaics in gold and blue and green. The dome and roof are of a wonderful deep sky blue resplendent with stars. The most lovely of all these decorations is the mosaic over the entrance doorway of *Christ the Good Shepherd*. He is seated on a hillock and holds the Cross high in His left hand and with His right He fondles one of the sheep that surround Him. Delicate flowers and shrubs grow from the grassy ground and are silhouetted against the sky. The cathedral Baptistry also dates from the fifth century with its lovely mosaic of the Baptism of Christ, and in the archbishopric is a restored chapel of the fifth century and the wonderful carved ivory throne of St Maximianus.

Nothing is left of Theodoric's great palace, but the magnificent church of Sant Apollinare Nuovo which he built close to it, remains as a glorious work of the early part of the sixth century. The portico and façade were added in the sixteenth century. The interior of the great basilica is divided into three by twenty-four pillars of Greek marble. The most lovely thing in the church, though, is the series of mosaics that decorate the wall space in the nave above the arcades. On one side a radiant procession of virgins is led by St Euphemia and the three Magi to the throne where sits the Virgin with the Child on her knee, guarded on either side by standing angels. The swift forward movement of the Magi, their gorgeous eastern robes flowing behind them, contrasts satisfyingly with the upright figures. Delightful flowers spring up beneath their feet and palms decorate the background. On the opposite side, coming from the city of Ravenna, a procession of martyrs treads a flower-strewn way to the Throne of Christ. Above the processions and between the windows are majestic figures of the prophets and above again are the scenes from the life of Christ. These glorious decorations were probably not all created during the time of Theodoric. It is possible that some were carried out later in the time of Belisarius.

Theodoric's great two-storied tomb made from huge blocks of stone outside the city is too clumsy to be beautiful, and has none of the interest of the wonderful tomb of his sister Galla Placidia.

But to come back to the mosaics, there is still the unforgettable experience of visiting San Vitale. Octagonal in form, it was built on the same plan as St Sophia in Constantinople, though it was begun a few years earlier. It is here that we see the wonderful mosaic of Justinian and Theodora surrounded by their court, and here too are the lovely pink and cream-coloured marble columns with their delicately carved capitals.

The Piazza Maggiore is a delightful square. The Palazzo Comunale and the Palazzo Governativo were both built in the fifteenth century by the Venetians when they took over the city, and rebuilt in the seventeenth century. The solidly built pink and ochre palaces have wide arcades supported by pillars with carved capitals. Two Venetian columns which now carry statues of Sant Apollinaris and

San Vitale stand in front of the Palazzo Communale. It is no longer the empty, sad square of the early part of the century, but is packed with gay umbrellas and tables and chairs to accommodate the visitors. Here at least there is as much gaiety as in any other small Italian town. It is a delightful setting for the evening hours spent in strolling or talking and sipping a drink. A few yards away is the tomb of Dante who died here from a fever caught in the marshes in 1320.

Out beyond the town, some two and a half miles away, where the ancient port of Classis once stood, is the lonely great church of Sant' Apollinare, the last great undertaking of the Byzantines in Ravenna. Sad and desolate as is the exterior with its tottering campanile, there is a beautiful sixth-century mosaic in the Apse depicting Sant' Apollinare standing amongst flowers, strange little trees and rocks, and on either side a row of six sheep standing stiffly regimented. Above is a great cross, and higher still, the hand of God appearing through the clouds.

Beyond the Basilica the Corsini Canal winds through the shaded walks of the Pineta, the pinewood beloved of Dante, Byron and Boccaccio, which spreads to the sea.

The country that lies between Ravenna and Ferrara is a flat marshland with wide horizons, and when I first came here many years ago there was a strange ethereal quality about this landscape. When the weather is bad it is incredibly gloomy, but when the sun is shining, a silvery luminosity radiates from the flat fields, and the shining white clouds that sail over the firmament.

I do not like Ferrara, for it is a gloomy town, in spite of its magnificent monuments, its majestic palaces.

The huge red brick castle of the Estes rises out of the centre of the city and seems to cast a shadow over all the surrounding streets. For me the aura of a violent past pervades everything here, though in the Renaissance it was a past of great wealth and splendour, as we can see by visiting the art collections of the Schifanoia Palace, and those of the Palace of Ludovico il Moro, and the magnificent Romanesque cathedral.

I have to admit that I prefer to avoid Ferrara and take the secondary coast road along the spit of land that cuts off the huge lagoon of Comacchio from the sea.

Few people use this route because they find the marshland dull, and yet this region is not devoid of romance. The town of Comacchio is a kind of rustic Venice, full of canals and inhabited by a population of fishermen. These people derive the greater part of their livelihood from the eels that are so plentiful in the lagoon. I have been told that these creatures migrate to the Sargasso Sea in order to breed, and that eventually their progeny find their way to the Adriatic by instinct.

The ancient university city of Padua, domed and towered, with much of its surrounding wall still intact, lies buried in gardens and vineyards in the plain backed by the Euganean hills.

The university itself was founded in the early part of the thirteenth century, when the university of Bologna was dissolved, and it very quickly became famous all over Europe, especially in the field of medicine.

The streets of Padua are narrow, but many are arcaded; the main squares are spacious, and the principal buildings surrounded by gardens. In fact, it is a city of delightful squares and stately old palaces with large courtyards. The impression is of freedom and air and light; the soft golden light of the plain.

Perhaps one of the most delightful squares in the north of Italy is the Piazza Vittorio Emanuele, formerly more happily named the Prato della valle. It is surrounded by charming ochre-coloured houses, mostly arcaded, and the sixteenth-century church of San Giustina breaks the skyline with its eastern-looking domes. Opposite, the two storeys of pointed arches of the Loggia Amulea contrast with the broader rounder arcades. But what makes this unique as a square is the large garden in the centre with its shady trees. It is encircled by a canal, crossed by bridges, and peopled with a multitude of statues gleaming pale gold and white against the dark foliage. As if this were not enough, the oldest botanical garden in Europe, instituted in 1543, stretches back from the Piazza and increases the feeling of space.

Quite nearby is the Piazza del Santo with the huge Basilica of St Anthony. It was built as a shrine for the tomb of St Anthony of Padua, and was completed early in the fourteenth century, but has been added to and restored.

The confused grandeur of this immense church with its six domes, its turrets and spires, may be a little pretentious, but it is certainly an impressive building. The dimly-lit interior with its splendid monuments is awe-inspiring, especially when Mass is being sung and the lighted candles gleam on the wealth of exuberant decoration. The seventeenth-century Chapel of the Treasury, with its dozens of figures floating and twisting and dancing, supported by arches and pillars, has a glorious flow of movement. The wonderful Baroque candlesticks flow upwards in exuberant curves from a heavy base decorated with supporting figures.

But the Basilica is not only a monument to Baroque art; for those interested in the early schools of painting, there are some really beautiful frescoes by Altichieri and d'Avanzo, fourteenth-century painters of the school of Verona. In the background of another early fresco you can see a view of fourteenth-century Padua most decoratively carried out in fine outline, like a Moghul drawing.

Here, too, you will find the magnificent altar by Donatello with its wonderful crucifix and the panels of angels; plump, curly-haired winged children singing and piping with great enthusiasm. Outside the church in the square is one of the greatest equestrian statues of any period—the statue of Gattamalata.

The fifteenth-century sculptor had no traditional conception of a horseman on which to base his design, except the Roman statue of Marcus Aurelius on the Capitoline Hill, and the horses above St Mark's in Venice. The horse moves his left hind and foreleg at the same time—quite contrary to nature, but it seems to me of no importance since we are given the effect of powerful forward movement. The lack of any elaborate trappings and the simple treatment of the rider add to the impression of dignity and power. The fine head of Gattamalata shows him as a determined character—the man who succeeded in marching with his armies over the mountains of Garda in the depth of winter. The huge wooden model for this horse can be seen in the magnificent Sala della Ragione.

Besides Donatello there are two other great masters associated with Padua—the Florentine Giotto and Mantegna of the school of Padua.

To see some of the loveliest frescoes that Giotto ever painted, you must go to the other end of the town to the Scrovegni Chapel, or the Chapel of the Arena. This rather plain, red-tiled church set in a garden which was once the Roman Arena, has its interior completely covered with very well-preserved paintings telling the story of the life of Christ and of the Virgin.

Over the entrance is the splendid *Last Judgment*. Christ sits encircled by angels and flanked by the twelve Apostles. Hosts of angels fill the sky and, below, are the demons in torment on Christ's left and, to His right, the blessed rising up in a great throng to enter paradise. One of the most impressive of the twenty-eight panels on the side walls is, I think, the *Descent from the Cross*. With a few simple despairing figures mourning over the body, Giotto makes his picture more intensely dramatic than many later sophisticated conceptions of the scene. The grotesque little angels, overcome with grief, staggering about in the sky, and the stark, bare tree against the bright blue background increase the feeling of tragedy. How lovely, too, is the *Nativity*, peaceful and happy with the joyful angels and the stiff little Baby in its swaddling clothes.

The harmony of pinks and blues and greys in *Joachim and the Shepherds* is very beautiful, and the strange little rat-like sheep and the queer little lumpy trees growing from the bare rock have a great attraction for me. Every panel is worthy of prolonged study, but for most travellers it is only possible to get a general impression of the whole magnificent decoration. Do, though, spare time to see the carved *Madonna and Child* by Giovanni Pisano.

Here, in the city of Padua, within a few yards of each other, have worked two great masters who had such a far-reaching effect on Italian painting. Giotto, who influenced the Florentines and then the Italians, and Mantegna who influenced the Venetians.

Mantegna was born in Vicenza, but worked for some time in Padua, where he studied probably under Squarcione, who was a great traveller and deeply interested in Greece and in Ancient Rome. The numerous drawings he brought back from his travels served as a basis of study for his pupils who all tended to paint statues rather than warm human beings.

Mantegna himself was of course far greater than the school which begat him and though his figures do often look "carved", they have also tremendous vigour and their coldness is relieved by the numerous imaginative touches introduced into the landscape backgrounds. Beautiful little animals play in the sunshine; a lizard slithers swiftly over the crumbling stone of a ruin; a solemn little owl perched on a twig growing from a broken pillar watches the powerful executioner swing his mallet in the *Martyrdom of St James* with such force that he splits the sleeve of his tunic; a graceful young tree rises up in the foreground and its few leafy branches silhouetted against the sky sway above a delightfully detailed landscape rising to the walled and towered hill town. This fresco is one of the series he painted for the church of the Eremitani, quite close to the Chapel of the Arena. In all his paintings we can see tremendous knowledge of classical architecture. Many of the scenes take place inside classical buildings. Great pillars with elaborately carved capitals support pediments with bas-reliefs, and through Roman arches we look on to the countryside. Overhead, garlands of fruit and flowers, such as are found on ancient sarcophagi, are held aloft by cupids. But out of all these frescoes shines the tremendously forceful personality of Mantegna, whose work here and in Mantua had so much influence on the Venetians.

CHAPTER SIXTEEN

VENICE

I ALWAYS feel that Venice is one of the few places in the world that is certain not to disillusion the most blasé of travellers, for it is in fact far more beautiful than anyone can imagine.

The first impressions were, of course, better before the building of the railway, when voyagers were brought by gondola from Mestre, and so they approached the city slowly across the lagoon and could see it floating majestically on the smooth blue water.

We should really be grateful to Mussolini who was responsible for the construction of the motor road, as it is certainly more agreeable to drive in by car than to come by train. Even so, the two and a half miles that separate the town from the mainland are covered all too quickly, for it is quite impossible to dally.

Purists advise intending visitors to go to Chioggia at the southern end of the lagoon, and to take the steamer. They maintain that this is the perfect method of coming to Venice, especially if the arrival is timed for the late afternoon, and the whole landscape is enveloped in the mellow radiance of the sunset.

The Venetian lagoon is about twenty miles long and nine miles wide at its widest point, and Venice itself is only the largest of the half dozen groups of inhabited islands, not counting the long narrow spits of sand that enclose this large expanse of water.

These sandbanks, or Lidi, form a natural defence against attack from the sea, for the lagoon is very shallow—in places it is no more than nine inches deep at low tide—and the navigable channels follow strange and unexpected courses. Without the guidance of buoys it would be quite impossible for anyone but an expert pilot to steer a ship into the port of Venice, especially as there are currents that change from hour to hour.

Also, strangely enough in this inland sea, the flow of the tides is sufficiently strong to cleanse the water in the canals, and to ensure a relative state of hygiene.

These facts account for the foundation of the city, its development and survival. The first settlements were made when people from the mainland fled to the sandbanks of the lagoons in order to escape from the massacring hordes of Attila the Hun.

The descendants of these fugitives associated themselves together for self-defence, and they also sought the protection of the Emperors of Byzantium.

Eventually, the chief of the Rivoalto (Venice) became the head of the confederation of these states, with the title of Dux, or Doge as it was to be called later in the local dialect.

When Charlemagne decided to present the province of Venetia to the Pope, his son Pepin tried to subjugate the populations of the Lagoon, and the islands on which Venice now stands became their principal place of refuge, for the invaders were unable to reach them there.

For the next two centuries the Republic grew in strength and prosperity, in spite of the attacks of the Normans of southern Italy, the Saracens, and the Slavs of the east coast of the Adriatic.

In time the pressure from the Normans and the Saracens diminished, and in the year 1000, after defeating the fleets of the Slav pirates, Doge Pietro Orsoleo II established the supremacy of the Venetians in the Adriatic and assumed the title of Duke of Dalmatia.

With the coming of the Crusades, Venice played an even more important part in world affairs, for the fleets of the Republic were given the task of transporting the Christian armies to the Holy Land, and in doing so, they succeeded in annexing some Greek islands, and in establishing trading stations in various parts of the Mediterranean.

During the course of the Fourth Crusade, Doge Dandolo led the host that attacked and captured Constantinople. Though Baldwin of Flanders became Emperor, the Head of the Venetian State now took the style of "Lord of a quarter and of half a quarter of the Roman Empire", and Crete, some towns in Thessaly and some Greek and Dalmatian islands were added to the territories of the Republic. Now, more than ever, Venice had become the heir of Byzantium in the realms of art and of commerce, even though she had been repeatedly at war with the Eastern Empire, and did in fact contribute to its eventual destruction by her attacks.

The Venetian Republic survived, partly because of the impregnable situation of the mother-city in the Lagoon, and mainly because of the efficient and stable character of its constitution. Originally the administration was in the hands of an elected Grand Council, but later the members were selected only from the patrician families. Then to strengthen the authority of the Government and to expedite the authority of its decrees, the Council of Ten was created.

The State had an excellent intelligence service abroad, but within its territories an efficient espionage system watched over the internal security of the Republic, and subversive activities were severely punished.

In the fourteenth century the Venetians engaged in a life and death struggle with their principal commercial rivals, the Genoese. The fleets of the two republics fought in many parts of the Mediterranean, and in one of these engagements, the Battle of Curzola, Marco Polo was taken prisoner and interned in Genoa. To while away the dreary hours of his captivity he wrote the account of his journeys to China which have made his name immortal.

In 1380 the Genoese Admiral, Pietro Doria, succeeded in slipping past the Venetian fleet on guard in the Adriatic and established himself at Chioggia and on various islands of the Lido.

The capture of Venice appeared to be imminent, when Admiral Zeno returned unexpectedly from a cruise, and turned the tables on the attackers, who were besieged in their turn and forced to surrender with all their ships.

In the fifteenth century, Venice was at the height of her prosperity, power and glory. Her territories included not only the greater part of Istria and Dalmatia, islands off the coast of Greece and of Asia Minor, but upon the mainland of Italy, together with Brescia and Bergamo to the west, the region of the Dolomites known as the Trentino, and the hinterland of Trieste as well as of Istria.

The Turks, the Germans and the Greeks had their factories and their warehouses on the Grand Canal, and people wearing all the picturesque costumes of the Levant and of Eastern Europe could be seen parading in the Piazza San Marco.

The decline began with the fall of Constantinople and the discovery of America—on one side the Venetians were to be gradually dispossessed by the Turks, and the trade of the world was diverted to Western Europe.

In the eighteenth century the last of the Venetian colonies in the Levant fell before the onslaught of the Sultan's forces, but in Venice itself life was perhaps more urbane than ever.

Tiepolo painted his lovely portraits, and his splendid ceilings, Canaletto and Guardi immortalized the beauty of their native city on canvas.

At Carnival time the masked revellers frolicked gracefully in the palaces and on the piazzas, and all the year round, the unique pageantry of Venice was displayed to astonished and admiring travellers from all parts of Europe.

In 1797 the Trump of Doom sounded sharply and suddenly, when General Bonaparte decreed the end of the glorious republic that had flourished for over a thousand years.

By the Treaty of Vienna in 1814, Venice and her Italian possessions were handed over to the Austrians, whose sway was resented, but had to be endured.

During the period of anarchy that prevailed in 1848, the Venetians rebelled and restored the Republic, but after a siege that lasted over fifteen months they were forced to surrender to the Imperial General Radetzky.

In 1866, after being defeated by the Prussians at the Battle of Sadowa, the Austrians ceded Venice and most of Venetia to Italy, though they retained the Trentino and the region round Trieste.

In the mid-nineteenth century there was a movement afoot to modernize Venice: many of the canals in the vicinity of the station were filled up and the result is most unsightly. Then for a while there was a project to pull down St Mark's and to rebuild it in the neo-classical style so popular at the time in Austria. Altogether, under the Imperial régime, no less than two hundred historic palaces were demolished.

Nevertheless, in spite of much vandalism, Venice has preserved most of its basic features. There still remain no less than 118 canals which are crossed by close on four hundred bridges.

There are fifty islands, many of which have been built up on piles made from the pine trees which at one time covered the various strips of the Lido.

Steamboats carry passengers down the Grand Canal, the broad Giudecca Canal, and round the outskirts of the city. They also ply to the Lido, and to the maritime villages in various parts of the Lagoon.

These public services are now supplemented by the *motoscafi*, large motor-boats that can cut through the smaller canals and act as "express buses".

Venice: the Mint,
the Campanile and
the Palace of the
Doges

Venice: the Customs House and the Church of the
Salute seen from the Doge's Palace

Vicenza: Palladio's Loggia dei Capitani

Vicenza: a classical play at Palladio's Olympic Theatre

In recent years the number of motor-boats, in private hands and on hire, has increased considerably, and it is feared that their wash is damaging the foundations of many of the ancient buildings of the city.

Gondolas still survive, but they have become so expensive that they are patronized mainly by the richer tourists who are fortunately very numerous.

However, it would be unfair to blame the gondoliers for their high charges, for their craft are very costly to buy and to maintain.

The shape, size, colour and decorations of the gondola are established not only by tradition, but by regulations that have not been changed since the middle of the eighteenth century.

Skilled craftsmen are employed for the construction of these boats, which are tilted slightly to one side so as to counterbalance the weight of the gondolier, and curved so that they may keep a straight course in spite of the single oar.

The wood must be weathered and of the best quality, for the planks are very thin. Then the hull has to be scraped and waxed at least once in twenty days in the summer, a process which is expensive in time and money, but does ensure smooth and easy gliding through the water.

The life of a gondola is rarely more than five years, and that only if it is carefully sponged and scrubbed every day. The lovely fittings are usually inherited because the guild of boatmen is an ancient one, and the secrets of the trade are handed on from father to son.

The hatchet-like head with its six teeth is made of steel or of wrought iron and requires constant polishing, like the brass sea-horses, dolphins and harps that adorn the arm-rests and other parts of the boat.

In winter the passengers sit in a *felze*, a little house made of carved walnut wood and lined with wool. In the interior there is frequently a brass shrine for the picture of the patron saint.

Since there are only three bridges over the Grand Canal, there are ferries known as *traghetti* for the transport of the public from one side to the other, and this is done by gondola, though larger boats are sometimes used.

The Grand Canal follows an S-shaped course through Venice, which it divides into two unequal parts. The commercial port and the industrial quarter are in the western sector near the station and the terminal point of the road across the causeway in the Piazzale

M

Roma. The buses leave from this square, where there is an immense garage which is frequently too full to take in any more cars.

The motor-boats belonging to the larger hotels collect visitors at the station and at the Piazzale Roma, and there are, of course, plenty of gondolas for hire. If you are overloaded with luggage and wish to economize, the least expensive method of transport is to hire a porter to accompany you to your destination by steamer or by the *motoscafo*; he will not expect to be paid more than the official tariff.

The Giudecca Canal lies to the south of the southern and smaller sector of Venice, and this broad canal is used by ocean-going ships and fishing smacks.

On the far side of this channel, the two-mile-long island of the Giudecca is, in fact, almost a separate town with its own churches, shops and taverns, and is inhabited mainly by sailors and fishermen.

The Islet of San Giorgio is situated near the eastern extremity of the Giudecca, and faces the stretch of a mile and a half of water to the Piazza San Marco and the Doge's Palace.

Since I am a great believer in first impressions I would advise the newcomer to Venice to begin by going down the Grand Canal to get a glimpse of the majestic succession of palaces that line it on either side.

As you glide under the station bridge you see on the left-hand side the Church of the Scalzi, or bare-footed friars, a Baroque structure built by Longhena, the architect of the Salute. Then, a little way further on, on the same embankment, there is the Church of San Geremia, immortalized by Canaletto in one of his finest paintings. The ancient Ghetto behind this structure is infrequently visited, but it has lost most of its original character.

The much restored *Fondaco dei Turchi* on the right bank is a rather tasteless building in oriental style that was formerly the "Factory" of the Ottoman Empire.

Wagner lived for a while at the Palazzo Vendramin, one of the finest of the early Renaissance palaces in Venice, whose trefoiled windows are mirrored in the water on the opposite side of the Canal.

The Ca' Pesaro on the South Bank, and perhaps three hundred yards lower down on the Canal, is the largest and most beautiful of the Baroque palaces, in spite of its rather heavy marble façade.

Then, on the opposite side, the Ca' d'Oro, lavishly decorated in almost oriental manner, was built in the fifteenth century when the influence of the East was still strong. It was called the Golden Palace because the richly carved pillars and interlacing arches of the windows were gilded. The elaborate ornamentation has no relation to the structure of the building, but is, in fact, the most character-istically Venetian in the whole of Venice.

Nearby the over-renovated *Fondaco dei Tedeschi*, the former factory of the Hanseatic League, is now used as a post office. The fish market on the left bank opposite is full of life and movement in the morning, when the trawlers have brought in their night's catch.

Now the gracefully curved arch of the Rialto Bridge comes into view. It was for centuries the only bridge that spanned the Grand Canal.

It was built in the sixteenth century to replace the old wooden bridge that had been in use since the early days of the city. The Rialto quarter is the most ancient part of Venice, and it was formerly the commercial centre, with numerous warehouses and banks. There are cafés, restaurants and modest hotels on the open embankments. Just below the bridge, many of the houses have Gothic decorations, for they are among the oldest in the town.

On the right bank, a little lower down, the immense Renaissance Palazzo Grimani is now the Court of Appeal. The palaces of differ-ent periods and of different styles of architecture succeed each other so quickly that it is almost impossible to take in their principal features from the moving steamer. The elaborate Gothic façades alternate with the marble balustrades and the round arched columned windows of the late Renaissance and eighteenth century. One should take special note of the Palazzo Mocenigo, near the Sant' Angelo halt, for it was occupied for a while by Byron.

Beyond the Gothic Palazzo Foscari, on the left-hand side of the bend in the Canal, is the Palazzo Rezzonico where Robert Browning spent some months of his old age, and where he died in the year 1889.

A steeply curved wooden bridge links up the Campo della Carita to the Accademia, which houses one of the finest collections of old paintings in Italy.

A little way down on the same side is the domed church of the Santa Maria della Salute, which was built by Longhena as a votive offering to the Virgin for having brought to an end the plague which devastated Venice in the year 1630.

In the interior there are admirable paintings by Titian, including the Descent of the Holy Ghost, an altar piece of St Mark and four saints, and on the ceiling of the vestry, Cain and Abel, Abraham and Isaac.

However, the Salute is more justly celebrated as a fine architectural feature in the man-made landscape of Venice. To the simple harmony of the graceful dome are added the exuberant Baroque ornamentations of statues and carved buttresses below, and the cupola and the two tulip-shaped belfries at the back.

To the east of the church, the land narrows down to a point that projects into the open Lagoon, and on this point was built the Dogana di Mare towards the end of the seventeenth century. The colonnaded porch jutting into the sea is surmounted by a square tower on which two giants hold up a golden globe bearing the triumphant figure of Fortune.

The large palaces on the bank facing the Salute have for the most part been transformed into luxury hotels, each with its open terrace lapped by the waters of the Grand Canal. The lovely fifteenth-century Gothic Palazzo Giustianini, for instance, is now the Hotel de l'Europe. The Giustianini are a family of Venetian patricians who claim to be direct descendants of the Emperor Justinian.

Almost adjoining this palace was the Ridotto, the Casino of eighteenth-century Venice, where the rich merchants and aristocrats of the city used to gamble through the day and night for enormous sums of money.

The Piazza San Marco, the hub of Venice, serves as a kind of immense antechamber to the brilliantly coloured façade of St Mark's, and the tall Campanile that stands to one side of it.

The sixteenth-century Procuratie Vecchie on the north of the Square, and the Procuratie Nuove opposite, were the administrative offices of the Republic. Together with the Library they form one vast marble palace that encloses this outdoor saloon of Baroque architecture where the people of Venice and their visitors meet at all times of the day to stroll and gossip, or sit at one of the tables set out in front of the cafés.

One of these, the Café Florian, has preserved the delightful eighteenth-century decorations of the interior rooms where the aristocracy of the town foregathers in the winter-time.

Flocks of pigeons flutter round the Piazza and gobble up the grain from the hands of the tourists who never fail to feed them, though at one time these birds were maintained at the expense of the State.

The Campanile was originally erected in the year 900, but it collapsed no less than three times in the course of its existence.

The last time was at eleven o'clock in the morning in the year 1902. Though the Square was crowded no one was injured, and soon after, this historic tower was restored to its original form, but a lift was installed in the interior.

From the gallery at the top, three hundred feet up, one looks down at the clustered domes of St Mark's, the wide expanse of red-tiled roofs with their round carved chimneys, and all the towers and spires around. Palladio's Church of St George rises out of the gleaming blue waters a mile away, and behind it, stretches the long sandy Lido, with the white hotels and villas in a setting of trees.

To the north, and also across a mile or so of water, one sees the square island cemetery girdled by stone walls over which the black lines of cypresses appear like a procession of mourners.

Further still rise the towers and roof-tops of Murano, and in the far distance, those of Burano and Torcello, each of them miniatures of Venice in the midst of the Lagoon, with canals instead of streets and with boats as their principal means of transport.

On clear days, the northern horizon is bounded by the long rampart of the Alps, their crests glittering with snow and ice above the deep blue and violet of the lower slopes.

On the top of the clock-tower over an archway to the left of St Mark's, two bronze giants beat out the hours on a sounding bell. Below, the winged Lion of St Mark's is set above the blue and gold dial adorned with signs of the Zodiac.

The Church of San Marco was first built in 830 as a shrine for the bones of St Mark, which had been smuggled out of Egypt by some Venetian sailors. Destroyed by fire in the tenth century, it was rebuilt in the eleventh century in the Byzantine manner, so much so that it was said to duplicate the Church of San Sophia in Constantinople, but San Sophia was transformed into a Mosque, and so San Marco remains as the supreme expression of its style.

Above the five round arches of the doorways, the façade is decorated with blue and gold that forms a fitting background to the four bronze horses brought back by Doge Dandolo after overthrowing the Emperor of the East in 1204.

A balustraded terrace runs over the five doorways, and above it, the five archways are repeated, and the smaller ones serve as frames to mosaic pictures. Each of them is surmounted by a pinnacle and a statue, whilst stone angels stand at different levels around the dominating figure of St Mark on the central arch.

The interior of St Mark's is a glittering tabernacle of gold, bronze, marble and mosaics, for when the Republic was at the height of her prosperity her fleets seldom returned from a cruise without bringing back treasures to embellish the Metropolitan Church of their city.

So, though a mystic half-light prevails, the precious stones and metals, the pictures and mosaics gleam and give life to the darkness.

Under the green marble canopy of the High Altar are buried the bones of St Mark, and behind the altar is displayed the Pala d'Oro, a kind of gold casket of Byzantine work, ornamented with jewels, pearls, plates of gold and silver with enamel pictures of the Emperor John Comnenus, and of his wife the Empress Irene. There are also some twenty scenes depicting incidents from the Scriptures, and each of them is expressive of the grace, the dignity and the colour of the East.

The crucified figure of Christ rises up above the marble rood screen, and on either side of Him stand the Twelve Apostles and the Virgin Mary.

On the immense mosaic vault of the principal dome, Christ is borne heavenwards by four angels against a background sky of blue and of gold, and below, stand Archangels and Apostles.

Such scenes are repeated in each vault and on each wall, and though the decorations of statuary, carving and metal lamps and figures are so lavish, together they form a composition of singular harmony.

The treasures of St Mark's are so numerous that on each of my many visits I discover something new, or find a new aspect of something that I have seen before.

The Piazzetta to the left as one leaves St Mark's, is in a sense an extension of the main Piazza, and it is bounded on one side by the Doge's Palace and on the other by Sansovino's magnificent Library continued by the Zecca or Mint constructed by the same architect. The fourth side of the Piazzetta faces the open Lagoon with the island of St George right opposite and the Lido in the background.

On the left, behind the main buildings of the Square, there are public gardens where mothers sit and sew or gossip whilst their children play around them.

Near the Palace, the winged Lion of St Mark stands proudly on a tall granite column, and a statue of St Theodore is placed on a similar pedestal.

The first palace was built in 814, but the present structure was erected in the twelfth century and restored in the second half of the nineteenth century. In the fourteenth and fifteenth centuries an eastern wing was added and the inner quadrangle was completed.

The aspect of this building from the outside is so well-known that it scarcely needs to be described. The thirty-six columns with carved capitals on which the palace rests, appear to be short in relation to the height of the structure. This disproportion is due to the fact that the level of the Piazzetta and of St Mark's Square was raised in the eighteenth century to avoid flooding when the tides were unusually strong.

To enter into the courtyard is to pass from the early Middle Ages into the full florescence of the Renaissance, for everything that one sees inside is the product of the great genius of Sansovino, and the façades of the buildings are of marble with rich ornamentation of classical inspiration.

The access to the principal apartments is by the *Scala dei Giganti*, an outside marble staircase that takes its name from the giant figures of Mars and Neptune that symbolize the supremacy of Venice on the sea and on land.

The great wealth of the Republic is over-stressed by the lavishness of the decorations in the gilded halls—there is, strange to say, an excess of bad taste combined with great artistic achievement.

The panels and paintings by old masters depicting the history of Venice are in such profusion that they do in fact detract from the effect of harmony.

Yet one cannot fail to marvel at the splendour and achievements of this maritime race in every field of human activity, and there is real interest in visiting the Halls where the Great Council and the Council of Ten held their deliberations.

High up under the roof are the "Leads", the prison where political prisoners were incarcerated, and from which Casanova made his wonderful escape. Below, at water level, were the cells for criminals, and spanning the small canal at the back is the Bridge of Sighs, perhaps the most famous of all Venetian monuments.

CHAPTER SEVENTEEN

VENICE (*Continued*)
THE ACCADEMIA : THE FRARI : THE SCUOLA DI SAN ROCCO

THE Riva degli Schiavoni, the embankment where the Slavonic crews from Dalmatia used to berth their ships, is one of the busiest places in Venice.

If the Dalmatians have vanished, the moorings are now occupied by the landing stages of the steamers leaving for the station, the different beaches of the Lido, Chioggia, Murano, Torcello and Burano.

There is also a very useful service to the Island of San Giorgio, the Giudecca, and the Fondamento delle Zattere, the waterside that lies on the north of the wide Giudecca Canal.

The nearest of the Lido islands and the most fashionable is only a quarter of an hour from San Marco by steamer or motor-boat, and the price of bathing varies according to the type of establishment that you select.

There is also dancing and gambling to be had at the Casino. But to return to Venice itself, the Hotel Danielli on the Riva degli Schiavoni is of sentimental interest to those who love poetry and romance. It was to this ancient Gothic palace that George Sand came with Alfred de Musset, and during his illness she met the doctor with whom she fell in love, an affair that led to her separation from the young poet and to the endless battle of words that caused so much commotion in the literary world in Paris.

From their room the lovers could look over the water at the tall campanile of the Palladian Church of St George, and at the big ships gliding gently towards the Giudecca Canal.

To the east of the Riva degli Schiavoni is the Arsenal where the immense fleets of the Republic were built and fitted out.

The yards are still closed to the public, but the Naval Museum at the entrance contains models of ships of all periods, and in particular of those that were used by the Venetians in the past.

About half a mile to the east of the Arsenal the buildings that house the Biennale Exhibition of Art have been erected in pleasant public gardens on the waterside.

I am often asked where to stay in Venice. My reply is always the same: for a first visit of two or three days the large hotels on the Grand Canal provide all the amenities that anyone can require. If their prices are steep, why, surely one must be prepared to pay for the privilege of staying in a beautiful old palace, of watching gondolas glide by whilst breakfasting, and of obtaining some conception of how patricians lived before the fall of the Republic.

For those making a longer stay and wishing to economize, there are pleasant and comfortable pensions on the Zattere, such as the Seguso, or the Calcina where Ruskin lived whilst he was writing *The Stones of Venice*.

Here is less noise, though it is noisy everywhere in Venice, and the neighbouring quarter is more Venetian in character than the purlieus of St Mark's Square where the tourists abound.

I have sometimes stayed on the Zattere, because from the windows of my room, the one that Ruskin occupied, I could watch the liners and the fishing smacks sailing down the Canal. At night, half a mile away across the water, the lights on the Giudecca would begin to shine, and the beautiful Palladian Church of the Redeemer would be clearly outlined against the starry sky.

In the morning I took my breakfast on the terrace outside, with the wash of the passing ferry-boats lapping almost at my feet.

The Zattere quarter is unpretentious, but there are canals which reflect the churches, pink-washed houses and crumbling palaces on their smooth green surfaces. In diminutive shipyards men work at building or repairing gondolas, whilst small barges glide by with their loads of brilliantly-coloured fruit and vegetables.

The shops cater for the local population, and so even the foreigner is served with the simple friendly courtesy that you find in a remote provincial town. I remember particularly the chemist because of the coloured antique jars on his shelves, the counter carved with the emblems of pharmacy, and the same emblems repeated in the plaster mouldings of the walls.

Some of the taverns in this quarter serve excellent food in shady gardens with arbours of vines and creepers, and here, as elsewhere in the Zattere district, contacts with charming and cultured Italians are easily established.

By plunging through a maze of narrow *calle*, as the lanes are called, you can reach the Campo San Margherita, a large square where some of the simple cafés are frequented by painters and students, and here again the receptive traveller is welcomed with ready courtesy.

Although I am fond of wandering through the remoter districts, I do not by any means despise the liveliness and movement of the quarter round St Mark's Square. Here the tourists abound, as they always have abounded in the centre of Venice for the past thousand years, and it is certain that by their presence they have brought not only prosperity in their train, but they have given life to a place which might otherwise have been in a complete state of decay.

The palaces and monuments of Venice were constructed by the wealthiest people of their age, and it is only by the expenditure of vast sums that these buildings can survive.

Similarly, it is conceivable that the traditional crafts would not be flourishing now without the publicity given to them by the foreign visitors who have carried Venetian products to the ends of the earth and kept them before the public eye.

Glass, silk, painted furniture, wrought iron, lace and embroidery are being produced in greater quantities than ever, and not only are the old traditional patterns and models being used, but also modern designs of great originality and beauty.

It would be difficult to pass through Venice without seeing at least one of the large glass factories and their exhibition rooms. Tourists are invited to visit these places wherever they go.

Although prices have risen, I am quite sure that with due discrimination and care it is a good investment to buy glass, and especially to order table sets which can be made to the purchaser's own specifications, for there are scarcely any limits to what can be accomplished.

Venice is, I suppose, one of the few places in the world where glass has been made without interruption for over a thousand years, and the original workers learnt their craft from the Byzantines somewhere about the ninth or tenth century.

Indeed, the medieval Italians were far ahead of the rest of Europe, and the Venetians were the first to use glass for their windows, to sleep in real beds with sheets, and to take their food with forks instead of with their fingers.

These innovations were made in the twelfth century, but even in the eighteenth century Casanova remarked about the bad table manners of the English, who, he said, were apt to pick up pieces of meat with their hands, which they afterwards wiped on the cloth.

Unfortunately the Venetian women seem to be giving up wearing their beautifully embroidered shawls, and I suspect that it is mainly for reasons of economy. These lovely wrappings are still made, but in this case also, prices have risen unduly, though nothing better of the kind can be found in Europe.

Customs duties and high freights have placed the wrought-iron and painted furniture out of reach of all but the wealthiest at the time of writing these lines, but it is difficult to anticipate whether, in the near future, such things will be accessible to people of modest means.

Of the other goods displayed for sale, the gloves are always made of leather of superb quality, and are of excellent cut, and at reasonable prices.

For Anglo-Saxon men the ready-made shirts are frequently too small, because the Italians are usually slighter and tend to have smaller bones. So, for the same reason, I find the shoes too narrow for my broad feet. Both shirts and shoes can be made to measure quickly, and are delivered at the contracted time for a price that is not much higher than the manufactured product.

The best *calle* for shopping are the *Merceria Orologio*, reached by passing under the clock-tower in the Square, and the Calle XXII Marzo and the *Frezzeria* to the west of the Piazza San Marco.

In the *Frezzeria* and the Calle Vallaresso, its continuation to the Grand Canal, there are a number of restaurants of different categories, from the Colomba, where the film stars and successful artists congregate, to a kind of small grill room which bears the sign *Tavola Calda* to indicate that single dishes are served at a snack bar for reasonable prices.

The Pilsen, a *brasserie* specializing in German beer, and beer of the German type, has a terrace on the edge of the Bacino Orsoleo, a wide canal just to the north of the Piazza San Marco.

Trattorie and cheaper eating places are for the most part away from the tourist centre, but there are exceptions to this rule.

Roughly speaking, there are no regional dishes in Venice, but the scampi and most kinds of fish are exceptionally good.

The best of the local wines on draught are white, but the Soave, a vintage of the Graves type from the province of Vicenza, is among the best products of the Italian vineyards, and in Venice it is always sold in bottles.

The visitor making a short stay rarely has difficulty in finding entertainment in the evening, for it is always agreeable to sit at a café terrace in the Piazza, to go out in a gondola or to explore remoter quarters when the moonlight and the darkness combine to lend enchantment to the Venetian scene.

How pleasant it is to wander at venture through the narrow *calle* and suddenly come upon an immense square with a Baroque church at the far end! Shadows and moonlight pattern the façade bringing out into relief the chubby *putti*, the flowing garlands and the swags. Stone saints and apostles stand on the balustraded roof and are silhouetted against a starry sky.

Then if you stroll on a few yards further, you will be glad to stand on one of the bridges and gaze at the black silky surface of a small canal. From time to time there is a shout, a sound of rippling water, and then the steel hatchet head of a gondola glides forward at the corner of a crumbling wall.

Certainly the night is the time to take in the detail of the traditional ornamentation of Venice, the wrought-iron lamps, the twisted stone chimneys, the doorways, and the gaily painted mooring posts outside the ancient palaces.

This aimless wandering is an agreeable pastime, but it is easy to get lost in the maze of tortuous little alleys that twist and turn so that all sense of direction vanishes.

Then, strange to say, the Venetians do not know their way about their own city, except, of course, in their own quarter, which they seldom leave. Until quite recently each district had its own customs, its own traditions and even its own dialect. So I have often found that people who have sought to guide me would lose their bearings, and in the end I have been surrounded by a group of individuals, each of whom had his own theory as to the route I should take to go home.

However, with a good map, it is possible to go for a walk without these agreeable mishaps. I do like to spend an evening at one of the cafés overlooking the Grand Canal near the Rialto Bridge, for here the clientele is Italian, and the scene is typically Venetian and full of movement.

I do not recommend a visit to the Giudecca at night, for after sunset it is practically deserted and, apart from Palladio's Church of the Redeemer, there are no buildings of sufficient majesty to make up for the atmosphere of gloom and melancholy that prevails. Most of the taverns and the *trattorie* are nearly empty, and all of them are unpretentious, though devoid of much local colour. The one attraction is the view from the eastern extremity of the wharf when the moon is shining, and the Church of the Salute, the Doge's Palace and the Riva degli Schiavoni can be seen clearly in its silver radiance.

By day the Giudecca is pleasant enough, mainly because of the effects of light and shadow on the waters of the small canals, the crumbling old houses, and the complete absence of tourists and of the commercialism that is bound to follow in their train.

It is a place for the painter rather than for the indefatigable sight-seer, the seeker after smartness and sensational monuments, and so I can only recommend it to those who have leisure, and wish to spend a few hours in relative solitude.

If you are spending several days in Venice, do not fail to go to the Fenice, one of the most beautiful eighteenth-century theatres in Europe. In the summer season there are performances of Goldoni's plays, and sometimes also by some of the best of the international ballet companies, and in this setting the impression of their virtuosity is much increased.

Since many people are allergic to picture galleries, or at any rate prefer to stay out of doors, I have reserved my descriptions of the Accademia, the Church of the Frari, and the Scuola di San Rocco for the end of this chapter.

You must visit the galleries of the Accademia if you do not want to miss the only chance of seeing a completely representative collection of the works of the Venetian School. About a century later in its development than the other Italian schools, once established, it reached its highest peak very swiftly. Reduced to their simplest terms the origins of the Venetian school are as follows:

Gentile da Fabriano, whose lovely *Adoration of the Magi* is one of the great treasures of the Uffizi, and Pisanello, who worked in Verona, were both active in Venice in the early part of the fifteenth century. One of Fabriano's most important pupils was the Venetian, Jacopo Bellini. Of his two sons and pupils, Gentile and Giovanni, the latter was to have a great influence on Giorgione and Titian. Giovanni Bellini was also very much influenced by the work of the School of Padua, and he spread this influence through his pupils.

Broadly speaking, the main difference between the two greatest

Italian schools of painting, Venice and Florence, is that the Florentines were pre-eminently architects, sculptors and goldsmiths, and
therefore superb draughtsmen and more interested in form than
colour, and the Venetians from the very beginning were essentially
painters and magnificent colourists—more interested in colour than
in draughtsmanship and form. Secondly the peace of Florence was
constantly being disturbed, and she was not large enough or wealthy
enough to absorb all her artists, so they sought commissions in other
states. Venice was immensely wealthy, not only compared to other
Italian states, but as a great power and a world centre of trade.
Finally, Venice was very much influenced by the Byzantines, by the
glowing art of mosaic and by the rich splendour and colour of the
Orient with which she had so much contact. Gold, silver, jewels and
rich merchandise poured into her port. Ambassadors came with
luxurious gifts; strange and rare animals were brought in as curios,
and Venice was one of the most colourful cities in the world and so
rich that she could employ her multitude of artists who did not need
to go elsewhere for commissions.

The Galleries of the Accademia are a reflection of all this colour
and luxury. There are not so many religious pictures as in Florence,
for this is an art of the palace and banqueting hall rather than of
the church, and when religious commissions were carried out, the
religious theme was usually of secondary importance and used as
an excuse to paint a magnificent procession or a great feast.

You will find the early painters have a good deal in common with
miniaturists in their love of detail and their decorative use of gold,
and with the Byzantines in their rich display. In Paolo da Venezia's
Coronation of the Virgin, the central figures are dressed in gorgeous
eastern robes and Jacobello del Fiore's interpretation of the same
subject is a glory of colour with its multitude of angels surrounding
the gilded throne.

Carlo Crivelli's *St Jerome and St Augustin* reminds us forcibly of
the art of Mantegna, by whom he was so much influenced. In another
room you will find the superb *St George* by the Paduan artist with
its sentimental-looking dragon, delightful landscape and garlands of
fruit and flowers swaying against a cloud-flecked sky.

Vittorio Carpaccio illustrates superbly the story of the life of St
Ursula. This legend of the daughter of the King of Brittany,
affianced to the son of the King of England and martyred by the
Huns at Cologne in company with eleven thousand virgins, is used

as a pretext to evoke the life of his time, in many cases with a background of Venice herself. These lovely paintings, so full of human interest, if you can separate fact from fancy, give a complete record of costume, architecture, shipping and many customs of the time. For the most delightful and completely satisfying of all Carpaccio's paintings, the dramatic and decorative *St George and the Dragon*, you will have to go to the Scuola di San Giorgio degli Schiavoni, where you will find many more of his best paintings.

There are two Madonnas by Jacopo Bellini, gentle and human in approach, showing a genius for line and flow of composition. He was a magnificent draughtsman and master of composition, and his sketch-book of ideas was to prove a great source of inspiration to his sons. Incidentally his delicate painting of *St Jerome in the Wilderness* is not here, but in Verona.

Gentile Bellini, the less famous of his two sons, like Carpaccio, shows us the life of his time, and we can get a very good idea of what the Piazza San Marco must have looked like in the sixteenth century during one of the many processions and festivals.

His brother, Giovanni, has a much less documentary attitude towards art. He is preoccupied with presenting warm, glowing flesh surrounded by air and light, and his numerous paintings of the Madonna and Child are never monotonous, for they are presented with a surprising variety of expression and composition. He is one of the greatest figures of the Venetian school, and links the early art of his father with the magnificent fullness of the greatest period of the Venetian school as revealed by Giorgione, Titian and Veronese.

You will want to make your choice from the works of these latter masters, for you cannot do them justice in one visit, and they are familiar to everyone through reproduction and through those originals which were shown in London at the Italian Exhibition before the war. You will certainly not want to miss Giorgione's *Tempest,* Titian's *Presentation in the Temple* and the *Pieta,* Tintoretto's *Adam and Eve* and *Cain and Abel,* or Veronese's *Marriage of St Catherine* and the *Feast of the House of Levi.*

For the best of Tintoretto's work you will have to go to the Scuola di San Rocco, some distance away, but it is close to the Church of the Frari which you will certainly want to visit as well. The Scuola was a religious association under the patronage of the saint, and was instituted to give aid to the needy and to care for the sick, more particularly those afflicted with the plague. The building was constructed in the middle of the sixteenth century, and its great reception rooms, decorated by Tintoretto where, as Burckhardt says, he was the first artist to treat the story of the Life of Christ from beginning to end in a completely naturalistic manner. But it is not mere naturalism which makes a visit to San Rocco such a great experience. Despite the intense dramatic force with which the stories are interpreted, there is always the human touch, the intimate incident, the warmth and glow of flesh, the radiance of light and gentle human affection.

How original are Tintoretto's conceptions—the *Nativity* in the hayloft with the cattle in the stable below; the *Flight into Egypt*; the donkey with his head bowed pushes his way straight towards us, Joseph grips him by the halter and Mary leans forward over the Child to protect him from the night air, and behind the group, a pink sunset envelops the distant hills in its radiance, tipping the trees and shrubs in the foreground with light.

But there is nothing in San Rocco, perhaps nothing in the whole of Italian Art, that approaches the awe-inspiring power of the huge *Crucifixion* in the Great Hall. Despite the fact that many minor happenings are going on amongst the multitude, nothing detracts from the tremendous importance of the tragic figure of Christ lifted high above the crowd against the dark, cloudy sky. Tintoretto's astonishing genius for representing the human figure in every attitude, and his subtle rendering of the foreshortening of a forward-poised head set superbly on the shoulders, never fail to delight me, as do his deep, strong, sometimes black, shadows contrasting with an almost theatrical lighting.

The nearby church of Santa Maria Gloriosa dei Frari was begun in the middle of the fourteenth century and completed early in the fifteenth. This, the largest church in Venice after St Mark's, is built entirely of red brick. It is of simple proportions and has little decoration outside, but the interior is almost a museum in itself, with its wealth of tombs and altar-pieces. There are many fine tombs, but it is the three great altar-pieces which have attracted people from all over the world to visit the Frari. There is the delicate *Virgin and Child* with saints by Bartolomeo Vivarini, then the *Virgin and Four Saints* by Giovanni Bellini—the famous painting known as the *Madonna of the Frari*, where Bellini has depicted her seated in a golden niche with the Child on her knees—and finally, the great

Verona: a fountain and palaces in the Piazza delle Erbe

Assumption by Titian, which alone is worth a journey to see. He also painted the Virgin shown majestic and triumphant on clouds upheld by adoring angels. On another canvas, the Pesaro family is shown at the feet of the Virgin, and here she benevolently leans forward to acknowledge their homage.

Away on the other side of the Grand Canal is a reminder of the pre-eminence of the Florentines as sculptors in the noble equestrian statue of Colleoni by Verrochio. It stands in the Square outside the Church of Santi Giovanni e Paolo. From some aspects, it is even finer than Donatello's *Gattamalata* in Padua, for the horse is moving more naturally. The rider is superb, yet I prefer the classic simplicity of the earlier monument, even though Ruskin said:

"I do not believe there is a more glorious work of sculpture existing in the world than the equestrian statue of Bartolomeo Colleoni."

The Condottiere had left his immense fortune to the Republic of Venice on condition that an equestrian statue was erected to his honour in the Piazza San Marco. This was contrary to Venetian law, but the inheritance was too large to miss, and the Senate cunningly found a loophole by placing the statue in the Piazza in front of the Scuola San Marco.

N

CHAPTER EIGHTEEN

THE VILLAS OF THE BRENTA RIVIERA :
VICENZA : THE CASTLES OF MONTICI :
VERONA : THE LAKE OF GARDA

I<small>N</small> a previous chapter I mentioned the *autostrada* that goes direct from Padua to Mestre—it is a dull road like most of these motorroads, and so it is just as well to return by the route that follows the course of the Brenta and see something of the Patrician Villas on the banks of that river.

In the past, many Venetians found the atmosphere of their city unbearable during the heat of summer and so they used to spend several months a year in their splendid residences on the mainland. Some of these mansions have been destroyed, but in the district of Treviso alone there are more than three hundred "palaces worthy of cities or sovereigns", as Goldoni expressed it. Further afield in Friuli, there are romantic-looking castles which are still in private occupation.

Other patricians favoured the neighbourhood of Vicenza or else they developed estates in the Euganean Hills, of which the highest are not more than two thousand feet. Though unsensational scenically, these hills have luxuriant loveliness and the views from the heights are typically Italian, as Shelley recorded:

> "Beneath is spread like a green sea
> The waveless plain of Lombardy,
> Bounded by the vaporous air,
> Islanded by cities fair."

The Euganean villages are neglected by travellers, and even by the Venetians, though a few landlords still cling to their villas, and to what is left of their estates after the redistribution of land to the peasants, inaugurated after the Second World War.

Living is still relatively cheap, and in the remoter regions houses can be bought for a song. The climate is good, and with a car

Venice, Padua, Vicenza and Verona are all within easy reach. The
peasants are courteous, well-mannered and friendly—for those who
like a peaceful country life, the Euganean Hills would be ideal for
retirement or as a place in which to write or paint.

The road along the Brenta is all too short, and there are so many
villas that I cannot enumerate them all. Palladio's Villa Malcontenta
stands at the water's edge, and the wide colonnaded portico is
mirrored in the still surface of the river.

The Villa Pisani at Stra is surrounded by extensive gardens and a
beautiful park. As you drive past you can catch a glimpse of a
miniature Versailles through the magnificent and monumental
wrought-iron gates.

It is a short and easy run from Padua to Vicenza, a town where
Palladian palaces are intermingled with buildings of the thirteenth
and fourteenth centuries and of the Renaissance, but in essence
Vicenza belongs more particularly to Palladio.

This great architect was born here in 1518, and he died in his
native city in 1580. Though he built churches in Venice, splendid
villas in various parts of the countryside, he constructed palaces in
Vicenza—for the Basilica, with its superimposed arcaded galleries,
has all the aspect of a magnificent patrician mansion.

The work of Palladio was much criticized by the Victorians, who
considered that his style was dull and lacking in originality, and yet
he was a source of inspiration to the architects of some of the finest
eighteenth-century buildings in England. His influence can be traced
indirectly in many of the American colonial mansions and churches
with their wide colonnaded porches.

Certainly he pursued the formulæ and designs of the Classical
Age, and did owe a great deal to his predecessors Michelangelo,
Sangallo and Sammichele, but in his conceptions he realized perfect
harmony, at the expense perhaps of the elaborate ornamentation that
was used by many of his contemporaries and most of his immediate
successors.

The peculiar feature of his style is that it was designed for
northern Italy, yet it has proved perfectly suitable for the pastoral
English countryside and even, with modifications, for Virginia. At
Chiswick Lord Burlington constructed an exact reproduction of the
Villa Rotonda, which is near Vicenza, and Burlington House is
directly inspired by Palladio.

Vicenza is situated in the plain, a few miles to the south of the lower ranges of the Alps. Monte Berico, a small wooded hill, rises up on the southern outskirts of the city.

The famous Teatro Olimpico is situated near the Porta Settembre, the gate of the main road to Padua. This most famous of all theatres was built by Palladio and has permanent scenery representing a colonnaded piazza with vistas of streets through monumental archways. Here we see a succession of palaces whose roofs are surmounted by tall statues, statues fill innumerable niches between the pilasters with richly carved capitals—in fact the architect gave free rein to his fancy, and created in wood and plaster the embryo of the town of his dreams. Here is none of the severity noted by his critics, for to a classical design he has added much of the ornamentation used by the exponents of pure Baroque.

On occasion during the summer season, there are performances of plays in this theatre, and to see them in this setting is an unforgettable experience.

The long narrow Corso, lined with palaces of different ages, cuts right through the centre of Vicenza. At the entrance of this street, the Palazzo Chierati is now the civic museum, containing some fine pictures and also, it must be added, some works of secondary importance. With its open colonnaded gallery on the ground floor, and two large open loggias with Ionic pillars above, this palace is among the best of Palladio's works. Here again as in the Teatro Olimpico, statues line the edge of the flat roof, and soften the classical severity of the plan.

In the Corso, the mansions of all periods succeed each other— there are Venetian façades with elaborately carved windows, Renaissance buildings with the motifs of the period, Palladian palaces and neo-classical palaces.

About halfway down the Corso, a narrow street on the left leads into the Piazza dei Signori with Palladio's Basilica on one side, and facing it, his neo-classical Loggia del Capitanio. The Basilica, in fact, encloses an earlier Gothic building whose dome rises from the centre of the outer structure.

In the centre of the Piazza, as in the Piazzetta in Venice, the winged lion of St Mark and the figure of St Ferdinand stand on high granite columns. Opposite to them, on the right-hand side, rises the tall slender watch-tower of the city.

I have not the space to describe the other features of Vicenza—it is a town admirably suited for wandering and exploration. Within a small compass there is so much to see, many magnificent palaces hidden away in narrow streets, unexpected medieval fortifications and towers, a castle, and beautifully shaded public gardens at the western extremity of the city. Then, if there is time, it is worth while walking or driving to the summit of Monte Berici for the sake of the view of the Alps across the valley, and of the varied monuments of Vicenza almost at one's feet.

.   .   .

Soon after leaving Vicenza, the road passes through low hills, and the vegetation becomes more abundant, the air softer with the mists that Shelley noted in his poems. A slight deviation leads to the Castles of Romeo and Juliet which stand on two steep eminences facing each other as if to emulate the age-old rivalry of the Capulets and the Montagues, or as they were known in Italy, the Capelli and the Montecchi.

These strongholds have been restored, and one of them, Juliet's Castle, has been turned into the semblance of a medieval tavern.

It is easy to carp at such renovations, but in this case the ruins were in a complete state of decay and would in course of time have practically disappeared. Then the restaurant serves excellent food and has been decorated with taste, and the "Olde Worlde Look" has not been exaggerated. From the terrace outside, there is approximately the view that Shelley described so well in his poem, though it was not the same prospect.

Now it appears that the Montagues and Capulets may not have lived here and we know that Romeo and Juliet are probably legendary figures. Since Shakespeare gave these two lovers immortality, I see no reason why we should not accept the story that they lived in these two castles without ever meeting until the fateful night of the ball.

At any rate, I, like many others, have stood on this terrace and enjoyed the spectacle of the rolling hills and misted plains, and of the tiers of blue mountains and snowy peaks far away to the north.

In the lowlands, the castles and villas, the villages and towns are scattered in the strange pattern of meadows and woods, olive groves, vineyards and orchards.

The road from Montecchio to Verona runs westwards and parallel to the foothills of the Alps, passing through the vineyards of Soave which produce one of the best and most agreeable white wines in Italy—Val Policella, another of the regional vintages, comes from a valley near the southern extremity of the Lake of Garda, about thirty miles further on.

The landscape is a pleasing one, and the countryside is fertile and productive.

Verona is certainly one of the most beautiful and attractive towns in Italy, for despite its wealth of monuments it has not yet been submerged by tourists, though every amenity is provided for the foreign visitor.

The town is of great antiquity, for it is situated in an important position strategically and commercially, since it guards the access to the Lombard Plain from the Brenner Pass and is halfway between Milan and Venice.

Under the Romans it was a city of some standing with a large garrison, a capitol, a forum, and the huge arena which has remained almost intact until the present day. In the Middle Ages, Verona was a small republic, but by the thirteenth century, a Captain of the People named Massimo della Scala became overlord of the city, which he and his descendants ruled for nearly a hundred and fifty years. For a while under the Scaligers, as they were called, the state of Verona prospered and even extended its sway over many neighbouring cities.

Cangrande della Scala may be considered the precursor of the Renaissance tyrants who ruled over various parts of Italy. In his reign and in those of his two immediate successors, the arts flourished, and skilful architects built some of the finest monuments of the city.

Towards the end of the fourteenth century, Verona found that her independence was endangered by the Visconti of Milan on one side and by the Republic of Venice on the other, whilst there was intermittent pressure from the Holy Roman Emperor. Thus situated between three fires, the people of Verona placed themselves under the protection of Venice in 1405 and their territories became an integral part of the Republic.

During the fifty-two years of their occupation in the nineteenth century, the Austrians fortified the city strongly, making it the part of their defensive system in northern Italy which was known as the Quadrilateral.

In the Second World War, Verona suffered from devastating

aerial bombardments by the Allies, and from severe destruction by the Germans, who blew up the medieval Scaliger bridge, and all the other bridges, including one that had been built by the Romans. A swift and intelligent reconstruction has removed most of the traces of this unfortunate devastation.

The jade-green fast-flowing waters of the Adige envelop the greater part of the old town, but the fortifications built by the Austrians enclose another ancient quarter that is situated on the heights to the north of the river.

If you arrive by road from Venice you soon come upon the immense Piazza Brá with crowded café terraces on one side and the huge Roman amphitheatre on the other.

This arena is one of the few of its type that has been in almost constant use from the time of its construction—in the Middle Ages there were tournaments and pageants—later there were tournaments and bullfights. In the fifteenth century, on festive occasions, the gentlemen of Verona would besiege the most beautiful women of the city in a festooned pavilion that was called "The Castle of Love".

In the late seventeenth century, a small theatre was erected in the ring and plays and ballets were performed.

Every summer since 1913 operas have been presented to audiences of over 11,000 people. The singers are among the best in Europe and the staging is superb.

On the south side of the Piazza Brá, a strip of the fifteenth-century ramparts runs from the magnificent Palazzo Gran Guardia to the Ponte Aleardi. In the Via del Pontiere on the right-hand side, just before reaching this bridge, is the little monastery where the marriage of Romeo is believed to have been celebrated.

A stone coffin in a small vaulted crypt is presented as Juliet's tomb —to touch it, you are told, is to ensure the eternal love of the one that you love. Such is the strangeness of human nature, that everyone does so, openly or surreptitiously, including, I may add, myself, when I thought that no one was looking.

On the ground level, a simple cloister of Roman arches surrounds a small garden planted with flowers, vines and orange trees, and in one corner is the little window where Juliet placed her letters for Romeo.

Besides this charming piece of sentimentality, Verona has so many art treasures of all periods to offer that I am forced to be selective.

On the far side of the river, for instance, there is the Roman theatre, where Shakespeare's plays are presented in the summer. The terrace of the modernized Castel Pietro, just a little higher up, has the finest view of the city and of the river—then a few hundred yards away to the east the gardens of the Villa Giusti are small but as beautiful in their own way as those of Tivoli.

One agreeable feature of Verona is that in certain streets all traffic is barred, and so one may stroll from the Piazza Brá to the centre by the Via Giuseppe Mazzini, which has some excellent shops.

The Piazza delle Erbe, on the site of the Roman forum, is still the centre of the city—fountains play amid the market stalls with their white awnings, and the winged lion of St Mark on a column still testifies to the sway of Venice in the past. Palaces of different periods range along the sides of the square, and at the far end, lines of statues in graceful postures stand at the top of the Baroque façade of the Palazzo Maffei.

The tower of the Lamberti rises nearly two hundred and eighty feet above the Palazzo Comunale—the bells of this watch-tower have sounded the tocsin and peeled in celebrations for six hundred and fifty years.

The Piazza Dante, still known locally as the Piazza Signori, has kept its aristocratic character, for it is surrounded by the former administrative offices of the Scala lords.

The architecture belongs to the Middle Ages and the early Renaissance. On one side the Comunale Palace, which also faces the Piazza Erbe, is linked up by arches to the Council Hall and to the Scaliger Palace. Unlike its neighbour, which is always full of movement, this square is usually nearly empty save for the few people who sit at the tables outside the two solemn-looking cafés.

A little further on, the Gothic tombs of several of the Scala family are grouped together in front of a small church. Elaborately carved and surrounded by tall wrought-iron grills, they are much admired by Ruskinians. . . .

In the vicinity the house of the Montagues is pointed out to tourists, and not far away, one is shown Juliet's balcony in a small palace which belonged to the Capulets.

The cathedral, which is also in this quarter, has features of Romanesque, Gothic and Renaissance architecture—badly damaged during the last war, it has been skilfully restored.

As I have already said, Verona is a place of great charm, with its ancient squares, its quiet streets, its palaces of different styles and different periods, but best of all perhaps I like the river bank, and the views of the country on the other side of the Adige.

The Scaliger Castle on the southern embankment is a massive structure of red brick with odd cleft Guelf battlements which are continued on the adjoining bridge, for the fortress was intended to guard the bridgehead.

The interior has been carefully restored and furnished with antique furniture and pictures.

The Scaliger Castle is now used as a museum and it possesses not only a series of rooms sumptuously furnished in the style of the period, but a very good collection of medieval arms, and some interesting fourteenth-century bronzes and marble reliefs. Of even greater interest are the rooms full of paintings, for the most part by natives of Verona or its environs.

Inevitably, as in every provincial gallery, there are a number of works of little or no value, but it is astonishing how many first-class works are here which might so easily have found their way into the galleries of Venice or Milan. There are even works by the native Paolo Veronese: a superb full-length portrait and *The Deposition*. There is also a *Portrait of a Gentleman* by Titian. But it is not to see the paintings by these Venetian masters that we have come, but to find Jacopo Bellini's moving *Crucifixion* with the lonely figure against a bleak sky and this artist's delicately-coloured and decorative *St Jerome*, so full of imagination and delightful natural touches. Then there is Crivelli's *Madonna of the Passion*, with the gorgeously attired Virgin and the grotesque Baby with a realistic garland of fruit hanging from pillars and two downy birds perched upon it.

But the greatest treasure of the collection is the wonderful *Madonna of the Rose Garden* by Stefano da Zevio, one of the most fascinating paintings in the whole of the north of Italy. Against a heavenly golden background the Madonna with the Child in her lap is seated in a mystical golden garden of roses and peacocks and little coloured birds. Winged angels flutter over the surrounding pergola, plucking roses to strew at Mary's feet. Even if you have no time to see anything else, rush through the other rooms just to take one look at this enchanting picture. You will never regret it.

In the same room is Pisanello's *Madonna of the Quail*, another gilded delight. The Virgin is seated gracefully with the Child on her knee, twisting His head around to watch the quail on the ground, while other birds perch on bushes behind Him. The line of the Virgin's hair is continued along the flowing curve of her gown in a perfect arabesque, and two diminutive angels gently lower a jewelled crown onto her head.

If you find this painting makes you long to see more of Pisanello's work, go to the Church of S. Anastasia, where you will find a large fresco of St George delivering the Princess from the Dragon, as impressive in its grandeur of composition as it is fascinating in its almost oriental detail.

You will find plenty of other things to interest you in this fourteenth-century church, including some early frescoes whose authorship is unknown, and a remarkable series of reliefs in the Pellegrini Chapel, in particular, the rather naive *Birth of Christ* with toylike heads of an ox and an ass suspended above the Baby's crib.

The Romanesque church of San Zeno was built in the eleventh century on the site of an even earlier edifice. It was enlarged and added to in the twelfth and fourteenth centuries. The façade is pure Romanesque in style and its lovely rose-ochre portal is borne on two pillars rising from the backs of lions carved in pink marble. In the Tympanum is a relief of the *Last Judgment*. Flanking the superb bronze doors are twelfth-century marble reliefs depicting scenes from the New and Old Testaments. Each individual panel both in the doors themselves and in the flanking decoration is worthy of close attention. The immense interior is divided into three naves by alternate massive and slender pillars supporting rounded arches leading forward to a wide flight of steps descending to the tenth-century crypt with its ancient tombs and frescoes.

Another double flight of steps ascends to the choir uplifted above the lower church and here we find the magnificent altar-piece by Andrea Mantegna. Set in an elaborately carved golden frame, the three panels are divided by pillars. In the centre the Virgin sits enthroned, the Child on her knee, surrounded by adoring angels. The flanking panels contain groups of saints. In all the brilliance of colour perhaps the most exciting is the deep red cloak and the primrose-yellow robe of the saint on the left. The three panels are happily linked by garlands of flowers and fruit and beneath them the predella is formed of three small pictures, the *Agony in the Garden*, the *Crucifixion* and *Christ rising from the Tomb*. Those in the predella are copies, the originals being in the Louvre, but they are excellent copies and full of the most fascinating details of flowers and birds and animals.

The road from Verona to Milan is uninteresting save for the few miles along the broad southern extremity of Lake Garda. Peschiera is a summer resort, but it has still the massive fortifications of medieval times.

At Sirmione there is a well-preserved Scaliger castle on a small headland and Desenzano is the terminal point of the steamers that ply to all parts of the lake.

The highway passes through the industrial suburbs of Brescia, an ancient town with monuments that would be of real interest anywhere but in Italy—in the centre there are old churches, a museum and some Roman remains—but why see the second rate when you have seen or are going to see the best?

I have made many omissions in this book, but I have done so of a set purpose, for in the present day few people have the money or leisure to spend months seeing such places as Florence or Rome, though I have been fortunate enough to spend eight years in Italy, and I still go there very frequently.

So I venture to make one final suggestion: instead of going a second time to Milan, it would be pleasanter to leave Italy by the Brenner Pass, taking the eastern road along the Lake of Garda, for the coast on this side is still unspoilt, and the little fishing villages such as Bardolino, Torre del Benaco and Malcesine have kept much of their original character.

The western highway passes through the resorts of the Gardone Riviera, which has a mild climate and has some resemblance to the Côte d'Azur. There are avenues of palms along the waterfronts, and the gardens of the luxury hotels are full of bougainvilias, oleanders and other semi-tropical plants.

The little town of Salo was for a few months the capital of Mussoline's Fascist Republic after the Armistice of 1943.

Near here is the house where that strange genius Gabriele d'Annunzio spent the last years of his life. His apartments reveal his really eccentric ideas of decoration, and the relics displayed are for the most part connected with numerous amours, or his year as dictator of the short-lived State of Fiume, the town that he seized with his army of volunteers.

The two highways meet at Arco, three or four miles beyond the far end of the lake, and then the route continues as far as the ancient and highly picturesque town of Trento on the trunk road from Verona to the Brenner.

At Bolzano, the majority of the inhabitants are German-speaking, for until 1918 this was the chief town of an Austrian province, and the architecture of many of the older houses and buildings is indeed Tyrolese.

Here again the road forks and there is a choice of routes. The right-hand one offers more views of high mountains and rugged scenery. The left-hand road passes through the fertile valley of Merano, whose mild climate produces some of the finest and largest fruit in the world.

There are castles perched on the hill-tops above the spreading orchards, and the cottages in the villages are half-timbered like those of Kent or of South Germany. Meran itself is a pleasing resort with numerous hotels of every category, for visitors come here to see the flowers in the spring, and in the autumn there are patients for the grape cure, which is one of the best known ways of slimming.

The two roads meet again at Vipiteno, a little town with crumbling fortifications and gaily painted houses, only a few miles from the frontier. Once over the Isarco Pass, all traces of southern vegetation vanish—on all sides there are pinewoods, and bubbling torrents rush through green meadows that are full of gentians or crocuses. The dark grim-looking mountains to the north bear little or no resemblance to the jagged peaks of the Dolomites, whose red granite crags glow like fire in the rays of a southern sun.

APPENDICES

TRANSPORT AND GENERAL INFORMATION

In this section of General Information, I have ventured to quote a number of prices for fares, hotel rooms, porterage charges and so on. In doing so I fully realize that these prices may change. I am giving these statistics because they may afford some guidance as to relative prices. For up-to-date news, intending travellers should apply to the Italian State Tourist Office, Regent Street, London, W.1, who have supplied a large part of the information that I am giving here.

GENERAL INFORMATION

Italy can offer a holiday to suit every taste and requirement, at seaside resorts along the extensive coastline, on the shores of lakes in the North, in mountain villages on the slopes of the Alps and the Apennines, in the historical medieval towns of Tuscany and Umbria, and in cities where all modern comforts are blended with ancient and contemporary art.

The following brief outline includes the most popular centres:—

SEASIDE: WESTERN RIVIERA from the French coast frontier down to Rome: Bordighera, Ospedaletti, San Remo, Alassio, Spotorno, Celle, Varazze, Nervi, Portofino, Santa Margherita, Rapallo, Sestri Levante, Levanto, Lerici, Viareggio, Lido di Roma (Ostia).

EASTERN RIVIERA from North to South: Grado, Jesolo, Venice Lido, Cervia, Rimini, Riccione, Cattolica, Fano.

SOUTHERN RIVIERA: Isles of Capri and Ischia, Castellammare, Sorrento, Positano, Amalfi.

LAKES: LAKE MAGGIORE—Cannobio, Cannero, Pallanza, Baveno, Stresa.

LAKE ORTA—Omegna, Orta San Giulio.

LAKE COMO—Menaggio, Cadenabbia, Tremezzo, Lenno, Argegno, Cernobbio, Bellagio, Varenna.

LAKE GARDA—Sirmione, Salo', Gardone, Maderno, Bogliaco, Limone, Riva, Torbole, Malcesine, San Vigilio, Garda.

MOUNTAINS: WESTERN ALPS—Limone, Sestriere, Aosta, Courmayeur, Cervinia, Valtournanche, St Vincent, Cogne, Gressoney.

DOLOMITES—Arco, Molveno, Madonna di Campiglio, Mendola, Bolzano, Merano, Ortisei, Braies, Canazei, Carezza, Cortina.

HILL TOWNS: Siena, Perugia, Assisi, Urbino, San Gimignano.

CITIES (from North to South): Turin, Milan, Brescia, Verona, Vicenza, Padua, Venice, Genoa, Parma, Mantua, Ferrara, Ravenna, Bologna, Pisa, Florence, Rome, Naples, Palermo, Syracuse.

The Vatican City and the Republic of San Marino.

For all tickets and reservations application should be made to a Travel Agency.

Passports are necessary, but an Italian visa is not required by Nationals of Australia, Austria, Benelux Countries, Canada, Denmark, Eire, Finland, France, Greece, Iceland, Norway, Sweden, Switzerland, Turkey, U.S.A., West Germany, and holders of British (U.K.) passports (for a period up to ninety days). Visas are necessary in all other cases, including Ceylon, India, New Zealand, Pakistan, South Africa and British Mandated Territories, or Protectorates. Italian Consulates: In London (38 Eaton Place, S.W.1) and at Cardiff, Glasgow and Liverpool; also in Dublin (Eire).

Frontier Customs: Examinations take place on leaving and entering each country, as far as passports, currency and hand baggage are concerned. On international services the formalities are performed on the train. Examinations of heavy luggage may be deferred until arrival at destination, where a Customs Office exists (such as at Bolzano, Brindisi, Cortina, Genoa, Milan, Rome, San Remo, Taormina, Turin, Venice, etc.).

Free entry is allowed for personal effects, within a reasonable limit in quantity and value. Included in this category are: clothing, books, camping and household equipment, fishing-tackle, sporting gun, hand or cine-camera (5 and 2 spools respectively), binoculars, gramophone, typewriter, radio set (subject to a wireless licence fee of Lire 200), bicycle and manufactured tobacco up to 250 grammes (8¾ ozs. or average of 200 cigarettes).

Temporary free importation can be arranged for driven motor-vehicles by obtaining the requisite Customs Document (Tryptique or I.T.) at the frontier or in advance (International Carnet) through the recognized associations (R.A.C. or A.A.).

Customs Duties will be charged on excess quantities of personal effects and on those commodities scheduled as dutiable. Without an Import Licence some articles are prohibited and some are limited, e.g. maximum for tobacco is 8¾ lbs. with duty at about 20s. per 3½ ozs.

Export, without licence, limits the amount of Italian currency to Lire 30,000 and of souvenirs to a value of Lire 31,500.

Police Registration is required within three days of entering Italy. If staying at an hotel, the Management will attend to the formality, but the visitor is responsible for making the request at the first opportunity within that period.

Climate—Mean 24-hour temperature during each month (Fahrenheit):

	Jan.	Feb.	Mar.	April	May	June	July	Aug.	Sept.	Oct.	Nov.	Dec.
Florence	45	47	50	60	67	75	81	77	70	63	55	46
Genoa	43	46	49	57	65	72	76	75	70	62	54	45
Merano	40	42	45	55	63	70	75	74	66	57	50	42
Milan	36	40	46	55	65	71	75	75	67	56	45	39
Naples	50	54	58	63	70	78	81	80	74	68	60	52
Palermo	50	52	55	59	64	71	76	77	73	67	59	53
Rome	49	51	57	62	70	76	81	79	77	65	56	47
Venice	43	45	48	58	69	76	82	78	70	60	54	44

HOTEL ACCOMMODATION

Class		Single Room (one person) Lire		Double Room (two persons) Lire		Full Board (one person) per day Lire		Daily supplement for private bathroom (approx.) Lire
Hotel	Pension	from	to	from	to	from	to	
Luxury	—	1500	2500	2500	4200	4500	7000	2000
1st	—	1100	2000	1700	3600	3800	5800	1500
2nd	1st	800	1500	1400	2800	2900	3900	1000
3rd	2nd	600	1200	1100	1100	2300	3100	—
4th	3rd	400	900	700	1600	1700	2600	—

Supplements: Service (Tips) 15 per cent (in Rome 18 per cent, in Palermo 20 per cent). Revenue Tax 1 per cent. Local Tax: Lire 10 to 60 (a few pence) daily.

These extras increase the daily cost by about 3s. 9d. in the £.

Meals: As a separate item at hotel or restaurant can be calculated at from: Lire 200 (2s. 3d.) for breakfast and from Lire 600 (7s.) for luncheon or dinner.

High Season: During the peak holiday periods, maximum prices prevail.

Hotel Guide in two volumes: (1) North; (2) Central and South, at 5s. each.

Language: English is understood at most hotels and main stores. To ensure a speedy reply, letters to hotels or local Information Bureaux should be legibly written or typewritten, possibly containing a reply-paid coupon (9d. from Post Office).

Camping is assuming popularity in Italy and on principle it is sufficient for a visitor to ask the permission of the owner or occupier of the land in view. The Information Bureau of the nearest locality would give particulars on the most suitable local sites. The Touring Club Italiano (Milan) publishes *Campeggi in Italia* with English text and details of over 250 camping sites. London office at 10 Charles II Street, S.W.1. An abridged list of sites is issued by the Federazione Italiana del Campeggio, 30 Costa de Magnoli, Florence. The Camping Club of Great Britain (35 Old Kent Road, S.E.1) is in a position to give advice and details on camping on the Continent.

Correspondence can be addressed c/o Post Office by adding "Fermo in Posta" to the name of the locality. Delivery will be made at the local Central Post Office upon identification of addressee by passport.

Postal Rates :	Internal	Lire	Foreign	Lire
Letters	per each 15 grs.	25	first 20 grs.	60
			per extra 20 grs.	35
Post cards		20		35
„ „ (with 5 words or less)		10		12
Air Mail surcharge (per 5 grs)		10	(Europe)	25
Express surcharge (per 5 grs)		50	(„)	85
Registration		45		65

National Holidays are: January 1 and 6; St Joseph (March 19); Easter Monday; Liberation Day (April 25); Labour Day (May 1); Ascension of Christ (sixth Thursday after Easter); Corpus Domini (second Sunday after Whit-Sunday); Proclamation of the Republic (June 2); SS. Peter and Paul (June 29); Assumption of the Virgin (August 15); All Saints Day (November 1); Victory Day 1918 (November 4); Conception of the Virgin (December 8); December 25 and 26.

Local Feast Days are held in honour of the towns' Patron Saints such as April 25 (St Mark) in Venice; June 24 (St John the Baptist) in Florence, Genoa and Turin; September 19 (St Gennaro) in Naples; October 4 (St Patronius in Bologna; December 7 (St Ambrose) in Milan.

Additional Traditional Festivals are celebrated in most towns and villages in commemoration of a local historical or religious event, the most notable and spectacular being the following:

AREZZO
"GIOSTRA DEL SARACINO" (Joust of the Saracen) *on the first Sunday in June and September*
A tilting contest in armour.

FLORENCE
"SCOPPIO DEL CARRO" (Firing the Chariot) *on Easter Saturday*
Setting off a pyramid of fireworks in the Cathedral Square by a mechanical dove driven from the Altar during High Mass.

"GIOCO DEL CALCIO" (Football Match) *first Sunday in May and 24 June*
Revival of a sixteenth-century game in medieval costume.

GENZANO
"INFIORATA" (Flower Festival) *on Corpus Domini Day*
A religious procession along streets carpeted with flowers in wonderful patterns.

GUBBIO
"FESTA DEI CERI" (Feast of the Candles) *May 15*
A procession in local costumes in which tall shrines are carried to the Church on the peak of Mt Igino.

NAPLES
"PIEDIGROTTA" (Festival of Piedigrotta) *7 and 8 September*
Parades of ornamented carts, illuminated boats and fireworks.

NOLA
"FESTA DEI GIGLI" (The Lily Festival) *third Sunday in June*
A procession in costume with allegorical towers.

PISA
"GIOCO DEL PONTE" (Battle of the Bridge) *Whit-Sunday*
Medieval parade and contest for possession of a bridge.

o

SIENA

"PALIO" (Horse Race) 2 *July and* 16 *August*
Parades and a race by members of the ancient city guilds in colourful medieval pageantry to win the Banner (Palio).

VENICE

"IL REDENTORE" (The Redeemer) *third Sunday in July*
Celebrations on the eve.

Calendars of Events are issued by some towns and districts with
details of their local theatrical and musical performances, exhibitions
and trade fairs, sport and social meetings, etc.

Publication: E.N.I.T. (Italian State Tourist Department) and
E.P.T. (Provincial Information Offices) publish leaflets, folders and
booklets which are given free of charge upon application by indicating town or district concerned.

TICKETS AND VALIDITY

Tickets from London and from British ports to many Italian
towns are printed and on issue by British Railways and agents with
a validity of two months (return journeys) or of one month for single
trips. Additional journeys or circular tours can be arranged in
advance through a Travel Agency with a validity of 60 days. The
journey can be commenced on any day within the period of validity,
calculated from midnight to midnight and inclusive of the issue date
stamped on the ticket.

Cost of tickets for any itinerary or form of transportation may be
prepaid in sterling, including fees for reserved seats, sleeping
accommodation and meals on trains, without affecting the travel
allowance.

Break of journey is allowed at any number of intermediate stations
without formality.

Children under four years of age (not occupying a seat) travel free;
between the ages of four and ten years at approximately half-rate.
On local Italian tickets the half-rate is extended up to the age of
fourteen.

Fast Trains. Special supplements are charged for travel on certain
trains such as the "Golden Arrow" between London and Paris and

on the "Rapido" trains in Italy; seats thereon are limited and must be booked.

Seat Reservation on the British Continental boat-trains and in the international coaches from Continental ports or towns to Italian destinations should be secured in advance (London/Italy from 4s.). On some Italian trains a limited number of seats are reservable (fee, Lire 150) at the station booking-offices from 15 days to two hours in advance or through a local Travel Agency up to six hours previously. At Milan and Rome stations three and five hours respectively is the minimum notice.

Luggage. Hand-luggage is carried free and limited to an amount as can be conveniently placed over one's seat. Heavy luggage, without limit, is registered on departure and charged for accordingly. Free allowance, between London and the Franco-Italian frontiers, up to 66 lbs. per adult or 44 lbs. per child. In Italy the charge is calculated on the gross weight. Example: London-Calais-Modane frontier (adult) 66 lbs. free and 17s. 1d. per 22 lbs. in excess. Modane frontier to Genoa 2s. 7d., to Florence 4s. 2d., to Rome 5s. 5d., to Naples 6s. 3d. per each 22 lbs.

Journey time (approx.) by the most direct routes (First and Second Class):

via Calais-Paris-Mt. Cenis Tunnel: London dep. 10.00 arriving next day at:

Uzio-Sestriere 6.08, Turin 7.37 (Aosta 11.03), Genoa 10.46 (Alassio 14.02), Rapallo 11.49, Viareggio 13.45, Pisa 14.06 (Florence 15.50, Siena 18.17), Rome 18.35 (Naples 22.15).

via Calais-Paris-Simplon Tunnel: London dep. 10.00 arriving next day at: Stresa 6.24, Milan 7.47 (Florence 14.37, Perugia 17.46, Siena 18.17, Rome 19.07), Brescia 9.28, Desenzano Garda 9.54, Verona 10.30 (Bolzano 13.54, Merano 15.03), Vicenza 11.20, Padua 11.47, Venice 12.24, Trieste 15.19 (Bologna 11.22, Rimini 13.17).

via Calais-Lille-Bale-St Gothard Tunnel: London dep. 12.30 arriving next day at: Como 11.33, Milan 12.15 (Florence 17.14, Rimini 17.24, Rome 21.10), Desenzano 14.59, Verona 15.36 (Bolzano 19.45, Merano 21.10), Padua 16.31, Venice 17.47, Trieste 21.32.

via Calais-Paris-Riviera Coast: London dep. 10.00 arriving next day at: Bordighera 12.20, San Remo 12.31, Alassio 13.30, Genoa 15.25.

via Calais Lille-Bale-Brenner Pass: London dep. 12.30 arriving next
    day at: (Innsbruck 12.11, dep. 12.25), Colle Isarco 14.11, For-
    tezza 14.44, Chiusa 15.17, Bolzano 15.57 (Merano 18.12, Cortina
    21.20), Verona 18.20 (Venice 20.44).

Third-class ⎧ via Newhaven-Dieppe at 9.05 (daily); 20.20 (August).
departures: ⎨ via Folkestone-Calais at 12.30 (daily).
            ⎪ via Folkestone-Boulogne at 9.00 (June/September).
            ⎩ Dover-Ostend at 9.00 (daily).

N.B. It is advisable to seek confirmation prior to date of departure.
    On and from April 22 (introduction of Summer Time) depar-
    tures from London will be 1 hour later (via Folkestone or
    Dover) and 25 mins. later (via Newhaven).

Fast Train Supplements on Italian "Rapido" trains can be
included in the ticket at the time of booking, or collected on board.

Italian Local Tickets can be obtained in advance through a Travel
Agency to supplement an itinerary not already covered by a direct
ticket, under the same conditions as to intermediate stops, with a
validity of sixty days.

Tariffs, both for passengers and luggage, are based on a differ-
ential mileage scale which decreases in proportion to the increase in
the distance covered by the ticket, e.g. (passenger second class) 50
kms. at Lire 500; 500 kms. at Lire 4870; 1,000 kms. at Lire 8770.
Reductions on the Italian State Railways:—

    Families (minimum four people, including servants): 25 per
    cent.

    Parties: 25 per cent (10 to 149 people); up 40 per cent for larger
    groups.

    Individuals: 25 per cent in connection with special events, fairs
    or seasons as may be advertised from time to time.

Two children between four and fourteen years count as one adult
passenger.

LOCAL coach and airline fares :

From :	To (or v.v.)				£	s.	d.	Hours	Miles
By MOTOR-COACH									
Bolzano	Carezza	..	..	..		7	0	1½	19
,,	Cortina	..	..	..	1	9	0	5½	71
Florence	Perugia	..	..	..		17	0	6	104
,,	Ravenna	..	..	..		11	0	4½	85
,,	Siena	..	..	..		4	9	2	45
,,	Venice	..	..	..	2	1	3	8	194

LOCAL coach and airline fares :

From :	To (or v.v.)				£ s. d.		Hours	Miles
By MOTOR-COACH								
Genoa	Alassio	..	..	..	8 6		2¼	63
„	Florence	..	..	..	1 13 6		7½	171
„	Rapallo	..	..	..	2 6		1¼	22
„	San Remo	..	..	..	12 0		3½	94
„	Viareggio	..	..	..	1 0 0		5	106
Milan	Bolzano	..	..	..	1 11 0		6	186
„	Gardone	..	..	..	14 6		2¼	90
„	Genoa	.	..	..	13 6		3	99
„	Menaggio	..	..	..	8 3		2	48
„	Rimini	..	..	..	1 11 0		6¼	208
„	Venice	..	..	..	1 3 6		5	175
„	Verona	..	..	..	13 6		3	99
Rome	Naples	..	..	..	12 0		5	157
„	Perugia	..	..	..	18 0		7¼	129
„	Positano	..	..	..	1 2 6		7¼	191
„	Siena	..	..	..	13 0		8	168
Venice	Cortina	..	..	..	1 3 6		4½	104
„	Ravenna	..	..	..	14 3		4	118
„	Rimini	..	..	..	18 0		6	148
International Services :								
Aosta	Bourg. S. Maurice	..	..		14 0		5	56
Alassio	Nice	..	..	..	13 6		4	65
San Remo	Nice	..	..	..	7 6		2¼	38
Bolzano	Innsbruck	..	..	..	16 0		6	87
„	St. Moritz	..	..	..	2 15 0		11	121
Cortina	Lienz	..	..	..	18 0		3½	52
By AIRWAY								
Milan	Pisa	..	..	..	3 19 3		1	—
„	Rome	..	..	..	7 17 3		2	—
„	Venice	..	..	..	4 2 3		1	—
Rome	Catania	..	..	..	8 13 3		3	—
„	Naples	..	..	..	2 13 0		1	—
„	Palermo	..	..	..	7 13 3		2	—
„	Venice	..	..	..	7 17 3		2	—

Sixty-Day Rail Tickets are issued for any desired itinerary and rated according to distance covered (minimum 500 kms.). Intermediate breaks of journey allowed.

Short-term Seasons for travel-at-will over the whole Italian Railway System are now available as follows:

	1st Class	2nd Class	
	£ s. d.	£ s. d.	
10-day period	17 13 0	11 15 6	approx.
20-day period	26 9 9	17 13 0	approx.

Each period can be extended for further days up to double the original validity on payment of the proportionate value. Change to superior class on single journeys by paying the difference at the normal tariff. No extra for travel on fast trains. To calculate cost from London add the return fare to one of the frontier stations.

TRAIN RESERVATIONS (*Fees*):		*First*			*Second*		
In England (*Continental boat-trains*) :—		£	s.	d.	£	s.	d.
SEATS (ordinary) ..	.. ..		1	0		1	0
„ (Pullman) ..	via Dover or Folkestone		5	6		—	
„ („) ..	via Newhaven		4	0		—	
„ („) ..	per "Golden Arrow" London/Dover		5	6		4	6
SLEEPERS ..	.. London/Paris per Dunkerque Ferry	3	17	5	2	16	7

On the Continent :—

SEATS (ordinary) ..	in through-coaches on International trains		2	0		2	0
„ (Pullman) ..	per "Golden Arrow" Calais/Paris ..	1	1	8		14	2
„ („) ..	Rome/Florence		15	6		—	
„ („) ..	Rome/Milan		1	6	6		—
„ („) ..	Rome/Naples		12	0		—	
SLEEPERS ..	Paris/Florence	9	4	2	5	13	11
„	„ /Genoa	7	6	6	4	15	10
„	„ /Milan	7	5	5	4	16	5
„	„ /Pisa	8	10	5	5	8	5
„	„ /Rome	10	4	9	6	7	8
„	„ /Trieste	10	9	8	6	11	3
„	„ /Turin	5	19	1	3	18	3
„	„ /Venice	9	9	1	6	1	8
„	Calais/above towns add extra ..		16	0		11	6
„	„ /Bale	5	1	1	3	6	6
„	Ostend/Milan	9	14	7	6	18	4
„	Rome/Palermo or Syracuse ..	6	1	3	3	13	9

	France		*Switzerland*		*Italy*	
	s.	d.	s.	d.	s.	d.
RESTAURANT CARS: Breakfast .. .. from	4	3	4	3	4	7
Lunch or Dinner .. from	22	1	11	3	16	10

MISCELLANEOUS TARIFFS

Hire of Pillows on Italian trains: Lire 200.

Luggage Deposit at Italian railway stations: Lire 50 per piece per day.

Porterage within the precincts of Italian stations: Lire 30 or 50 per piece according to size.

Taxi Hire varies according to locality, but the average rate is Lire 190 (2s. 3d.) per 1680 metres (one mile) for two people, with a minimum of Lire 90. Extras: Lire 10 on the tariff per additional passenger; Lire 10 to 100 for luggage according to quantity; Lire 150 after 9 p.m.

Private Car Hire (chauffeur driven) at the average rate for a four-seater car of Lire 95 per km., equivalent to about 1s. per mile; plus cost of meals or night accommodation for driver when necessary. For Self-Drive Hire apply to A.C.I., 14 Via Po, Rome (from Lire 5000 daily for 62 miles).

Gondola Hire (two people): Lire 1200 for first hour and Lire 600 per additional hour (extras: Lire 300 per hour after 10 p.m. and Lire 100 per extra passenger. From Venice station to hotel: Lire 700 (after 10 p.m. Lire 900). By the Canal Steamers the fares are Lire 15 per stage (Lire 20 after 10 p.m. and on holidays).

N.B.—All the above rates are liable to alteration.

Currency: Monetary Unit is the Lira. Notes are issued by the Banca d'Italia for Lire 10, 50, 100, 500, 1000, 5000 and 10,000. Coins are of Lire 5 and 10.

Note: On Express trains along the main Italian routes foreign currency up to the value of Lire 40,000 will be accepted at the prevailing rate of exchange for the convenience of travellers.

COACH SERVICES

Public road transport has developed considerably in Italy in the last ten years. In most cases the bus stations are near the railway stations, but seats are not bookable for short-distance routes.

There are long-distance services to remote districts from all big cities, and there are also long-distance services between the principal towns of Italy.

ROUND TRIPS AND INTERNATIONAL SERVICES

The Ciat Company operates an extensive *de luxe* bus system for visitors who wish to travel at ease and admire the beauties of the countryside.

Travellers sit in two-seated divans that are padded with foam rubber.

The visibility is increased by roof windows, and there is an efficient heating system.

There is a bar so that refreshments may be taken *en route*.

The drivers are highly skilled, and the hostesses speak at least two languages besides Italian.

The Company operates circuits of Italy from April to October each year. The circuits cover the principal art cities of Italy, and in winter the service is continued with modifications for the change of climate.

There are halts or town drives at the principal places of interest on the itinerary, and it is worth noting that passengers may break their journey at any of the towns passed in the circuit.

There is also a service between Genoa and Nice, and the Europabus Company have buses running between Venice and Innsbruck, and Milan and Innsbruck.

TIPS FOR MOTORISTS

When the Mont Cenis or the Simplon passes are blocked with snow it is possible to ship cars by rail through the tunnels.

Motorists who have not provided themselves with the requisite documents, may obtain temporary import permits at the offices of the Italian Automobile Club, which are installed at each of the principal frontier posts.

Petrol Coupons. Can be obtained at the offices of the ENIT (Italian Government Tourist Bureau) abroad or at the frontier, or at the offices of the Italian Automobile Club. These coupons allow the purchase of motor fuel with a reduction of 30 per cent of the prices prevailing in Italy. For cars there is an allowance of up to thirty litres a day, for large motor-cycles the allowance is ten litres a day and for light motor-cycles the amount is five litres a day. This concession is granted for a maximum stay of ninety days in a calendar year.

Ferries transport cars from the mainland to Sicily, Elba and also to Ischia.

Repairs. Generally speaking spares for well-known makes of British and American cars are obtainable in large centres, but it is well to remember that Italian mechanics are skilful and obliging. When spare parts are unobtainable, it is sometimes possible to have them made on the spot, even in remote places.

LIST OF HOTELS ON THE ROUTE OF THE GRAND TOUR

In compiling this list, I have made a selection of hotels and pensions that are conveniently situated on the route that I have described in this book.

Many of these places are known to me. Others I have set down from recommendations that have been made to me, but in no case can I guarantee that they will suit my readers.

The figures before the names of the hotels indicate the category and are an indication of the prices charged and of the amenities provided.

Amalfi
(1) The Cappucino Convento. In a thirteenth-century monastery with cloisters, a little way up the hill.
(2) The Luna. Also in a thirteenth-century convent, but nearer the sea.
(3) The Italia e Svizzera. In the town, facing the sea.

Arezzo
(2) Continentale. Piazza G. Monacco.
(3) Chiavi d'Oro. Piazza San Francesco.

Bolsena
(3) Al Lago. On the lakeside.

Bracciano
(4) Casina del Lago. On the lakeside.

Bonassola
Locanda Delle Rose. Very unpretentious, but very cheap.

Camogli
(2) Italia.
(4) Pesce d'Oro. Near the sea, unpretentious but cheap.

Capri
Quisisana. Luxury hotel.
(1) Cæsar Augustus. Near Anacapri with cliffside garden.
(1) Tiberio Palazzo. At Capri, high up with garden and terrace.
(2) Ercolano Palace. At Capri.
(2) Pagano. At Capri.
(4) Maresca. At the Marina Grande. Inexpensive and very good.

Florence
Excelsior, Luxury. Piazza Ognissanti, on the river.
(1) Grand. Piazza Ognissanti, on the river.
(2) Balestri. Piazza Mentana, on the river.
(2) Berchielli. No meals. Lung Arno Acciaioli. On the river.
(2) Helvetia. Via de Pescione. Central.
(3) Universo. No meals. Piazza Santa Maria Novella. Near station. Inexpensive, unpretentious.
(3) Pensione Norchi. Lungarno Zecca. On the river.
(3) Pensione Bandini. Piazza Santo Spirito. In a pleasant square.

Formia
- (1) Miramare. On the sea.
- (2) Grand. On the sea.
- (3) Marino.

Portofino
- (1) Splendide.
- (2) Piccolo.
- (3) Lina.

Positano
- (2) Miramare.
- (3) San Caterina.
- (3) Savoia.
- (3) Vittoria.
- (4) Margherita.

Rapallo
- (1) Bristol. Large garden, private bathing beach.
- (1) Europa. Large garden.
- (1) Excelsior. Large garden, private beach.
- (2) Astoria. On the front.
- (2) Grande Italia. On the front, small private beach.
- (3) Fausto. On the front.
- (3) Rapallo. On the front.

Ravenna
- (1) Jolly.
- (2) Touring. Via XIII Giugno.
- (3) Nuovo San Marco. Via XIII Giugno.

NOTE—Since there is a shortage of hotels in Ravenna, it is advisable to book rooms before arrival.

Rimini, Riccione and Cattolica

There are so many hotels in these three places that I cannot make a selected list. Prices on this Adriatic Coast tend to be lower than on the West Coast.

Rome

There are so many hotels in Rome that I have contented myself by noting those that are known to me or to my friends.

    Luxury. The Bernini Bristol. Piazza Barberini. Central.
- (2) The Alexandre. Via Veneto.
- (2) The Dinesen. Via Porta Pinciana. Pleasant situation.
- (1) The Eden. Via Veneto.

(1) Flora. Via Veneto.

(1) Hassler. Piaza Trinita de Monte. At the top of the Spanish steps.

(2) Inghilterra. Via Bocca di Leone. In the old town near the Piazza di Spagna.

(2) Internazionale. Via Sistina. Very central.

(2) Londra E Cargill. Via Collina.

(1) Piazza di Spagna. Via Mario de' Fiori. Very cheap, no meals.

(3) Sistina. Via Sistina. Cheap, no meals.

Pensione Hansen. Via Sistina.

Pensione Shelley. Corso d'Italia.

Genoa

(4) Americano E Della Stazione. Via A. Doria. Very cheap, very unpretentious, near station.

(2) Britannia. Via Balbi. Central.

Luxury, Colombia. Near the Main Station.

(1) Bristol. Via XX Settembre.

(3) Doria. Via Garibaldi. Central, no meals, rooms with private baths.

(2) Londra. Via Arsenale di Terra.

Ischia

At Porto d'Ischia—(2) Lido. Near Beach.

(3) Floridiana. Near beach.

At Casamicciola — (2) Bellavista.

At Forio—Small pensions only.

Levanto

(2) Excelsior.

(3) Europa.

Lerici

(3) Shelley E Delle Palme. On the sea.

(4) Italia.

Lucca

(2) Universo. Piazza Puccini.

(3) Luna. Via Filungo.

Naples

(3) Bologna Gran Bretagna. Via Agostino de Pretic, near bus station and steamers for Capri and Ischia.

(1) Continental. Via Partenope. On the sea front.

(3) Diana. Via Santa Lucia. Quiet quarter near front.
Excelsior. Luxury. Via Partenope.
(1) Londres. Piazza Municipale. Opposite bus stop and very near
steamers for Capri.
(2) Metropoli. Via Partenope. On the sea front.
(2) Torino. Via Agostino de Pretis, near bus terminal and
steamers for Capri and Ischia.

Orvieto
(1) Grand Hotel. Piazza del Popolo.
(3) Italica. Via Piazza del Popolo.

Orta
(1) Belvedere. Lakeside.
(4) Due Spade. Off the main square.

Perugia
(1) Brufani Palace.
(3) Della Posta. Corso Vanucci.
(2) Rosetta. Corso Vanucci. Central.

Pisa
(1) Nettuno. Lung Arno Pacinotti. On the river.
(2) Vistoria. Lung Arno Pacinotti. On the river.
(3) Roma. Via Casteletto. Inexpensive, simple.

Santa Margherita
(1) Eden. High up with large garden.
(1) Imperiale. Gardens down to the sea.
(1) Laurin. On the front.
(2) Continental. Gardens down to the sea. Rock bathing.
(2) Fiena. Outside the town. Private cabins on gravel beach.

Siena
(1) Continentale.
(3) Toscana. Via Angiolieri. Simple and inexpensive.
(3) Pensione Chiusarelli. Via Chiusarelli. Cheap and very good of
its kind.

Sorrento
(1) Cocumella. In an old monastery on the edge of the cliff, lift to
private beach.
(1) Vittoria. On the cliff, large garden, lift to private beach.
(1) Tramontana. On the cliff, gardens, lift down to private beach.
Pleasant old-fashioned atmosphere.
(2) La Terrazza. On the edge of the cliff. Private beach.

(2) Sirene. Garden and private beach.

(3) Loreley. On the front. Private cabins.

Venice

Luxury. Bauer Grunwald. On the Grand Canal.

Danielli. Riva degli Schiavoni, next to the Doge's Palace.

Grand Hotel. Grand Canal.

First Class. Europa. Grand Canal.

Luna. Grand Canal.

Second Class. Regina. Grand Canal.

Cavaletto. On a small side canal.

Savoia. Riva degli Schiavoni.

Pensions. Dinesen S. Vio 628.

La Calcina. Zattere 780.

Seguso. Zattere 779.

These last two pensions face the Giudecca Canal and are in a relatively quiet quarter.

Verona

(1) Colomba D'Oro. Via Carlo Cattaneo.

(3) Bologna. Near Piazza Bra. Very good of its class.

Vicenza

(1) Jolly. Viale Roma.

(2) Roma. Corso Palladio.

(3) Basilica. Piazza Erbe.

WINES AND SOFT DRINKS

Wine is produced in every province of Italy, and generally speaking, it is a good plan to drink the wine of the region that you are in because it is likely to be cheaper, and it will certainly harmonize with the local food.

So, for instance, if you happen to be in Tuscany and more especially in Florence, you will find that the Chianti makes an admirable accompaniment to the excellent beefsteaks that are served in the restaurants and the *trattorie*.

In Naples, the Capri, Vesuvio, Lachrima Christi and the Sorriso d'Ischia should be drunk with the fish or the *pizze*.

Frascati and other wines of the Roman Castles do not travel, but they are really refreshing and in prime condition in the taverns of Rome—the best of them are white, which is just as well, for red wine is too heating for the summer climate of Rome.

On the coast of Liguria from Genoa to Spezia, the white wines of the Cinque Terre and the Coronata suit the fish dishes that are served in most hotels and restaurants. Another excellent vintage is the Albenga that is procurable in Alassio.

In the Veneto, the district that includes the provinces of Venice, Verona, Vicenza, Padua and Treviso, wines such as the Bardolino and the Valpolicella (red and white), the Soave and the Riesling (both white, the former sweetish, the latter dry), can compare favourably with many of the products of the German or French vineyards.

LIST OF WINES IN ALPHABETICAL ORDER

Albano (red, dry, 12–13 deg.) Ravenna, Ferrara.

Aleatico (red desert wine, sweet) Elba.

Barbera d'Asti (red, dry, 8–13 deg.) Piedmont.

Bardolino (red, dry, 11 deg.) Veneto.

Barolo (Red, dry, 13–15 deg.) Piedmont.

Caldaro Lego (red, medium sweet, 10–12 deg.) Trentino, Garda.

Capri (white, dry, 11–13 deg.) Capri, Naples region.

Chianti (red, dry, 10–12 deg.) Florence, Tuscany.

Cinque Terre (white, sweet, 18 deg.) Spezia, Levanto.

Coronata (dry, white, 13 deg.) Genoa.

Corvo (white and red, 12–14 deg.) Sicily, procurable anywhere, the white Corvo stands icing.

Est Est Est (white, medium sweet) Bolsena and district.

Falerno (white and red, dry, medium sweet, and sweet) Naples.

Freisa (red, dry, 10–12 deg.) has a slight flavour of strawberries.

Grignolino (red, medium sweet) Lombardy.

Lachrima Christi (white, dry, 12 deg.) Naples.

Lambrusco (red, sweet and dry) Ravenna, Forli, Ferrara.

Marsala (amber, very sweet, 18 deg.) procurable everywhere, a Sicilian dessert wine.

Montepulciano (red, dry) southern and central Tuscany.

Moscato (sweet, very light) a dessert wine produced in most provinces. Try it with ice.

Orvieto (white, dry or sweet) Orvieto, procurable everywhere.

Prosecco (white, medium sweet) Veneto.

Ravello (red, 12–14 deg.) Ravello and Amalfi.

Riesling (white, dry) produced in most countries. North of Italy.

Rufina (red, dry) Tuscany.

Sangue di Giuda (red with a bitter sweet taste) "Blood of Judas", is
 produced and drunk mainly in Lombardy (Milan).
Soave Bianco (white, dry or medium sweet) Verona and Vicenza.
Sorriso d'Ischia (white, sweet, 11 deg.) Ischia and Naples.
Valpolicella (red, dry, 13 deg.) Veneto.
Vernaccia (white, dry, 15 deg.) Eastern Central Italy.
Vino Santo (sweet white, low alcoholic content) most parts of Italy.

SOFT DRINKS

There are springs of mineral waters in most parts of Italy, and
these waters are sold in bottle everywhere, and in bars they are also
obtainable by the glass.

Many of these mineral waters are bottled with fruit juices, usually
orange, and they are unbeatable as thirst quenchers.

Coca-Cola is on sale everywhere.

Incidentally, the water in all the big towns is pure and can be
drunk quite safely.

Tea is still rather expensive, and as a rule it is made too weak for
English tastes.

Tonic water is now being made in Florence and in Milan.

APERITIFS AND SPIRITS

The *Americano* made with vermouth, bitters, orange bitters and
a drop of gin is an excellent aperitif in hot weather. There are many
recipes for the making of this drink, but the result is more or less the
same. The *Negroni* is a potent and more expensive variant of the
Americano, which needs to be treated with caution.

When asking for a cocktail, it is necessary to specify whether
English or Italian gin is to be used. The latter is less expensive.

Italian brandies are improving, but have not yet caught up with
French brandies.

In northern Italy, a white grape spirit called *aquavite* is made. It
is strong and frequently rather rough.

Of the liqueurs, the *Certosa*, green and yellow, is more or less as
the French Chartreuse. The *Strega* is another popular sweet liqueur.
Whisky can be obtained nearly everywhere but the price is high.

Beer, German and of the German type, is sold in bottles, and also
in some bars on draught. In bottle it costs nearly as much as the
equivalent quantity of wine.

GLOSSARY OF FOOD TERMS

Abbachio: Baby lamb. An excellent Roman speciality.

Agnolotti: A kind of Ravioli.

Anguille: Eels.

Anitra: Duck.

Arrosto: Roast, e.g. *Arrosto di Vitella*. Roast veal.

Baccala: Dried cod. Prepared in the right way it is very good.

Bistecca: Beef steak. A Florentine speciality.

Burro: Butter. *Al burro*, cooked with butter.

Caciucco: Fish stew.

Calamaio: Cuttle fish. An acquired taste, but a taste worth acquiring.

Capretto: Kid. Excellent provided that the kid is not grown up.

Carciofi: Artichokes.

Carciofi alla giudia: Jerusalem artichokes.

Ciliege: Cherries.

Datteri: Dates. Sometimes also mussels.

Fagioli: Beans.

Fegato: Liver.

Fegato alla Veneziana: Liver and onions.

Fettucine: Ribbon-like pasta made with eggs.

Fichi: Figs.

Fonduta: Melted cheese prepared with butter, eggs.

Frittata: Omelette.

Fritto Misto: Mixed fry of meat or fish.

Frutti di mare: Shell fish.

Funghi: Mushrooms or edible fungus.

Lasagne: Flat ribbon-like pasta of good quality.

Maiale: Pork. Avoid it in the summer.

Manzo: Beef. Manzo bollito or boiled beef. Avoid it.

Mela: Apple.

Merluzzo: Fresh haddock.

Mozzarella. Soft cheese made from buffalo milk.

Mozzarella in Carozza: Italian Welsh rabbit. Quite edible.

Nespoli: Medlars.

Ostriche: Oysters. Careful!

Parmigiano: Parmesan cheese. Very hard, very good ungrated.

Patate: Potatoes.

Pesche: Peaches.

Pesche spada: Sword fish.

Pesto: A sauce made with strong cheese, garlic and pine kernels. Excellent, but to quote a guide book, the flavour is unmistakable.

Pichione: Pigeon.

Piselli: Peas.

Polenta: Maize flour used as a vegetable.

Polpettine: Rissoles. Let sleeping dogs lie.

Risotto alla Milanese: Risotto cooked with saffron and chicken livers.

Rombo: Turbot.

Salsiccie: Pork sausages flavoured with garlic and spices.

Sogliola: Sole.

Tacchino: Turkey.

Tonno: Tunny fish.

Trifolota: With truffles. The white truffles are cheaper than the black.

Triglie: Red mullet.

Uva: Grapes.

Zampone: Highly seasoned sausages. Only for strong stomachs.

P

INDEX

227